*CHINESE SENIOR MIGRANTS
AND THE GLOBALIZATION
OF RETIREMENT*

CHINESE SENIOR MIGRANTS AND THE GLOBALIZATION OF RETIREMENT

NICOLE DEJONG NEWENDORP

STANFORD UNIVERSITY PRESS
Stanford, California

Stanford University Press
Stanford, California

© 2020 by the Board of Trustees of the Leland Stanford Junior University. All rights reserved.

No part of this book may be reproduced or transmitted in any form or by any means, electronic or mechanical, including photocopying and recording, or in any information storage or retrieval system without the prior written permission of Stanford University Press.

Printed in the United States of America on acid-free, archival-quality paper

Library of Congress Cataloging-in-Publication Data

Names: Newendorp, Nicole DeJong, author.
Title: Chinese senior migrants and the globalization of retirement / Nicole DeJong Newendorp.
Description: Stanford, California : Stanford University Press, [2020] | Includes bibliographical references and index.
Identifiers: LCCN 2020008450 (print) | LCCN 2020008451 (ebook) | ISBN 9781503611726 (cloth) | ISBN 9781503613881 (paperback) | ISBN 9781503613898 (ebook)
Subjects: LCSH: Older Chinese Americans—United States. | Older immigrants—United States. | Retirement—United States. | United States—Emigration and immigration—Social aspects. | China—Emigration and immigration—Social aspects.
Classification: LCC E184.C5 N49 2020 (print) | LCC E184.C5 (ebook) | DDC 305.26086/912—dc23
LC record available at https://lccn.loc.gov/2020008450
LC ebook record available at https://lccn.loc.gov/2020008451

Cover design: Rob Ehle
Cover photograph: "Dancing Solves Everything," Cambridge Senior Center in Cambridge, MA, photo by Gabe Taylor

CONTENTS

	Acknowledgments	vii
	Timeline of Historical Events	xi
1	Chinese Senior Migrants in the United States	1
2	Why Seniors Move	31
3	Generational Belonging in the Nation-State	53
4	The Meaning of "Retirement" for Chinese Senior Migrants in the United States	76
5	Negotiating Family Value(s) in the United States	99
6	Aging in Place?	122
7	My Chinese Heart	146
8	Reconfiguring Retirement	170
	Notes	183
	References	195
	Index	209

ACKNOWLEDGMENTS

As is often the way of things, this project grew and developed in ways that were impossible to imagine when I showed up in the waiting room of a Chinatown social service organization with modest hopes of meeting a few Chinese American senior citizens in 2007. In the process, I have accrued substantial debts to many more individuals than I am even able to name here.

None of my fieldwork for this (or my previous) book would have been possible without the full year of intensive Cantonese language training I did in Hong Kong in 2000 and 2001 funded by the Blakemore Foundation. I remember having to defend the relevance of learning Cantonese (as opposed to Mandarin) at my selection interview and remain thankful to this day for the foundation's support. Funding for this project was also provided by the Research Fellowship Program at the University of Massachusetts Boston Institute of Asian American Studies and an Oral History Project Grant from Harvard University's Schlesinger Library.

I don't have sufficient words to express my substantial gratitude to the many members of the Chinese American community in and around Boston who have taken time and effort to meet with me and tell me their stories over many years. I owe a particular debt to Tunney Lee, whose consistent willingness to engage in conversation with me about the history and development of Boston's Chinatown has mattered greatly for my understanding of its community today. Other individuals who were crucial to the completion of this project include Kun Chang, who facilitated my initial volunteer work in Chinatown; Kye Liang, who provided personal introductions to key actors throughout the area; and David Chang, who pushed me to look beyond Chinatown to more fully consider the lifeworlds of Chinese seniors residing in Boston's remote suburban locations. The Chinese Historical Society of New England (CHSNE) was an important site of information when I was first beginning this project. Members of the Chinese American Women in New England Oral History Project, particularly

Stephanie Fan, Ruth Hill, Connie Wong, and Dorothy Yep, allowed me to come to meetings to learn about Chinatown's historical and contemporary community. Betty Yau, of the Quincy Mayor's Asian American Advisory Committee, facilitated my introduction to community centers and housing estates in Quincy. Additionally, I was made welcome at various times over the past decade by staff and clients at many organizations in and around Boston's Chinatown, including: the Asian American Civic Association, the Asian Community Development Corporation, the Boston Chinese Evangelical Church, the Boston Chinatown Neighborhood Center, the Chinese Consolidated Benevolent Association, the Chinese Progressive Association, the Greater Boston Chinese Golden Age Center, the North Quincy Community Center, the Philips Brooks House Association Chinatown Citizenship and ESL Programs, and Wollaston Senior Center.

I relied on the help of Harvard undergraduate and graduate students at many stages of the research and writing for this project. Yan Yang, John Lee, and Patricia (Patty) Zhong transcribed my interviews from Cantonese into English. Patty also served as an interpreter for several interviewees who could understand Cantonese but spoke only Taishanese. Debra Chang and Linda Zhang each spent an entire summer doing research with me as mentees through Harvard's BLISS program. Debra shadowed me in Boston's Chinatown, while Linda accompanied me to Quincy. Both contributed significantly to my understanding of seniors' lives in those areas by developing their own relationships with Mandarin-speaking senior migrants in the largely Cantonese-speaking areas we most often frequented. Amy Cheung performed the Herculean task of creating a database of all my interview transcriptions and fieldnotes. Conversations with Jesper Ke about his thesis research on Chinese-born senior migrants in the greater Boston area confirmed recent demographic shifts in Boston's Chinese American senior population which I did not have time to investigate myself. Jin Park assembled the bibliography, and Yong Han Poh assisted with a host of odds and ends as I prepared the final manuscript for publication. The students who have taken my engaged learning seminar on Boston's Chinatown over the past four years have greatly influenced my understanding of contemporary Asian American social and political concerns, which has been important to my ability to write about some of those concerns here.

To complete this project, I had to learn entire new areas of scholarly work. Wing-kai To, Madeline Hsu, Emma Teng, Heather Lee, and Thomas Chen shaped my learning about the history of Chinese in Boston and the rest of the United States. Paul Watanabe, Michael Liu, and Shauna Lo at the University of

Massachusetts Boston Institute for Asian American Studies provided substantial guidance about Asian Americans in New England while I was a research fellow in 2009–2010 and have always been willing to answer my many questions since that time. Ken Chih-Yan Sun introduced me to literature situated at the nexus of aging and migration many years ago and remains my primary interlocutor on the subject of Chinese senior migration today. Different bits and pieces of this book have been presented at numerous locations, including multiple annual meetings of the Association of Asian Studies and the American Anthropological Association, as well as Harvard University's Center for Population and Development Studies; Brown University's Population Studies and Training Center; the University of Illinois (Urbana-Champaign); the University of Massachusetts Boston; the University of Hong Kong; Hong Kong Baptist University; and the Massachusetts Historical Society. I am deeply grateful to all of the organizers and audience members of these events for their insightful comments that have helped to strengthen my work.

I am extremely fortunate to have benefited from the mentorship of Rubie Watson and James L. Watson since I entered Harvard University as a graduate student. They have consistently provided unwavering support on all of my professional and personal endeavors for almost 25 years. Over the years, conversations with many other mentors and colleagues have sharpened my understanding of particular aspects of the social phenomena I discuss here. For those insights, I thank Nancy Abelmann, Andrew Brandel, Manduhai Buyandelger, Kevin Caffrey, Melissa Caldwell, Nara Dillon, Vanessa Fong, Sara Friedman, Marilyn Halter, Michael Herzfeld, Charlotte Ikels, Philip Kao, Andrea Louie, Katherine Mason, Young-a Park, Sonja Plesset, Elizabeth Remick, Tracey Rosen, Jeanne Shea, Priscilla Song, Tulasi Srinivas, Reed Ueda, Elanah Uretsky, Mary C. Waters, Hong Zhang, and Min Zhang.

I owe a huge thank-you to all my fantastic colleagues over the years at Harvard University's Committee on Degrees in Social Studies. I am particularly grateful to the members of our administrative team who have never failed in their unwavering collegial support and friendship over the past decade: Kate Anable, Anya Bassett, Katie Greene, Nicolas Prevelakis, Bonnie Talbert, and Don Tontiplaphol. Lauren Doan, Shane Iverson, and Heather Jacques provided much-needed, good-humored administrative help to keep me going. I am also lucky to have worked with so many incredible students, whom I thank for their enthusiasm and encouragement of this project over many years.

Laura J. Miller, my writing partner, has been there at every stage of my research and writing—providing sage advice, reading innumerable drafts, and always encouraging me to keep going. I would never have completed this book without her tremendous help. Marcela Maxfield and Sunna Juhn at Stanford University Press have provided crucial expertise, support, and guidance. Several anonymous reviewers offered excellent feedback on earlier versions of this book that greatly helped with the shaping of the final product. Sue Gilroy, at Harvard University's Lamont Library, tracked down elusive sources that I couldn't locate on my own. Andrew Brandel provided the final word on my last-minute editorial changes, for which I cannot thank him enough.

Last but not least, I thank all members of my family, near and far, for their loving support and encouragement all these years. Zeke and Gabe, who have grown up alongside this project, I dedicate this book to you.

TIMELINE OF HISTORICAL EVENTS

1839–1842	First Opium War
1841	Hong Kong ceded to Britain after first Opium War defeat
1848–1855	California Gold Rush
1856–1860	Second Opium War
1875	Page Act prohibits entry of Chinese women to the United States
1882	Chinese Exclusion Act prohibits all immigration by Chinese laborers to the United States
1924	Johnson-Reed Immigration Act of 1924 limits immigrants' entry to the United States by national origins quota
1939–1945	World War II
1943	Chinese Exclusion Act repealed
1949	Founding of the People's Republic of China (PRC)
1949–1976	Maoist period
1965	Hart-Celler Immigration and Naturalization Act abolishes national origins quotas from 1924 Immigration Act
1966–1976	Cultural Revolution
1978	Beginning of the PRC's reform era under Deng Xiaoping

CHINESE SENIOR MIGRANTS AND THE GLOBALIZATION OF RETIREMENT

1 CHINESE SENIOR MIGRANTS IN THE UNITED STATES

Ten years ago, I had just finished writing a book about Chinese migrant families in Hong Kong and was looking for a new project.[1] I decided, as a temporary measure, to learn something about Boston's Chinatown, where I figured I could use my Cantonese language skills to get to know older Chinese Americans, including individuals originally from Hong Kong.[2] So one afternoon, I rode the T (Boston's subway line) a few stops from my workplace in Cambridge to downtown. From there, I walked several more blocks and ended up in the waiting area of a local service organization, where I asked at the desk if there was someone I could talk with about becoming a volunteer English teacher. After ascertaining that I had some relevant teaching experience and collecting information for a routine CORI check, I was assigned to provide weekly English as a Second Language (ESL) instruction to a group of Chinese American senior citizens who were participants in a government-subsidized work training program aimed at helping low-income adults aged fifty-five and older learn skills to enter (or reenter) the workforce.[3]

At the time, I had no expectations about where my volunteer teaching would lead. My goal was simply to learn something about this community of Chinese-speaking older individuals—and, I hoped, provide some useful English language training for them in the process. What I had not foreseen was how attached to my students I would become. Despite having to wake up at 4:00 a.m. (or earlier) to take care of my other work and family responsibilities on the days I would leave Cambridge after lunch and head to Chinatown, I taught my classes on a volunteer basis for one afternoon every week for three years. During this time, I tried my best to help my older students learn some English, but—as they freely talked about—it was hard going, and I was frustrated (as were they) that despite our significant efforts, it was difficult for them to make much progress. Yet the conversations that resulted, in a mixture of English, Cantonese, Mandarin, and (although I don't understand it) Taishanese, were fascinating.

One of the first things I learned about my ESL students, much to my initial surprise, was that most of them, in 2007, were relatively new arrivals to the United States. As I investigated further, I learned that one-third of all Chinese-born residents in the United States have arrived here since 1990, and Chinese are now among the three largest immigrant groups in the country, following Mexicans and Indians.[4] Moreover, Chinese immigrants are on average older than all other foreign-born immigrants in the United States, and in recent decades, more than 30 percent of them have come at age sixty or older.[5] Yet when I searched for ethnographic studies that would shed light on why senior migrants were coming in such numbers at the turn of the millennium and what life was like for them after migrating to a new country for the first time in the latter decades of their lives, I found almost nothing. It was this information that I cited to colleagues to justify my attention to this population once my data collection began in earnest in 2009. Yet the real fascination for me was their stories. Through the snippets I first heard in class and later through substantially more detailed narratives that I collected and recorded from 2009 to 2012, I was drawn to stories of hardship, hard work, good fortune, family stress, and desire—stories that helped me begin to understand why so many older individuals would pick up and move to a new country, leaving behind family, friends, and lifelong social networks to grapple instead with a new language, new ways of life, and a host of other obstacles just at the stage of life when many individuals also begin navigating the effects of mental or physical decline associated with natural processes of aging.

Emigration from China is not a new phenomenon. Chinese make up what is arguably the world's oldest diaspora, dating from around 200 B.C.E.[6] By 2010, overseas Chinese—that is, ethnically Chinese individuals who may be many generations removed from living in China—numbered over 40 million in 148 countries worldwide.[7] However, recent migration trends differ from past practices in scale, scope, and intensity. Patterns of settlement outside China over the past 150 years have shifted away from original routes to Southeast Asia and are now increasingly oriented toward North America, Europe, and Australia, in addition to East Asia's powerhouse economies of Japan, South Korea, and Singapore.[8] Following the past several decades of rapid economic and social transformation in China, record numbers of Chinese now travel abroad every year, engage in investment emigration, enroll as university and secondary school students outside China, and move abroad to work, join family, or establish new citizenship claims.[9] In 2015, almost 11 million Chinese citizens were living outside China.[10] Over one-fifth of those individuals resided in the United States—the "top destination for Chinese immigrants" as estimated by the United Nations Population Division.[11] The vast scholarly literature on Chinese migration, past and present, mostly predates this recent boom in international migration trends from China and, along with its basis in China's long-standing diasporic networks, largely emphasizes Chinese migrants' rootedness in territorial China. Whether viewed as "reluctant" emigrants, "sojourners" rather than settlers, or "flexible citizens" looking out for their own personal interests, Chinese migrants are depicted as maintaining a lifelong, primary orientation toward China, downplaying the possibility that they may also develop a sense of belonging elsewhere in the world.[12]

Chinese migration literature also makes clear that the desire to engage in global flows of movement influences individuals across the social and economic spectrum in China, including working-class and peasant women who marry across borders; Fuzhounese villagers who often follow clandestine networks to migrate to Europe and the United States; Chinese entrepreneurs who establish businesses abroad; and youth who work or study internationally.[13] Chinese seniors are engaged in global mobility processes in significant ways. Rapidly increasing economic inequality in contemporary China has left many older Chinese financially insecure at the same moment that changing social and cultural values have destabilized Chinese seniors' traditional place of authority in family life and opened up new possibilities of active aging oriented around "autonomy and intergenerational independence."[14] As a result, Chinese seniors with diasporic family networks, desires to fulfill lifelong dreams to "see the world," and awareness of opportunities to experience idealized retired lifestyles abroad have increasingly been activating their family-based networks to engage in retirement migration beyond the borders of territorial China, including to the United States. In this way, their moves—whether within an Asian regional sphere or across the Pacific—are in line with those of increasing numbers of seniors worldwide for whom retirement migration has become an important means to navigate the challenges posed to their traditional expectations for retirement by increased longevity, demographically aging populations, and global neoliberal trends reducing state welfare support for aging individuals.

This book is about what I learned from listening to recent Chinese senior migrants' stories about their engagement in transnational lifeways and global mobility processes—that is, how Chinese seniors made sense of relocating to the United States in the latter decades of their lives. I draw inspiration from a fledgling body of recent qualitative work examining ethnically Asian seniors as active contributors to—rather than passive recipients of—the migration processes of which they are a part. For example, Sarah Lamb focuses on the lifeworlds of retired Indian American seniors who follow adult children to the United States, and Ken Chih-Yan Sun traces the paths of Taiwanese American seniors who return to Taiwan for retirement once their professional working life in the United States ends.[15] In both cases, seniors navigate familial and social ties in multiple locations, confronting challenging decisions to engage in migration trajectories, even as the possibilities they have for participating in contemporary mobility flows are directly related to a political and economic ease of travel between Asia and the United States that did not exist even a few decades ago. These works, like many other accounts in the anthropological scholarship of migration, reinforce our understanding of migrants as individuals with complex motivations, desires, and goals.[16] This crucial interpretative lens seeks to disrupt many of the durable misconceptions that continue to haunt much popular writing on immigration today, including views that reduce immigrants' complex lifeworlds to one-dimensional perspectives portraying them as drains on the U.S. economy, disrupters to social well-being, and otherwise undeserving of sympathetic treatment by the communities in which they reside.[17]

Of course, anthropologists have always aimed to humanize the actors at the center of our intellectual inquiries. As early as the 1970s, anthropologists portrayed migrants as multifaceted individuals strategically engaged in social and global processes of travel, displacement, and cultural interaction.[18] My ethnography—which both builds on these long-standing anthropological humanizing portraits of migrants and also goes against predominant scholarly portrayals of Chinese overseas as forever rooted to territorial China—highlights recent Chinese senior migrants as complex actors with a strong sense of affinity to and active engagement in the United States, where they perform crucial roles that foster the well-being of American communities. Their lives have most often been filled with decades of hardship and political and social upheaval, but their outlook on life in the United States remains strongly positive, even in ongoing situations of significant daily challenges.

My interviewees' stories are grounded in long-standing processes of global movement, including the deeply interactive histories of trade and transnationalism between the United States and China during the nineteenth and twentieth centuries.[19] At the same time, their stories are also entangled with national policies of restriction and structural disempowerment that sought to curtail the entrance of Chinese migrants to the United States and the exit of citizens from China over that same period of time. As a result, these stories reflect the complexity of contemporary flows of movement—of people, information, and ideas—that make up an ever-changing backdrop to my interviewees' long lives and to which my interviewees are active contributors. Overall, my approach foregrounds how paying attention to the life experiences of a particular group of relatively overlooked individuals, navigating unexpected delights and difficulties, sheds light on seniors' strategies for achieving later-life goals within a context of rapidly aging population demographics and global neoliberal trends that simultaneously render seniors' lifeways more precarious. Thus, I begin with a story that highlights some of the many seeming paradoxes involved with the migration processes of my Chinese senior migrant interviewees. It's also the story that initially hooked me—transforming a more casual interest in my Boston Chinatown ESL students' lives into a more serious academic project. This story challenged many of my preconceived ideas about my ESL students. It also highlighted for me the interaction between historical and contemporary processes of global mobility and migration and, in so doing, started me down the path of investigating how seniors' memories and subjective experiences of movement within and beyond China in past decades have continued to influence their contemporary migration trajectories.

MR. LEE'S STORY

In 2008, I got to know a man I will call "Mr. Lee," a member of the ESL class that I was teaching as a volunteer to Chinese-born senior citizens in Boston's Chinatown. At that time, Mr. Lee was in his late eighties. Originally from Guangdong Province—like most other Chinese immigrants who have the longest historical ties to the United States—he was physically active and eager to learn. He was a diligent student who read English at a high intermediate level, all the while peering closely through a large magnifying glass. Each week, he came to class with meticulously prepared notes on vocabulary and grammar written in his careful and clear cursive writing. Like his classmates, Mr. Lee had trouble speaking conversational English, so our discussions took place in a patchwork of English, Cantonese, and Mandarin.

Through Mr. Lee's participation in my class, I learned that he had been sponsored to come to the United States by an adult child about a decade earlier. However, I also learned that his grandfather had migrated to the country during the period of Chinese exclusion, probably sometime in the early 1900s. Although most Chinese nationals were formally barred from entrance following the enactment of the Chinese Exclusion Act in 1882, individuals found ways—both legal and clandestine—to immigrate despite the act's goals to completely curtail Chinese nationals' entrance to the United States. Because Mr. Lee's grandfather lived in San Francisco, it's possible that he arrived as a "paper son" following the destruction of the San Francisco public records office in the great fire of 1906, when the loss of public birth records provided an opportunity for would-be Chinese immigrants to prove through other means, including witness testimony, that they had been born in the United States and, as citizens, were exempt from the exclusion laws. While in San Francisco, Mr. Lee's grandfather worked in a laundry, one of the few occupations available to Chinese immigrants in the early twentieth century. Later, he returned to China with deep resentment of the difficult labor and humiliating treatment that he had endured. As Mr. Lee explained, his grandfather's arms and hands were covered in burns from the hot irons he used to press clothes, and he was in constant physical pain. Wanting to protect his descendants from the hardships that he had experienced in San Francisco, Mr. Lee's grandfather forbade his sons, and later his grandsons, from ever going to the United States, an order that carries particularly strong weight in the Chinese cultural context and continued to influence Mr. Lee's father throughout his life. Mr. Lee told me:

> My dad remembered all the sufferings that my grandfather experienced. [My grandfather] said that the [Lee] family would never go to America ever again because he went through so much suffering, and he didn't want anyone to ever have to go through what he went through. He was looked down upon. He had to pick up the clothes underneath people's beds, and he had to crawl [on the floor]. He was kicked around. He was very embarrassed. My dad said that our family would never go back to America.

Nevertheless, here was Mr. Lee, almost one hundred years later, sitting in my class, intently working to build on his already substantial English language skills—at once smiling broadly when he was able to answer my questions correctly in English but also conveying his sense of deep distress at his grandfather's experiences.[20]

The fact that Mr. Lee was living in the United States where his grandfather and father had forbidden him to go, rather than in China, where he had lived for the first seventy-five years of his life, was just one of many seeming paradoxes in Mr. Lee's life. In China, Mr. Lee had performed important work as an engineer overseeing the development of China's railways. In Boston, he lived in obscurity, unable to communicate many of his routine needs in English. Despite his advanced age at migration and relative lack of English fluency, Mr. Lee worked in Boston's Chinatown for several years after his arrival, until he was mugged on the job and felt his physical safety was threatened. One primary reason that he moved to Boston was to be near his adult children who lived in the United States, but when I met him, Mr. Lee lived alone, in a small public housing unit in an urban area far removed from Chinatown, and he saw his children only on special occasions. Moreover, despite his low-income status, Mr. Lee traveled to China once each year to celebrate important milestones with his adult children and numerous grandchildren still living there as long as his health allowed him to make the long plane journey. Finally, despite the many difficulties that had accompanied his immigration to the United States in the latter decades of his life and his active acknowledgment of these difficulties, Mr. Lee described his life now in largely positive terms. In particular, his migration in his seventies fulfilled a long-held desire to see the world beyond China and experience its marvels firsthand—a sentiment many of my other interviewees voiced as well.[21]

CHINESE SENIOR MIGRANTS IN THE UNITED STATES,
PAST AND PRESENT

As I learned over the period of my research, many aspects of Mr. Lee's life were typical of other Chinese senior migrants in the Boston area and the United States more generally. First, significant numbers of Chinese seniors have been migrating to the United States as relatively young and healthy (yet senior) adults—in part because of an earlier age of retirement in China (fifty-five for women and sixty for men) compared to the United States. Second, many of these senior migrants, particularly those from Southeast China, have long-standing ties to the United States. Even when sponsored by adult children, they may also have parents, uncles, aunts, cousins, or siblings already living here—or who lived here at some point during the twentieth century. Third, many of these seniors are actively engaged in social, familial, and work activities in the United States—both in and also beyond Chinatown enclave areas, where they have many opportunities to perform paid and unpaid labor. Fourth, Chinese-born seniors encounter significant hardships in the United States, where poverty rates for Chinese American senior citizens are very high[22] and many struggle with basic communication, claiming that in the United States, it is as if they are "blind, deaf, and dumb." Moreover, senior migrants may also experience social alienation through tense racial relations and practical difficulties negotiating bureaucratic and medical institutions.[23] Even so, many seniors describe their lives in the United States in positive terms, most commonly using the Mandarin Chinese term *xingfu* (C. *hahngfuk*)—to reference the sense of well-being and social stability that they have achieved by moving here.[24] And fifth, those who can afford the expense travel back and forth to China as long as their health allows, often staying a few weeks each year in China to visit with the family they left behind and, in this way, engage in contemporary transnational migratory trajectories that are more commonly associated with younger adult migrants.

These characteristics, which were the norm among my interviewees, are not necessarily true of all Chinese-born seniors in the United States, particularly those who migrated here at a significantly younger age or recent migrants who hail from parts of China north of Guangdong Province. Nevertheless, by drawing attention to the long-standing family connections that far predate seniors' physical moves to the United States, along with the multiple ways that recent immigrant seniors are intensely engaged with and embedded in their new living environments, these characteristics provide a significant challenge to preconceptions that often continue to dominate accounts of migration and its social effects. This is true particularly of economic-driven analyses that link international wage differentials with rational choice theory to assume economic gain as the primary motivating force for all immigration. This view also focuses primary attention on younger, working-age adults while relegating older immigrants' engagement in global migration processes to a passive role determined by seniors' caregiving needs. While many studies take a more complex understanding of migration motivation as their starting point, a presumed passivity of older adult migrants is also exacerbated in other ways, including by scholarly efforts to document and quantify seniors' social marginalization and discomfort—that is, their inability to assimilate into their new host society.

My point here is not to claim that economic gain is completely irrelevant to Chinese seniors' migration goals—or that their lives in the United States are not fraught with difficulties, including the social marginalization that many older immigrants in fact regularly experience. Rather, my point is that paying attention to seniors' migration stories—with all the richness, complexity, ambiguity, and depth of personal hardships and desires that animate individual decisions to participate in global mobility processes at an advanced age—allows for the development of a much more nuanced portrait of seniors' goals and experiences as migrants and highlights the many important contributions recent senior migrants make as social and political actors in the United States. As a result, these stories ultimately help to explain why seniors make up such a large percentage of the recent Chinese immigrant population to the United States despite the many social and economic disadvantages they face here. Moreover, these stories also help explain why seniors—as grandparents—are crucial actors in current debates on U.S. immigration policy, although their own voices are rarely heard. Grandparent migrants may not be a prominent contemporary news headline, particularly in comparison to other migration-related concerns such as granting a pathway to citizenship for Dreamers or the potential abuse of high-skill visa allotments by corporations seeking to replace American resident workers with lower-cost immigrant labor. These debates nonetheless share a common origin through the family preference categories that have been a linchpin of U.S. immigration policy since the Hart-Celler Immigration and Naturalization Act was passed in 1965. Grandparents are at the center of this debate. They are not eligible to come to the United States through employment categories; at the same time, they are not recognized as nuclear family—although they provide important labor that contributes to the economic and emotional well-being of their families in America. Thus, in contemporary debates about whether and how to reform the family-preference categories that dominate the legal possibilities for entrance in favor of more "economically productive" immigrants who will actively contribute to national economic growth, grandparents sit in a vulnerable position—potentially becoming a wedge to dismantle the very policies that they and their families have depended on for economic survival. Chinese American seniors, who are significantly positioned at the intersection of many long-standing contradictions in U.S. immigration policy, are therefore (as anthropologists like to say) good to "think" these debates.

The contradictions inherent in my interviewees' experiences are threefold. First, as *immigrants*, they embody an important paradox in our common perceptions of what it means to be American today. As a nation, we privilege narratives of immigrant hardship and sacrifice as crucial to the American ethos of survival and success. That historical imagery is woven into all aspects of our national ideology, particularly around the possibility of freedom from oppression, best symbolized by the Statue of Liberty. Yet the relative ease of immigration to the United States, particularly for categories of non-Western migrants, is recent, dating to the Hart-Celler Act of 1965. Before that time, U.S. immigration policy was characterized by alternating periods of welcoming inclusion and significant restriction, with much of the twentieth century oriented toward exclusionary policies.[25] Second, as *seniors,* whose migration sponsorship depends on family members already legally resident in the United States, my interviewees' increasing demographic significance in the country today may be at least in part an accident of history. That is, it seems likely that the American policymakers who penned the Hart-Celler Act underestimated just how radically it would reshape American demographics because the previously restrictive entrance policies that had been largely in place since 1924 hid much of the dynamism inherent in migration processes and the networks that support them.[26] Today, the continued reliance on the family preference categories established through the Hart-Celler Act for granting legal entrance criteria of immigrants to the United States sets it apart from all other developed nations, which have increasingly sought to more closely tie legal entrance requirements to professional skills and education over family ties. Finally, as *Chinese Americans,* my interviewees' experiences highlight the uniquely important place of Chinese immigrants in American immigration history. When the Chinese became the first group to be denied entry to the United States on the basis of their race through the Chinese Exclusion Laws enacted in the late nineteenth century, that legal precedent opened the door to racially based immigration policies that closed the door to Southern and Eastern Europeans as well as non-Western immigrants for much of the twentieth century and continues today in racialized portrayals of immigrants from all non-Western areas of the world.[27] Although the Chinese Exclusion Laws were lifted following China's role as an American ally in World War II, leading to increased possibilities of immigration, particularly for well-educated individuals and their families, Chinese Americans continue to be subject to a long-standing pattern of lack of recognition as American citizens through continued social positioning as "forever foreigners" despite their almost two-hundred-year history in the United States.[28]

The contemporary demographic composition of Chinese American seniors directly reflects this history. The low-income, Taishanese- and Cantonese-speaking first-generation immigrant elderly population dominating Chinatown enclave areas for the majority of the previous century as a legacy of the Chinese Exclusion Laws has given way to a much larger and diverse population of Chinese

American seniors in this century. These populations of Chinese seniors spread far beyond the confines of ethnic enclaves and include native U.S.-born Chinese Americans who came of age during or just after World War II, retired professionals who migrated through Cold War refugee categories privileging well-educated Chinese, Taiwanese seniors who came to the country for advanced education and stayed throughout their adult working lives, and retired professionals from China who have moved to take care of their Chinese American grandchildren. Today, Chinese American seniors may be first, second, or third generation in the United States; they may speak English, Mandarin, Cantonese, Taishanese, Fujianese, Shanghainese, Taiwanese, or another Chinese dialect; they may have worked their whole lives cooking in a restaurant kitchen or designing world-class architecture; they may have never traveled beyond one city's Chinatown's borders or comprise part of the ethnically Chinese globe-trotting elite described by Ong as "flexible citizens."[29] In short, the many changes in American immigration policy during the twentieth century paved the way for the rich tapestry of ethnic Chinese seniors' lives in the United States today and fundamentally shaped the personal lives—from childhood to parenthood to retirement—of the specific demographic of Cantonese-speaking recent Chinese senior migrants whose experiences I examine in this ethnography. Like Mr. Lee, whose grandfather first came to the United States during the period of Chinese exclusion, whose daughter migrated here through marriage to a Chinese American descendant of early twentieth-century Chinese immigrants, and whose own immigration was made possible through the family preference categories established by the Hart-Celler Act, the majority of my Cantonese-speaking senior migrant interviewees' lives have been intertwined with American immigration policy since at least the early twentieth century.

In this way, the primarily Cantonese-speaking elderly Chinese I focus on here share certain similarities with previously examined groups of Chinese American seniors who dominate earlier scholarly portrayals of American Chinatowns and their low-income residents. Work on San Francisco and New York Chinatown enclave areas has long included accounts of aging Chinese American seniors, highlighting in particular the bachelor societies that predominated during the first half of the twentieth century and continued to influence Chinatowns' social and economic needs well into the latter half of that century.[30] Most relevant is Charlotte Ikels's ethnography, *Aging and Adaptation: Chinese in Hong Kong and the United States*.[31] Focused on Cantonese- and Taishanese-speaking seniors, Ikels's work provides an important portrait of the comparative challenges elders faced during the late 1970s and early 1980s in both Hong Kong and Boston. Certain community attributes that she examines continue to resonate with experiences of recent senior migrants in Boston's Chinatown today, including the presence of a handful of particularly active women who serve as helpers to less fortunate community residents, as I discuss in Chapter 3. However, more noticeable are the differences. Over the past thirty years, similar to the increasing numbers of Chinese immigrants throughout the United States, Boston's Chinese community has changed substantially—not only demographically but also in terms of primary areas of residence in suburban areas, increased access to resources and support services, and decreased levels of racial tension, creating an entirely different context of reception for Chinese seniors who have arrived in the area since 1990 than for the elderly whom Ikels studied.

Also noteworthy is how substantially life in the People's Republic of China (PRC) has changed over the past three decades. This is true for all PRC citizens but especially for contemporary seniors who lived through the devastation wrought by the Japanese in China and Hong Kong during World War II, the establishment of the PRC in 1949, the resultant social and political turmoil during the Maoist years, and China's return to a capitalist- and consumption-oriented society at the end of the twentieth century. These rapid political changes, and their accompanying social effects, have created a radically different platform for Chinese seniors' experiences today, whether in China or the United States, as compared to the late 1970s. New scholarly work on Asian American senior citizens has begun to reflect the recent demographic shift in Chinese American elderly and registers growing attention to seniors' experiences of mental health and well-being, particularly in terms of their caregiving needs, their roles as grandparent caregivers, and their experiences of dementia.[32] Mostly quantitative, however, many studies obscure much of the diversity of contemporary Chinese senior migrant experience and often combine survey data of Chinese Americans with Asian American seniors more generally. One notable exception is Zibin Guo's *Ginseng and Aspirin: Health Care Alternatives for Aging Chinese in New York*.[33] Guo's ethnography documents how Chinese American elderly use both Western and Chinese medicine as they age. Focused on Chinese American seniors who have been long-term residents in New York City as well as more recent immigrant arrivals, Guo's careful attention to how seniors navigate their health care needs in Flushing, New York's Asian ethnic enclave, speaks to the complex cultural negotiations that accompany aging individuals' attempts to access and reconcile different health care options in new and diverse residential environments—a theme that resonates with the growing literature on retirement migration worldwide.

AGING AND GLOBALIZATION

This demographic shift in Chinese American seniors over the past few decades, facilitated by U.S. immigration policy changes in latter decades of the twentieth century, is also a direct result of the increasing engagement of contemporary Chinese seniors in global mobility processes. In this way, Chinese seniors' migration patterns reflect their embeddedness in national and global power structures that are changing the possibilities for their life outcomes all over the globe—not just in China. Across East Asia, seniors are increasingly activating new strategies of support for their older age.[34] Whereas European countries, the United States, and Canada have all developed (more or less) robust social welfare infrastructures to support senior citizens, East Asian countries have generally depended significantly more on family than on institutional support for their elderly. As nations across the globe, including those in East Asia, have increasingly experienced the withdrawal of the state from many forms of public welfare support over the past decades, seniors' living situations in China, Korea, and Japan have been rendered even more precarious through the apparent breakdown of traditional family support.

In China, the problem is particularly acute: one-fifth of the world's older population lives in China. Between 2011 and 2014, the Chinese population aged sixty and over grew from 185 million to 212 million. By 2050, the elderly are expected to comprise close to a third of China's overall population.[35] Moreover, the transition to a demographically aging society has been particularly compressed in China, with life expectancy at birth increasing from about forty-five years to seventy years over a few decades.[36] China's much-noted one-child policy has exacerbated this transition and contributed to growing fears about the social and economic feasibility of supporting such large numbers of senior citizens.[37] As a result, providing for China's elderly is an almost impossible task, although the Chinese state has taken concrete steps to address the pressing problem of senior support through improving pensions, increasing access to health care, and even passing legislation mandating that adult children provide emotional and financial support to their aging parents. Nevertheless, particularly in rural areas, these resources are still inadequate, with one in four seniors living in poverty.[38] The Chinese state has been working to fill this gap between what seniors need and what support is provided through the promotion of "active aging" and in recent years has created thousands of "old-age universities" for retirees aged sixty and older.[39] In this way, the PRC is acting as a leader on the global stage in promoting opportunities for seniors to live healthy, active lives. At the same time, this approach to supporting seniors' well-being—echoing globally fashionable trends for "successful aging"—is criticized among many scholars because it places the burden of senior citizens' well-being on seniors themselves by encouraging them to adopt a Westernized ideal of personhood and be independently responsible for keeping themselves healthy, well fed, and engaged in socially meaningful activities whether or not they receive necessary financial support from the state or from their family.[40]

Focusing on these and other concerns, much of the literature on globalization and aging emphasizes the negative effects of globalization on seniors' lives, particularly in terms of the marginalization and poverty that can result from the inadequate expansion of services for the elderly and in relationship to rapid modernization processes that have undermined traditional nonstate—particularly family-based—forms of elder support.[41] These processes can propel seniors to engage in global mobility flows when aging individuals seek to follow adult children who have migrated before them to new locations where they may not have friends, networks, or other forms of community support they would have experienced had they stayed in their country of origin.[42] In other cases, seniors' lives are most affected by their inability to participate in the same possibilities for global mobility afforded to their adult children. While sometimes this inability is an individual problem related to aging and its accompanying physical limitations, more often seniors are unable to join families abroad because of immigration restrictions that prevent families from migrating together as intact units.

In a recent ethnography, anthropologist Kristin Yarris trains her ethnographic lens on grandmothers left behind in Nicaragua to take care of grandchildren when their adult children migrate abroad.[43] Yarris examines the roles of these seniors as central actors in transnational caregiving chains, which are reliant on grandparents' daily caregiving work of the children parents must leave behind—either because as low-wage workers in first world countries they cannot afford child care, or because the states where they've found work to sustain their families at home do not allow for children to travel together with parent laborers.[44] Yarris recounts how Nicaraguan grandparents justify the emotional and physical hardships they endure through cultural expressions of "solidarity and sacrifice," and in that way, she deflects attention away from the actual disempowerment that results from their embeddedness in global power structures to instead emphasize the potential for seniors' agency and self-definition.[45] Yarris thus effectively harnesses the ambiguities inherent in migration processes for individuals and families—ambiguities that provide powerful challenges to traditional debates about power and agency in migrant family life.

Yarris's work is one of a number of recent publications that reflect a move away from the primarily negative portrayals of senior migrants as disempowered by global power structures stacked unfavorably against them. Instead, scholarly works situated at the intersection of aging and transnationalism increasingly highlight the nuanced ways in which seniors work to negotiate favorable life circumstances despite the many challenges they encounter through social, political, and economic constraints that affect their lives in complex ways.[46] Scholars note that seniors, like the grandparents Yarris studied, are often involved in transnational practices even when they aren't themselves migrants: they grandparent from afar and may depend on remittances sent by adult children or family members living in other countries. Sometimes, though, it's those in the older generation rather than their adult children who are the primary movers, as individuals cross borders in search of affordable health care or to stay in touch with friends and family left behind in their countries of origin.[47] Seniors also engage in retirement migration, in which they relocate abroad in order to ensure support as they age—a process that many scholars differentiate from what social geographers call "lifestyle migration," which instead indexes younger adult migrants' quests to experience new forms of self-realization abroad.[48]

Most often, scholars characterize retirement migration as taking three main forms: assistance migration, return migration, and amenity migration. *Assistance migration* describes the migratory patterns of the old-old who move in order to receive needed care as they become increasingly infirm. In most cases, these patterns involve migrating to be near adult children who live elsewhere, and it's this model that has dominated most scholars' past investigations of Chinese senior migration to North America.[49] *Return migration* references seniors' decisions to relocate following retirement to a place of previous residence, often where they lived as younger adults. In these cases, individuals experience multiple moves and cultural negotiations throughout their lives—first to pursue education, work, marriage, or other opportunities abroad and then later as seniors adjusting to new lifestyles in their previous place of residence, where they may or may not be welcome after decades of living elsewhere. This pattern is newly emergent in the literature on Asian senior migrants. For example, Taiwanese-born seniors who spent their working adult lives as professionals in the United States have begun returning to Taiwan following retirement in the United States.[50] *Amenity migration* focuses on the process of moving to a new location to gain access to beneficial resources and lifestyles—most commonly characterized by the snowbelt-to-sunbelt migration that takes place internationally, when seniors retire from the global North to the global South. Amenity migration is facilitated by an increasingly wide-ranging network of services supporting senior citizens' travel, exploration, and retirement abroad, thus creating possibilities for senior migrants to negotiate new livelihoods and realize lifelong dreams as older adults—and blurring lines with the migration patterns of younger, well-off adults whose participation in global mobility flows is motivated through the real and imagined benefits of alternative lifestyles possible elsewhere. While these advantages are most readily accessible to well-off individuals, amenity migration is increasingly practiced by Northern European and American senior citizens who cannot afford to retire in their home countries and thus migrate to a sunbelt location as a means of both stretching meager resources through access to lower-cost housing and medical care and experiencing new forms of community engagement and active retirement lifestyles available through cultural interaction and volunteer opportunities.[51] Similarly, the retirement migration of Chinese seniors to the United States demonstrates a strategic navigation of similar lifestyle concerns for individuals without significant financial capital.

Throughout the rest of this book, I engage with these newly complex views about the global mobility pathways and migration experiences for aging adults. My account takes a granular approach to examining the lives of Chinese-born recent senior migrants like Mr. Lee, with whose story I opened this discussion on the increasing global mobility of Chinese seniors and the many contradictions that we see epitomized through the life experiences of Chinese American senior citizens like him. Reflecting on his presence in the United States one hundred years after his grandfather's humiliation as a laundry worker in San Francisco, Mr. Lee explained his primary motivation for migrating for the first time in his seventies to a land he had never visited earlier in his life and had been prohibited by his family to visit:

> In the past one hundred years, America has changed a lot. It has changed to a point where the development of science is amazing, the economy is doing well, and it is the most democratic country in the world. . . . I wanted to know if [this] was true. I had to experience [America] for myself. I had to see it myself. . . . I wanted to see America.

Encompassing aspects of all three patterns of global movement described by previous scholars, the retirement migration of many of my interviewees in and around Boston's Chinatown was fueled as much by goals to strategize for support in old age as it was by dreams of forging new pathways to long-desired ways of life. Hence, I describe the complex historical, social, and economic conditions in China and the United States that form the backdrop to Chinese seniors' moves in the latter decades of their lives and, in so doing, highlight the depth of integration and engagement many Chinese retirees experience after moving—despite their relatively short terms of residency and their social marginality. In this way, low-income migrants whom we might otherwise assume to be relatively powerless take on roles as both active contributors to their communities and innovators of new ways of belonging to the American communities in which they reside, even as they retain strong feelings of pride in being ethnically Chinese. This approach coincides with that of a handful of scholars who focus on the mundane experiences of older migrants as a lens to understanding subjective processes involved with aging in new locations and reconfiguration of identities within transnational processes.[52] Like them, I highlight the interactive nature of questions around aging migrants' vulnerability, well-being, identity, and agency by moving away from standard senior migrant typologies to a more holistic account foregrounding Chinese-born seniors' engagement with global mobility processes and their accompanying transformative possibilities. To do this, I focus on the globalization of retirement as a reframing lens to highlight aging migrants' engagement with power structures at multiple levels and, in so doing, demonstrate the contingent and transformative nature of social processes in which vulnerability and well-being are intertwined, agency and disempowerment sit side by side, and globally circulating ideas about idealized retirement lifestyles are influential in enabling our understanding of the many possibilities for Chinese-born senior migrants to connect Chinese and American ways of being and belonging in the world.

STUDY LOCATION AND DEMOGRAPHICS

Most research on Chinese migration to the United States has focused on California and, more recently, New York, but the Chinese American community in the greater Boston area, including Boston's downtown Chinatown and Quincy and other nearby areas, is worthy of attention because of its long history and its current rapid growth. In 2015, the greater Boston metropolitan area was the fourth largest area of residency for Chinese immigrants in the country.⁵³ Massachusetts is an attractive destination for Chinese-born immigrants because of long-standing family connections to the area and well-developed Chinese-language service infrastructures easily accessible by public transportation from both urban and suburban areas physically removed from Boston's downtown Chinatown location. The many well-known institutions of higher education in the area also appeal to both Chinese immigrants and visitors, evidenced in part by the new nonstop airline connections established between Boston and Beijing, Boston and Shanghai, and Boston and Hong Kong by multiple airlines.

Recent Chinese migrants to Boston reflect similar demographic shifts in Chinese immigrants across the United States that are oriented toward professional, well-educated Mandarin speakers. Nonetheless, many new immigrants rely on the well-developed service and commercial infrastructure of Boston's Chinatown, the fifth largest in the country and a thriving neighborhood in Boston's downtown that has been continuously settled by Chinese immigrants since the 1880s.⁵⁴ The original two-block location offered boardinghouses, entertainment venues, and stores serving Chinese laundrymen who were scattered across the region in the late nineteenth and early twentieth centuries and congregated together on their days off. By World War II, Boston's Chinatown had grown and transitioned to a family-oriented residential area with significant business interests and strong social supports, primarily in the form of traditional Chinese immigrant surname and regional associations but also through non-Chinese institutions such as the YMCA. Over the past sixty years, Boston's Chinatown has faced substantial challenges. In the 1950s and 1960s, the neighborhood was almost destroyed when two major highway projects linking downtown Boston to suburban communities were routed directly through the area. Current residents worry about gentrification and being priced out of the area. However, unlike many other midsized Chinatowns that were demolished or lost their residential populations through a combination of urban renewal and residents' relocation to suburban areas during the second half of the twentieth century, Boston's Chinatown has survived because of the activist efforts of a postwar generation of Chinese Americans and the creation of several hundred units of subsidized housing that continue to form the core of Chinatown's residential community. Today, Boston's Chinatown has over nine thousand residents—of whom 47 percent are of Asian descent.⁵⁵

Quincy's history as an ethnic enclave is considerably more recent. Chinese immigrant families began moving to the city in the early 1980s, following the extension of a subway line directly linking Quincy to Boston's Chinatown. Affordable to immigrants priced out of more upscale suburban locations, Quincy, on the South Shore of Massachusetts Bay, is just a twenty-minute subway ride from Chinatown—with its continuing rich infrastructure of Chinese-language services, restaurants, and markets. Quincy's Asian American population has grown so rapidly that it has taken the city by complete surprise. In 1980, only 750 of Quincy's 85,000 residents were ethnically Asian. In this way, it seems to mimic the exponential growth of suburban Chinese locations in other parts of the country.[56] Yet unlike Mandarin-dominated suburban areas like Monterey Park in California, Quincy's population has remained substantially more working class and Cantonese oriented through its direct connections to Boston's downtown Chinatown—a status Tom Chung has called a "one step up enclave," since Quincy's residents differ demographically from those in Chinatown and from Asian Americans in substantially wealthier suburban areas.[57] Today, Quincy has the highest per capita Asian population in Massachusetts, with more than 22,000 residents, comprising at least a quarter (and probably more) of the city's population.[58] It is a significant ethnic crossing, with newly established Chinese-language service organizations as well as Asian-owned restaurants and businesses that attract Asian American clientele from suburban areas all along the South Shore.[59] In Quincy, as in Boston's downtown Chinatown, the density of Chinese residents and services creates important infrastructures and networks that support seniors' lifestyles and daily needs.

While both Chinatown and Quincy are significant hubs for Chinese migrants throughout the greater Boston area, Chinese immigrants and their Chinese American families are spread out across urban and suburban locations in and around greater Boston. In general, however, adult migrants who came to the United States from China to pursue graduate studies and professional careers have settled in many of the wealthier suburban areas north and west of the city, where there are fewer direct transportation links to Boston's downtown Chinatown. The senior migrants who come to join their Chinese American families in these suburban residential locations tend to speak Mandarin but not Cantonese and are more likely to have been professionals themselves in urban areas of China. They most often migrate specifically to help with child care for their American-born grandchildren and may be fully occupied with that task, particularly if their grandchildren are young. On weekends, when their adult children are home from work, many of these seniors try to get out of their relatively isolated living situations to socialize with others—as participants in the Harvard Chinatown ESL programs, by visiting Chinatown restaurants with friends, or through engagement with suburban groups of Mandarin-speaking seniors. In contrast, immigrants who settle in Boston's Chinatown or in urban areas easily accessible by public transportation to Chinatown, including Quincy and increasingly Malden, are likely to be lower income, Cantonese speaking, and have long-standing familial connections to the area, with the kinds of complex family migration histories epitomized by Mr. Lee.

My focus on Cantonese-speaking seniors in this ethnography has been a deliberate methodological choice. It trains attention on the continuing socioeconomic diversity of contemporary Chinese Americans who, like Asian Americans overall, "are overrepresented at both ends of the educational and socioeconomic spectrum of privilege and poverty."[60] It also allows me to trace the migratory trajectories unique to this regional group—characterized by long-standing engagement in diasporic pathways beyond territorial China, dense networks of family and friends in North America, and generally lower levels of income and educational attainment when compared with non-Cantonese-speaking (that is, Mandarin speaking) seniors. However, these groups are not mutually distinct, and throughout my research, I encountered individuals who straddled both or interacted with each other despite their different backgrounds. Moreover, many seniors, even those residing in suburban locations, travel monthly, weekly, or even daily to Boston's Chinatown or to Quincy for shopping, dining, working, exercising, socializing, or seeking resource help. As a result, although Chinatown and Quincy were the primary sites of my field research and the majority of my interviewees spoke Cantonese, I draw on observations and conversations with a diverse range of Chinese speakers (most often Mandarin or Taishanese) who make up the larger Chinese American senior community in and around Boston. The Chinese residential communities of Chinatown and Quincy have important differences—most obviously, that Chinatown is recognized as a distinctive neighborhood in downtown Boston, while Quincy is a separate city without a clearly bounded geographical area known as "Chinatown." Nevertheless, both locations are desirable for Chinese seniors—as residents and also as regular visitors from suburban locations—because of the significant networks that support their lifestyles and daily needs. They were ideal locations for me to learn about recent Chinese senior migrants' life experiences through my interactions with migrants and area leaders at senior community centers, housing estates, and social service organizations.

DATA COLLECTION: TIMELINE AND FOCUS

The research that directly informs this book took place over three distinct periods of data collection between 2009 and 2012, totaling about sixteen months of participant observation and interview-based research in the greater Boston area. Yet none of this research would have been possible without the experiences I had and relationships I developed over the three years from 2007 to 2009 when I was a volunteer ESL tutor in Chinatown before beginning my data collection. When it came time to stop my volunteer teaching and focus instead on data collection, volunteers from among my English-language learners made up my first group of interview subjects. After learning about my research goals, seven individuals were willing to meet with me outside class for a series of five focus group interviews of up to an hour each, in which they responded conversationally to a different theme each week. Because the group members trusted me and were already familiar with each other, those first interviews were filled with banter and personal commentary that were unique within my data collection process—and added substantially to what I learned through subsequent data collected through both individual interviews and participant observation over the next few years.

Even more important, my long-term interactions through my volunteer teaching allowed me to develop strong personal relationships with support staff at Chinatown-area community service locations who were then willing to introduce me to additional contacts that made my research possible. Some of these contacts led to interviews that I would never have been able to collect otherwise without the mutual connection, and they diversified my interview sample; others provided the references I needed to access new locations for participant observation. As I traveled across different locations in Boston and Quincy over the next few years, these previous interactions continued to pave the way for my encounters with new groups of Chinese-born seniors. For example, in 2012, when I walked for the first time through the door of a community center for Chinese senior citizens in Quincy and introduced myself, the center's director surprised me by saying, "Oh! You're Nicole!" To my delight, she had already heard about me from one of her friends and, as a result, was happy to approve my visits to her center over the following weeks.

In all, I completed formal interviews with over fifty interviewees and compiled over two hundred single-spaced pages of notes from my many hours of participant observation in different locations of Chinese senior life in and around Boston. This data collection consistently focused on Chinese seniors who had immigrated to the United States after 1990 at the age of sixty or older—that is, following their age of retirement in the PRC.

The first period of data collection, beginning in summer 2009 and lasting through most of the winter into 2010, allowed me to explore seniors' motivations for their later-life migration trajectories, along with how their experiences relocating to the United States were influenced by their earlier life experiences in China. Data collection during this period included focus group interviews and individual life story interviews averaging two hours each. During fall 2009, I also spent one day each weekend at the Chinatown ESL and citizenship classes run by Harvard students through the Phillips Brooks House Association, where I was able to both recruit additional interviewees and learn firsthand about how older migrants experienced the citizenship exam process. The second stage of research took place from May to September 2011 while I sought to understand how Chinese senior migrants—whether or not they lived in Boston's downtown Chinatown—interacted with the specific support networks, job opportunities, and friendship circles available to them. My data collection included individual interviews with senior migrants recruited through my Chinatown and Harvard contacts, individual interviews with support professionals across a range of Chinatown service organizations, and participant observation at gatherings of Chinese seniors at different locations, including a subsidized senior housing complex recreational space, several NGOs and local community organizations, and the ballroom dancing club, which met two or three times each week in Chinatown and had additional meetings at other Boston-area locations on other weekday afternoons. My final period of research, during summer 2012, built off what I had learned during the previous two stages. I investigated Chinese senior migrants' experiences in Quincy to trace interconnections between the social networks and residents in Quincy and Boston's downtown Chinatown. In Quincy, all my data collection was through participant observation. Over four months, I spent one day each week at two senior centers (one primarily Chinese and one primarily white but with some activities for Chinese seniors) and two subsidized public housing complexes, each with 50 percent Chinese senior residency. I also continued to attend the ballroom club's weekly meeting in Quincy.

BEING AN OUTSIDER IN BOSTON'S CHINATOWN

When I began interacting with Chinese senior migrants in Chinatown, I was unsure as to how I would be received. Indeed, as a volunteer ESL instructor, I was acutely aware of my status as a white, non–Asian American individual connected to a prestigious university that has not always been on good terms with its neighbors in surrounding communities. Despite having been a resident of the greater Boston area since 1993, I was no less of an outsider in Boston's Chinatown than I had been in Hong Kong in 2000, when one local scholar overtly dismissed my chances of conducting fieldwork in the low-income, red-light district that was also home to a large population of recent immigrants from mainland China, telling me that I would "stick out like a sore thumb." Yet that fieldwork was ultimately successful, and so I was no stranger to being both an outsider and a curious oddity as a white person who can speak and understand Cantonese. As I had learned from my Hong Kong–based research and experienced again while interacting with Chinese senior migrants in the Boston area, many people were excited to have the opportunity to talk with me because their limited English-language skills usually prevented communication with non-Chinese individuals.

Of course, people in Chinatown and Quincy expressed surprise at my initial presence—sometimes ignoring me, sometimes politely but superficially responding to my conversational overtures. But just as had been the case in Hong Kong, my consistent engagement over time resulted in significant relationships of trust, sometimes even with individuals who had been highly skeptical of my initial presence. For example, one staff member at a community center who had not interacted at all with me over my first few months of weekly visits took to joking with me by substituting Cantonese words I had used with homonyms that altered questions I had asked—resulting in funny, sometimes shocking, but always good-natured twists of meaning. In another case, a gruff, wheelchair-bound elderly man watched me conversing with others for weeks before finally asking me in Cantonese where I was from. When I replied that I am American, he asked where I grew up, to which I answered "Texas." Not content with that response, he asked in detail about my parents' ethnic backgrounds, suggesting that they must be Chinese, which is not the case. After a few minutes of continued puzzling, he finally blurted out: "I know! You're from Taiwan!" In other words, he heard me say that I was not Chinese, and yet he couldn't understand how I couldn't actually be Chinese because of my ability to converse in Cantonese. Thus, he lit on an explanation that made categorical sense to him within the kinds of Chineseness that he could conceptualize. While these encounters and others indicated that my interviewees were always aware of my difference from them, they also demonstrated the substantial ways in which ties could form across and despite that difference through shared interactions over days, weeks, months, and years.

Throughout this time, I was consistently grateful for the generosity of everyone I interacted with, particularly through their willingness to spend the time to talk with me and answer the many questions that I asked them. In 2009 my Cantonese language skills were far rustier than they had been for my previous fieldwork in Hong Kong. My Mandarin language skills were even rustier still. Yet it turned out that my situation fit in better than I had expected to the community settings where I spent time with Chinese senior migrants in Chinatown and Quincy. In part, this was because almost all group-based interactions for older immigrants took place in a patchwork of different Chinese dialects. While Cantonese was the communal language most often spoken in institutional settings in Chinatown, there were always a handful of Chinese seniors who could not speak Cantonese. When someone in a group couldn't understand Cantonese, others would act as informal interpreters to explain what was being said to those who needed that information in another dialect. Many native Cantonese speakers couldn't speak Taishanese but could understand it, so it was also common for a senior to talk in Taishanese with a service worker, who would then answer in Cantonese. In other words, there was an everyday improvisational quality around dialect use and mutual communication that seniors were already accustomed to that substantially aided my interactions with them—primarily in Cantonese, less often in Mandarin, and sometimes requiring informal interpretation with Taishanese, Hakka, and Mandarin speakers with heavy regional accents.

Other aspects of my interviewees' lives as older immigrants also aided their acceptance of me. Most of them had tried hard to learn English, without much success, and were exceedingly aware of the challenges associated with learning a new language. As a result, they were particularly appreciative of my efforts, mistakes and all, to communicate with them. Moreover, many of them had American-born grandchildren, rendering them familiar with my accent. To compensate for any potential misunderstandings on my part, I was always careful to ask for clarification if I thought I did not fully understand conversations during my participant observation. I also hired students fluent in Cantonese and Taishanese to transcribe my recorded interviews. For the most part, though, my interviewees were simply relieved to be able to communicate directly with me and often asked me for help reading mail or other notices they had received or wondered if I could clarify questions they had about American life. They were also of course endlessly curious about how and why I had learned Cantonese in the first place.

Because I interacted with so many different individuals over the period of my research, I have made sure that only those who wanted to share their stories have information included in this ethnography. However, it's important to point out that many individuals were in fact quite eager to have their immigration stories known. Levels of frustration with adaptation to life in the United States were particularly high for some older individuals. When I first introduced myself at one of the Harvard program ESL classrooms and explained in Cantonese my goal to learn enough about seniors' experiences to write a book about what it's like to immigrate as an older Chinese person to the United States, one woman stood up and shouted in reply, "It's really hard!!" Her feelings were echoed by many others I encountered, most memorably by one man who responded to his ESL teacher's innocent query about whether anyone had questions about the lesson they had just learned by jumping up from his seat and shouting: "Problems? Yes, I have problems!" (C. *yauh mahntaih*; M. *you wenti*). In both Cantonese and Mandarin, *question* and *problem* are the same word (C. *mahntaih*; M. *wenti*). This recent immigrant seized on that double meaning to express his intense frustration about the difficulties and uncertainties that he was experiencing during his first months living in the United States.

ABOUT THIS BOOK: ITS ARGUMENTS AND CHAPTER SUMMARIES

In writing this ethnography, one of my goals has been to place the life experiences of senior migrants at the forefront of my analysis as a means of sidestepping what has historically been a dichotomous portrayal of migrants that situates immigrants as belonging either "here" (in their new country of residence) or "there" (the country from which they emigrated). Such portrayals are stubbornly persistent, particularly in popular debates on the subject, despite the fact that this often false divide has been rendered obsolete by academic work on transnationalism—a theoretical framework that highlights the multiple and overlapping ways that immigrants remain engaged socially, politically, and economically with their countries of origin even while living in new locations.[61] As scholars have demonstrated, transnational ties continue throughout decades, influencing the lives of immigrants and their children—sometimes even over generations of settlement in new locations.[62] Similarly, the vast literature on diaspora, with its emphasis on hybrid cultural forms, demonstrates the complexity of experiences surrounding identity and selfhood for migrants but even nonmigrants, especially in postcolonial locations where multiple and overlapping historical power structures continue to shape contemporary processes of identity construction.[63]

Scholars of Chinese migration have contributed in important ways to these academic conversations about how migrants experience, contribute to, and are affected by their various entanglements with multiple cultural forms and power structures. Chinese American historians in particular have been at the forefront of explaining the many ways that dense transnational ties between China and the United States were constructed and maintained throughout the twentieth century despite the hostility to Chinese immigrants enforced through policies of exclusion.[64] These ties not only shaped the development of Chinese American communities over the course of the twentieth century but also formed the backbone of my interviewees' contemporary migration trajectories, which would not have been possible without them—made clear through stories relating senior migrants' first interactions with the United States to their childhoods in early twentieth-century China. As echoed through seniors' stories, these historical accounts of Chinese and American transnationalism are important because they highlight how the United States has been a site of intensive social and political engagement for Chinese immigrants for well over a hundred years—a view seemingly in contrast to the literature on Chinese overseas, which instead acknowledges long-standing processes of Chinese emigration while simultaneously reinforcing emigrants' continued sense of orientation to China rather than to the locations Chinese emigrants reside abroad, including the United States.[65]

Beginning with the trope of the Chinese sojourner, historians and anthropologists writing about Chinese emigrants have stressed that migrants' sense of belonging in the world remains strongly tied to territorial China, no matter how long (or where) Chinese migrants reside beyond the borders of China's sovereign territory.[66] This sense of belonging has its basis in a cultural understanding of rootedness in and to China—an emic-centered perspective of inescapable attachment made visible through biological ties and economic and cultural connections to a migrant's place of origin.[67] Ties to China have also been reinforced and accentuated through the long history of racial hostility to Chinese abroad, including the history of Chinese exclusion in the United States but also in Southeast Asia, Latin America, and elsewhere.[68] Moreover, as increasing numbers of Chinese have left China for work or study destinations abroad over past decades, these ties have been further championed through the PRC government's portrayal of Chinese abroad as "heroes" of national development through the economic and cultural capital that they accumulate abroad and contribute to China's modernization efforts.[69] Recent ethnographies of Chinese migration demonstrate the continued salience of this point of view: whether describing Chinese entrepreneurs who travel to far-flung regions of the world to engage in business practices aimed at increasing their social mobility within China, or Chinese only children who move to urban areas in English-speaking regions of the world, Chinese migrants' primary sense of belonging is depicted as being in China and to China—just as the economic and cultural capital that Chinese migrants seek abroad is meant to help increase their social status as modern, cosmopolitan (yet) Chinese subjects who act in ever greater numbers and increasing sophistication on a global stage.[70]

Moreover, this literature on Chinese overseas underlines the central role played by the Chinese state as a moral and legal authority in defining the possibilities of belonging for Chinese migrants, no matter where in the world they live, and even as some Chinese citizens seek through migratory pathways to remove themselves from direct control of that state.[71] This perspective further obscures the fact that Chinese emigrants may have their own interests in establishing new forms of roots (and homes) abroad, as it ties "Chineseness" to nationalism through assuming that the various forms of capital (social, economic, cultural) that migrants accrue through their sojourns beyond China's sovereign territory will nonetheless contribute primarily to the continued development and modernization of contemporary China as a sovereign territory. Importantly, this view stands in contrast to Chinese Americans' own voices about their important history and long roots in the United States, where they have developed their own senses of belonging and attachment despite decades of racial hostility and social marginalization—beginning with overt hostility in the late nineteenth century and continuing today through the perpetuation of the "model minority" stereotype that both obscures the economic and cultural diversity of contemporary Chinese Americans and also prevents attention to the myriad ways Chinese Americans remain absent from mainstream American culture and discourse.[72]

The stories of my senior migrant interviewees disrupt these singular views of Chinese nationalism and territorial belonging. As recent migrants who have spent the majority of their adult lives—up to seven or more decades—in China before moving to the United States to live out their final years, my interviewees are situated at the crossroads of Chinese immigrant and Chinese American experiences, and in this way they embody many of the ambiguities and paradoxes that make migration such a compellingly humanistic topic of study. They are older individuals who in many cases have waited their whole lives to migrate to the United States to rejoin family yet often experience unanticipated family conflict when they finally do migrate. They are retirees who live at the economic and social margins of American society and yet nonetheless find significant opportunities to achieve meaningful retired lifestyles in a new country. They are members of a diaspora spanning vast regional and ideological differences that create significant fault lines among Chinese people today yet, perhaps unexpectedly, achieve personal well-being through social engagement with the diverse members of this community. As I argue over the next six chapters, these seniors' stories demonstrate the significance of age as a mediating factor that is fundamentally important for considering how migration is experienced and, in this way, provide an opportunity to rethink assumptions about seemingly familiar concepts—of migration, assimilation, identity, and so on. In particular, I discuss how these seniors' stories highlight the many possibilities for mutual engagement that connect Chinese and American ways of being and belonging in the world— what I refer to throughout this book as "affinity"—and in this process blur the boundaries of categories that all too often are reified in ways that obscure their very ambiguities. In other words, viewing processes of migration through the lens of these migrants' temporal positioning as seniors creates the opportunity to glimpse the seemingly unexpected alliances and senses of affiliation that allow for Chinese-born senior migrants' emotional attachment to and social and political engagement in the United States (that is, their affinity with it), even as they also retain a central pride in being Chinese and, when possible, continue to make return visits to China to visit family and friends there until they are physically unable to do so.

Chapters 2 through 4 foreground the complexity of recent Chinese-born senior migrants' motivations for migration as older adults to a new and often challenging environment that nonetheless presents important opportunities for living out culturally familiar Chinese lifestyles that are increasingly elusive for these same seniors in China today. In this way, seniors' migration stories highlight forms of affinity experienced by Chinese seniors in the United States —through family, nation, and community—demonstrating that, paradoxically, uprooting from territorial China is intimately connected with their ability to achieve "Chinese" ways of being in the world they desire as older adults.

In Chapter 2, I document my interviewees' long family histories of emigration and diasporic lifeways to show how movement itself is crucial to seniors' own sense of emplacement in the world, since it's only by participating in contemporary migration trajectories that they can fulfill dreams harbored since childhood of moving to the United States and rejoining family from whom they have been separated for decades. In Chapter 3, I show how Chinese-born seniors' nostalgia for the egalitarian values they experienced growing up in socialist China paradoxically lead to a strong sense of national belonging in the United States. In contrast to their critiques of the contemporary social and moral landscape in China today, these seniors praise what they see as a positive moral and social environment in the United States more generally and recognize their sense of affinity with ideals of fairness, humanity, and justice that they associate with the U.S. government's treatment of its citizens. In Chapter 4, I discuss how for recently migrated Chinese seniors, the well-developed infrastructure of welfare support and other services available for senior citizens provides an important context of reception for retirement as a stage of life through which Chinese senior migrants can craft a range of retired lifestyles that they find meaningful.

Chapters 5 through 7 then focus on Chinese-born recent senior migrants' negotiation of networks of support, space, and community in the United States. These chapters thus move beyond the question of motivation for seniors' later-life migration trajectories to that of adjustment to and engagement with their new places of residency. Following decades of scholarship on the acculturation of immigrants, I use these chapters to document how Chinese-born senior migrants' cultural norms and ways of life are renegotiated as they adapt to living in the United States as Chinese Americans. Yet in a twist on how migration scholars (and others) often discuss this process as one primarily involved with the shedding of cultural practices as immigrants acculturate into mainstream society, my ethnography instead depicts how, for these migrants, integration into American ways of life entails first and foremost being culturally Chinese— through practicing Chinese family values, aging as if in place in China, and taking part in Chinese cultural performances with other members of the Chinese diaspora in and around Boston.

In Chapter 5, I examine seniors' paid and unpaid work as caregivers in the United States to show how they are involved with the renegotiation of culturally Chinese family systems of value to ensure their own care from Chinese American family as they grow old. In Chapter 6, I document how recent Chinese senior migrants develop a set of routines and rhythms of daily life in Boston's and Quincy's Chinatown areas that mimic patterns of life already familiar to them from mainland China, creating an unexpected sense of affinity with the physical spaces they inhabit that are crucial to aging well. Finally, in Chapter 7, I situate my Cantonese-speaking recent senior migrant interviewees within the larger

Chinese senior diaspora through charting their daily practice of ballroom and other forms of Chinese dancing in and around Boston, where these forms of cultural performance are instrumental in the development of community ties that facilitate seniors' navigation of the challenges that accompany their experiences on the social and economic margins of American life. Taken together, these three chapters demonstrate that recent Chinese-born senior migrants find significant ways to root themselves as Chinese in physical locations well beyond the borders of territorial China, and that, at the same time, the renegotiations of Chinese cultural ways of being that take place through these processes create important possibilities for seniors' affinity to the United States as their primary place of "belonging."

I conclude in Chapter 8 by placing the experiences of Cantonese-speaking recent senior migrants whom I examine here in conversation with the situations of other demographic groups of Chinese retirement migrants and senior migrants more broadly. In so doing, I refocus on the multiple pathways to and forms of retirement as an important lens for understanding seniors' engagement with global migratory processes during the latter decades of their lives.

2 WHY SENIORS MOVE

One hot summer day in 2009, I sat down with a group of Chinese senior migrants I had been teaching as a volunteer in Boston's Chinatown for over a year. We talked about why they had decided to migrate to the United States as older adults. The group of three women and four men was animated; everyone had gotten to know each other well in my class as they all struggled with learning English-language phrases that they hoped to use in their daily life in Boston. Their answers to my questions were serious yet punctuated by moments of banter as members of the group called each other out on comments they found insufficiently straightforward and teased each other in good humor on the hidden meanings implied within their personal reflections. Together, they mused on their motivations for migration to the United States as retirees:

> Man 1: I'll talk first. The reason that I immigrated to the U.S. is because my daughter applied for me to come. I was in Guangzhou, and I had retired. I didn't have any work to do. So she applied for us to come and help her look after her children.
>
> Woman 1: I'll talk now. Our immigration was very simple. My husband's sisters were here. His father and mother were here. So, it was a simple case of family reunion [C. *tuyhn jeuih*].
>
> Man 2: For my family, I came—the application reason—was for family reunion. Because my father, mother, younger brothers and sisters, are all in the U.S. So

they applied for me to come. Actually, I didn't say that I wanted to come or that I didn't want to come. It was just that they told me to apply.

Man 3: My daughter got married and she left [China and came to the United States]. Then my son, he studied and he left [for the United States]. So, in the end, . . . my wife and I moved here.

Woman 2: [I came] because my daughter helped me come. The second reason was that all of my family has been here [in the United States] for a long time—both grandfathers [and] my husband's family have all been here from before the time that I was born.

What tied all these migrants' trajectories together was family, although that family was more diverse than I had expected, including not only children and grandchildren but also grandparents, parents, siblings, aunts, uncles, cousins, and in-laws. For me, the fascination in these seemingly straightforward accounts was how matter-of-factly multigenerational they were. Even in cases in which seniors had been sponsored to come to the United States by their adult children, most of those seniors also talked about their own parents or grandparents or in-laws as migrants who had come to this country well before them, often in the early twentieth century. In these ways, their talk highlighted both the connections between their forebears' experiences and their own, as well as the ways in which their moves were just the latest step in a long-standing family diasporic tradition.

That seniors' motivations for migration were bound up with talk of family life in the United States is not surprising. The geographic mobility of older adults has often been tied to the central roles that families play in motivating and facilitating seniors' moves abroad. Most often, seniors' later-life migration has been linked with the caregiving needs of older adults left behind when adult children relocate to new locations—what scholars call "assistance migration." This migratory pattern, which highlights a one-way move from a senior's original homeland to a new residential location, is most commonly associated with the oldest and most infirm migrants. Increasingly, it also applies to those who are left without other desirable forms of old-age support after adult children move away.[1] Recently, however, scholars have drawn attention to more complex pathways for seniors' interactions with family abroad, including transnational social linkages and the "pendular migration" that describes older migrants' trajectories between two locations when family members' primary place of residence doesn't coincide with the areas where seniors can access welfare and other support networks to sustain them as they age.²

Previous scholars' investigations of Chinese senior migration to the United States generally foregrounded assumptions that seniors' migration fell into assistance patterns.³ Nevertheless, it is likely that more complex pathways will become increasingly common for a younger generation of Chinese retirees who, because of China's one-child policy, in effect until 2015, have only one adult child and thus only one set of grandchildren. When those family members settle elsewhere, seniors may be more likely to follow them for varying periods of time, or perhaps even permanently, than when families have multiple children dispersed over different residential areas. In contrast, my Cantonese-speaking interviewees had established their families well before China's one-child policy was implemented in 1979, and thus they were likely to have adult children in multiple locations—including China, North America, and elsewhere around the world. These long-standing family trajectories, which are intricately connected to a Cantonese diasporic tradition dating from the nineteenth century and earlier, influenced seniors' migrant pathways in this century. As I argue below, seniors' moves to the United States were not just a result of their desires to interact with family, although reuniting with family abroad was a primary concern. Instead, their migration as older adults was also a result of their families' long-standing engagement in regionally specific diasporic lifeways that created not only the possibility of moving abroad but also highlighted engagement in global migratory trajectories as pathways Cantonese seniors should take.

Younger adult migrants from China have three main pathways to immigrate to the United States: they can migrate as students, they may migrate as white-collar workers, or they can make use of well-developed smuggling networks to settle illegally here.⁴ Yet for older adults who are at or near the end of their working careers and were educated—if they were educated at all—in an era before computers and without English instruction, family reunification is their only real pathway to migration and settlement in the United States. In most cases, Chinese seniors are sponsored by their working adult children who need help with child care. However, many Cantonese seniors—like those quoted above—also have other family in the United States from whom they have often been separated for decades and come to the United States through sibling or parent sponsorship to rejoin them and other family members already here. While these family-centered migration pathways enable seniors to rejoin family from whom they have often been separated for decades, these pathways also create new forms of separation from adult children, grandchildren, siblings, and aged parents left behind in China. In this way, Cantonese seniors, many of whom have family histories rooted in emigrant trajectories dating to the mid- to late nineteenth century, continue to replicate the historical pattern of Chinese split-family life across the Pacific Ocean that characterized Chinese emigrant life in the United States until the late twentieth century—from the time that Chinese exclusion laws were first passed in the United States in 1882 until the PRC reform period began almost one hundred years later.

The family-centered migration goals emphasized by Chinese-born seniors today echo findings by historians of Chinese migration who have documented the use of migration as a strategy for family survival and success for Chinese from Southeast China for several centuries.[5] These familial strategies are particularly noticeable for my Cantonese interviewees, who all have well-developed networks of extended kin in the United States (and often other areas in the world) that can be traced back to Guangdong's long history as one of the primary sending areas of Chinese emigrants and laborers abroad.[6] One result of this long history is that many Cantonese seniors today talk about migration to the United States as a "way of life," rooted in a Cantonese regional culture of migration that influenced them as children and younger adults in China and that even today continues to reinforce their globally networked ties through relatives living in far-flung locations around the world.[7]

SOUTHEAST CHINA'S HISTORICAL CULTURE OF MIGRATION

Guangdong's long-standing emigration history means that most Cantonese senior migrants are rarely the first members of their families to go abroad. Here, I use the term *Cantonese* broadly to refer to all emigrants from Guangdong Province, including regions where dialects are similar to but different from standard Cantonese, the language spoken in Guangdong's capital of Guangzhou (formerly Canton) and Hong Kong. As anthropologist Genevieve Leung explains, individuals from these regions still commonly "call themselves 'Cantonese' speakers" even as they also qualify their own dialect (in this case, Taishanese) as a "rural form of Cantonese."[8]

The paths that led residents of Guangdong Province to begin immigrating to the United States in the nineteenth century were just one piece of a larger history of emigration from Southeast China to other world areas. Today, when one travels to Guangdong—to those areas from which the earliest generations of Chinese emigrants made their way to the American West, where they worked as miners, railroad laborers, and laundrymen—the contemporary manifestations of the Cantonese orientation of engagement with a wider world beyond China are ever present. Fueled by a resurgence of emigration in the early 1980s, Guangdong's main cities of out-migration (Taishan City and Jiangmen City, among others) are home to monuments celebrating famous migrant ancestors and richly decorated hotels aimed at attracting returning overseas visitors.[9] Remittances support well-endowed schools with impressively up-to-date sports facilities and modern suburbs with beautiful housing. Additional contributions from overseas Chinese have built emigration-oriented museums featuring wall-sized maps with lighted, spider-web-like pathways connecting Guangdong—placed at the center of each world map—to all other populated regions of the world. On these maps, cities such as Taishan and Jiangmen are the bright red hubs from which Chinese emigrants radiated outward, like spokes on a wheel, to North America, South America, Europe, Asia, Africa, and Australia.

Historian Philip Kuhn documents a variety of historical factors that contributed to the development of Southeast China as "homeland of emigration."[10] Beginning with maritime exploration in the fifteenth century, continuing with the silver trade in the sixteenth century, and exploding into a culture of mass emigration by the mid-nineteenth century, Kuhn charts how a combination of population growth, internal strife, and devastation wrought by the Opium War in the mid-1800s served to push Chinese from this region to search for economic opportunities elsewhere despite imperial edicts that until 1893 prohibited emigration abroad. The most common destination for emigrants was Southeast Asia, where there were already well-established communities of overseas Chinese by the early nineteenth century. However, the gold rushes in North America and Australia and the need for cheap labor following the abolition of the slave trade from Africa contributed to the development of new pathways of migration from coastal areas of Southeast China to the Americas (including California, Canada, the West Indies, and Peru) and Australia—pathways that became as well established as those to Southeast Asia. One particularly well-worn pathway developed between the Pearl River Delta area of Guangdong Province and San Francisco after gold was discovered in California in 1848. Between 1849 and 1852, over 26,000 Chinese migrated to California; in the 1852 census, 10 percent of California's population was recorded as Chinese.[11] As Kuhn writes, throughout Southeast China, "migration was built into a pattern of life, in which labor spread spatially as opportunities permitted," developing "corridors" of interaction connecting particular sending areas in China to particular localities abroad.[12]

At the center of these migration corridors was colonial Hong Kong, ceded to Britain by China in 1841 following China's defeat in the first Opium War. Situated at the mouth of the Pearl River Delta, Hong Kong was a tiny outpost of the British Empire that served as the hub through which people, goods, and money flowed in and out of Guangdong to overseas locations all over the world. By the early 1900s, Hong Kong was a flourishing financial center with strong economic ties to international locations as the center of Chinese overseas transnational and diasporic networks.[13] The paths that led from villages, towns, and cities in Guangdong to Hong Kong were well traveled. Before 1949, when the PRC was founded, few barriers separated Hong Kong from the rest of Guangdong. Entrance to and exit from the colony to the mainland was routine. Families and businesses straddled both sides of the border. One Chinese senior migrant, a woman in her seventies who lives in Boston's Chinatown, emphasized the sense of meaningful connection to Hong Kong for Guangdong residents when she rhetorically asked me, "Who in Guangdong doesn't have a relative in Hong Kong?"

The family migration stories of the Chinese seniors in Boston bear witness to this long history of Cantonese out-migration—beginning first in Hong Kong and then radiating outward to other world areas. All the Cantonese senior migrants I've interviewed in the United States, whether from rural Guangdong (primarily Taishan) or larger urban areas, such as Guangzhou, come from families with long histories of movement. Typically interviewees narrate family histories in which grandfathers, fathers, or uncles first left their villages to work in Hong Kong but later ended up in the Philippines, Southeast Asia, or North America. In some families—often those involved in entrepreneurial or business-related activities—family members moved back and forth between China and Hong Kong, particularly during the Japanese occupation of China during World War II. For some emigrants, Hong Kong was a destination in and of itself; for others, it was an accidental destination—either because would-be migrants didn't end up leaving for international ports or because they elected to stay in Hong Kong rather than return to their home towns and villages in Guangdong after movement across the border was restricted. When the border closed between Hong Kong and Guangdong following the establishment of the PRC, there were significant repercussions for the families that had moved freely back and forth over that border before that time; in many cases, families, were split, with fathers and some siblings in Hong Kong and others in China.[14]

The migration history of Mr. Cheung's family presents a typical trajectory.[15]

It thus also shares many common features with the stories other senior migrants have told me, including long separation of children from fathers who emigrated when they were young, the dispersal of family throughout different countries in Asia and North America, and split-family life across the Guangdong–Hong Kong border. As with many of my interviewees, Mr. Cheung arrived in the United States only a few years before I met him, when he and his wife had retired from their jobs in China and were sponsored by their adult daughter to help look after their American-born grandchildren. However, their daughter was not the first member of their family to migrate. The first member of Mr. Cheung's family to come to the United States was his grandfather. Mr. Cheung never met his grandfather and told me that he didn't know many details about his migration history. Following a not uncommon pattern, Mr. Cheung's grandfather left Taishan and, as Mr. Cheung narrated, "[He] didn't really take care of his family. He came to [the United States but] didn't remember his family. All I know is that he came here, so my father only had his uncle and his brothers [to rely on]."

Typical of many Taishanese families in the late nineteenth and early twentieth centuries, the migratory tradition continued with the next generation. Mr. Cheung told me, "My dad's older brother is in the Philippines. He's not in America. So he didn't follow his father." Mr. Cheung's father also left their village for Hong Kong, where he lived and worked for almost all of Mr. Cheung's life. Mr. Cheung spent his childhood and most of his adult years in Guangdong Province, just a few hours away from Hong Kong by boat, bus, or train; nonetheless, because of restrictions on travel back and forth across the border (and perhaps for other reasons, not explained to me), Mr. Cheung had few opportunities for personal interaction with his father. Although his father did visit him from time to time, he stayed throughout his life in Hong Kong, where he is now buried. Today, many of Mr. Cheung's family members continue the region's diasporic tradition. In addition to his uncle, who still lives in the Philippines, the rest of Mr. Cheung's family lives in Canada and the United States, except for one adult daughter who has stayed in Guangzhou because she prefers the lifestyle and work opportunities there.

For today's Cantonese seniors like Mr. Cheung, it's not just the currently visible reminders of the region's history of out-migration that have been influential in recent decisions to migrate to the United States. Knowledge about the possibilities of travel and employment abroad were an intimate part of their daily life experiences as children growing up in an emigrant sending region with well-developed pathways to the United States and Southeast Asia. Moreover, that historical sense of interconnection to a world beyond China was not limited to urban areas. Many emigrants, like Mr. Cheung's grandfather, father, and uncles, originated from rural areas—tiny pockets of populated clusters in the middle of largely agricultural areas—creating bridges between those seemingly remote locations and cities in North America.[16] For much of the past, Chinese husbands and sons were the primary migrants abroad, too often leaving behind wives and children.[17] Their return visits to their villages introduced new cultural influences, including English-language words, to rural Chinese village life. One woman, who came to Boston for the first time in her early sixties in the late 1990s, described her surprise to learn that some common words she had known and used since childhood in her rural Taishanese village were actually English. For example, she told me, she and the other village children played "ball outside." For Taishanese villagers, an awareness of the greater world was constantly present not just through these traces of life abroad—through language, stories, and knowledge brought back to the village by returned emigrants—but also through the continual absence of village men, including fathers, uncles, brothers, and cousins, who had left their villages to pursue their economic livelihoods elsewhere.[18]

Anthropologists and other scholars refer to emigrant sending areas like these rural Cantonese villages as having a "culture of migration," meaning that emigration is routinized, with well-developed knowledge about pathways to particular receiving destinations, making migration both desirable and the predominant way to ensure economic security for oneself and one's family.[19] In areas with strong cultures of migration, individual opportunities for migration are supported through both connections with family abroad as well as institutional networks that provide the knowledge and other social capital necessary to enable new migrants to successfully journey, settle, and find work abroad. This infrastructure also provides the financial resources necessary to continue migration pathways into the future, primarily through remittances that not only support family members left behind and expand village resources but also subsidize the cost of new migrants' passage abroad.

The ways in which a culture of migration influences adult opportunities for emigration are clear; less studied are the impacts on children who grow up in these areas. One anthropologist who has investigated this question in relation to children in Ghana is Cati Coe. She explores in depth how growing up in a Ghanaian culture of migration socializes children into a migration mind-set—developing children's sense of connection to the outside world and their desire to migrate abroad at a young age. She explains:

Children conceived of the world as differentiated by the level of material resources present but connected through transnational linkages between people—particularly through the flow of those material resources necessary for social reproduction and expected through relations of entrustment.... Children consistently expressed the desire to go abroad, primarily because "abroad" was associated with work that would pay well. Children viewed "abroad" as similar to towns and cities in Ghana with the availability of beautiful things, cars, piped water, electrical fixtures and schools with resources and, just as many children preferred the town to the village, so, too, did many children want to go abroad.[20]

Like these Ghanaian children, the Cantonese seniors I know in the greater Boston area were similarly influenced by the culture of migration in which they grew up—fueling their desires to join family members abroad and experience a modern world interconnected with their home villages. One migrant in her seventies, today a U.S. citizen, talked about this desire to emigrate to the United States that she had harbored since childhood. She told me, "From my mom's generation we already thought that the families who went to America were good. [My mom] wanted to go to America too.... So sometimes when [my sisters and I] get together [in Boston], I can't believe that we're all in America together."

Unlike the children Coe writes about, Cantonese seniors did not have the opportunity to migrate as teens or young adults. Nonetheless, the desire to go abroad did not fade with time. That these seniors could maintain such a strong sense of connection to the United States over the course of their lives would seem to stand in contrast to the restrictive immigration policies that limited Chinese entrance to the United States even well before contemporary Cantonese seniors were born—dating back to their grandparents' and great-grandparents' generations. In 1875, only twenty-six years after the first Chinese emigrants began arriving in California, the United States passed the first legislation prohibiting the immigration of Chinese. Beginning with the Page Act, which excluded single women on the basis that they were likely to become prostitutes, and continuing with the Chinese Exclusion Act of 1882, which prohibited the legal migration of male laborers likely to work in agriculture, mining camps, or factories, U.S. immigration policy targeted the Chinese as the first group of prospective immigrants to be excluded from entering the country on the basis of their race.[21] As a result, overall numbers of Chinese immigrants dropped sharply after 1882, and many Chinese in the United States returned to China. Others, in much smaller numbers, succeeded in staying or migrating to the United States over the following sixty-one years, until the exclusion acts were repealed in 1943.

Writing about the history of Chinese in the United States during the era of Chinese exclusion, historian Madeleine Hsu has argued that rather than weakening transnational ties between China and the United States, the exclusion laws strengthened them through creating the need for networks supporting communication, financial transactions, and trade. These networks facilitated the movement of news, money, and goods between Chinese in the United States and Chinese in Guangdong, since Chinese individuals had few opportunities to make the journey across the Pacific themselves.[22] So even as Chinese exclusion prevented the immigration of many Chinese who might otherwise have chosen to leave China for the United States, it also served to keep villagers in Guangdong well aware of the United States as a potential destination through the integration of those villagers into global networks of trade and communication that could facilitate their future movement.

When the exclusion laws were repealed in 1943, following China's role as an ally of the United States during World War II, Cantonese who had family there hoped to join them abroad. However, both World War II and the establishment of the PRC in 1949 created new obstacles to joining family already overseas. Under the leadership of Mao Zedong, PRC state efforts to regulate and control China's population were strikingly effective at curtailing emigration from Guangdong (and China as a whole). As a result, individuals who had planned to make use of family networks to migrate to the United States after World War II had to reorient their goals. Instead of migrating as young adults, they had to postpone their plans of going abroad for thirty years or longer. In 2009, one immigrant in his sixties told me, "Actually, if it wasn't for liberation [that is, the Chinese Communist revolution in 1949, which resulted in the establishment of the PRC], lots of people would have left [China] a long time ago." For these migrants—my interviewees—their move to the United States at an older age represents the culmination of individual and family plans started many decades previously and only realized once exit from China became possible following the political and economic relaxation ushered in during China's reform period in the late 1970s and 1980s. While some individuals were able to flee China during the Maoist years, those exits were largely the result of individual refugees seeking to escape to Hong Kong (and from Hong Kong, possibly abroad). During the reform period, individuals and their families who had relatives abroad could be legally sponsored to emigrate, allowing couples, families, and older individuals to obtain exit permits and rejoin family members from whom they had been separated for most (if not all) of their lives.

Thus, today's Cantonese senior migrants' desires to engage with the world beyond China were kept alive through the continuing awareness of the possibility of migration as a way of life and the concomitant inability to visit (or sometimes even communicate with) family members abroad throughout most of their lives. As older adults, the combination of this lifelong desire harbored since childhood to engage in migration trajectories as their fathers, uncles, and grandfathers had before them and the desire to rejoin family members from whom they had been separated for decades served to fuel seniors' goals to move to the United States at the turn of the millennium as retirees.

MIGRATION AND CHINESE FAMILY SEPARATION THROUGHOUT THE TWENTIETH CENTURY

As I described in the previous section, the routinization of migration as a way of life for Cantonese from both rural and urban areas in the late nineteenth and early twentieth centuries continues to matter for contemporary Cantonese migrants' overseas trajectories. Like Mr. Cheung, the majority of my Cantonese senior migrant interviewees in Boston have family (including parents, siblings, uncles, aunts, and adult children) residing on multiple continents—most often Asia, North America, and Australia. Many others have families dispersed across many cities in North America, including Boston, New York, Chicago, San Francisco, Toronto, and Vancouver. These family networks serve as important resources for seniors, who depend on their relatives abroad to sponsor them to migrate to new destinations. Yet the presence of these networks, even combined with the desire to experience life abroad, is usually not sufficient in and of itself to ensure seniors' migration. For most seniors, the immediate catalyst for migration is to rejoin family members from whom they have long been separated.

Family dispersal has always been integral to Chinese diasporic practices. Given emigration's primary goal as a strategy for family support, particularly during the period of mass emigration from Southeast China beginning in the 1850s, the practice of sending males abroad as economic migrants allowed families as a household unit to survive in the face of limited economic opportunity in China.[23] More recently, the practice of dispersing families over spatial distance has continued through the practice of what Aihwa Ong has called "flexible citizenship"—when family members strategically pursue economic and political benefits through establishing residential locations in different world areas.[24] In both past and present migration practices, Chinese families have been viewed as social units that could function as an economic whole even when dispersed across significant physical distances.[25] On the one hand, this practice was pragmatic, enabling women to run households and farms in China while also taking care of children and elderly parents supported by remittances sent by their husbands working abroad.[26] On the other hand, split-family life was rarely as seamless as portrayed in much of the literature on the Chinese overseas. Distance led to economic and other disagreements among husbands and wives who had different goals for how remittance money should be used.[27] In some cases, split-family life resulted in the complete severing of family ties, such as when emigrants were unable to provide economically for their families in China or when husbands abroad married and established new families overseas.[28]

In the nineteenth century, family separations across the Pacific were born of practicality because of the high financial cost of traveling across the ocean, coupled with extreme uncertainty involved with the long journey abroad. Moreover, Chinese immigrants had few options for employment in the United States, with most working at hard labor to survive, living in mining camps and building railroads in the American West. These economic considerations that privileged males in the migrant journey from Guangdong to the United States in the 1800s were reinforced by cultural norms in which women's social roles were restricted to the family, whether as daughters, daughters-in-law, or servants.[29] Even when men had migrated to Southeast Asia, it was common to leave wives behind.[30] Women's lives were not easy when fathers and husbands left to earn a living abroad. Many wives were subjected to the whims of their in-laws and prevented from corresponding with their husbands; others took over backbreaking agricultural labor. As a result, many women also aspired to go abroad, with or without their husbands.[31]

The difficulties experienced through family separation were reinforced throughout the first half of the twentieth century, as Chinese exclusion laws in the United States made it virtually impossible for working-class Chinese emigrant men to return home to their families in China. Although some Chinese migrants had papers that theoretically ensured their ability to reenter the United States, the process was fraught with difficulty and subject to uncertainty, making it easier not to try to leave at all. Moreover, while some men were able to bring U.S. citizen children, primarily sons, from China to the United States, these children were also subject to interrogation and deportation to China. In the United States, there were few job opportunities outside of laundries and restaurants for men, and racism against Chinese was rampant. As a result, many eligible family members in China were never sponsored to join family in the United States prior to World War II, and many children grew up in China never knowing their fathers who were abroad.

Mrs. Chee, for example, remembers meeting her father only once before migrating to the United States when she was almost sixty years old in the late 1980s. Her father had lived in San Francisco throughout her childhood and adulthood, having followed his father to the United States as a boy. During the Pacific War, her father, who was worried about his family's safety in Guangdong, returned to China when Mrs. Chee was six years old. The purpose of that visit was to move the family to Burma, where Mrs. Chee's mother was born and her grandfather still lived, so that they would be safe from the encroaching Japanese army, which was devastating many areas of China and Southeast Asia.

Mrs. Chee described her life as a child in Burma as filled with work and hardship. By age ten, she and her sisters rolled cigarettes while their mother sewed piecework, so that the family would have enough money to survive. After the war, when Mrs. Chee was about sixteen, she and her sisters returned to Guangzhou, and she attended elementary school for two years before marrying a doctor ten years her senior. During the 1950s, Mrs. Chee trained as a nurse and enjoyed this opportunity to work while also raising three young children. When she retired in China at age fifty, she decided to emigrate. Her father told her that she would have a difficult time finding work in the United States and discouraged her from migrating, citing her family ties and husband's work in China as reasons to stay there. Even so, he was willing to sponsor her. So, in her late fifties, Mrs. Chee left her grown children and husband behind in China to go see her father for the first time since she was six years old. She told me:

> We weren't able to see each other for a long time, even though we always wanted to. . . . When I was little, I didn't really think about [not seeing my father]. But after I grew up and thought about it, I really wanted to see him. A lot of people were immigrating here [to the United States], so I wanted to come and see him.

After living in San Francisco with her father for a few months, Mrs. Chee moved to Boston, where an uncle helped her find work as a home health aide. Eventually Mrs. Chee's husband, followed by their children, joined her.

The economic hardship Mrs. Chee and her family faced in China as they struggled to provide for themselves with her father overseas was not unusual.

Many families benefited greatly from the remittances sent by men abroad, contributing to a general reputation of wealth for families with members overseas. However, throughout World War II, most communication and remittances were cut off. Moreover, some men never sent remittances, either because they were too poor to do so or because (like Mr. Cheung's father) they had abandoned their families in China—sometimes for new families in the United States. In these cases, families in China were left in precarious financial situations that were compounded by numerous social and political difficulties. Before 1949, hardships included routine extortion by both local bandits and government actors who refused to provide protection from bandits without bribes.[32] Financial difficulties were compounded by political hardships during the Maoist period.[33] From the late 1950s through 1978, when the Maoist period ended, families with members abroad were subject to significant economic and social uncertainty, since these families were ostracized by fellow villagers and persecuted by local cadres for their foreign connections.[34] One interviewee sought to convey to me the sense of isolation her mother-in-law faced during this period, when she experienced humiliating treatment by her fellow villagers and struggled financially to raise her sons after her husband had abandoned her for a foreign spouse in North America. With tears running down her cheeks, she told me, "I am crying for my mother-in-law. You have no idea how awful it was for her, what she had to put up with." Many of these left-behind family members were the first to leave Guangdong and rejoin family abroad once they had the opportunity to do so in the early 1980s.

The U.S. exclusion laws and World War II were not the only reasons senior migrants were separated from their family members. The same political ideology that created social and economic hardships for women and children with family abroad during the Maoist period also imposed restrictions on movement within and beyond China. One of the most common causes of family separation for my Cantonese interviewees was the closing of the border between mainland China and Hong Kong after 1949. Many seniors had stories about parents or siblings already working or married in Hong Kong, who stayed there rather than return to mainland China when the PRC was established. In other cases, some of my interviewees left their families in Hong Kong to go to school or work on the mainland and did not anticipate that they would not be allowed to return to their families later. Such was the case with Mr. Moy, who was seventy-eight years old and had been living in Boston for just over ten years at the time of our first interview in 2009. He told me:

> When I was born, my parents were running a business in Hong Kong, so I was born in Hong Kong. Elementary school, middle school were all in Hong Kong. When I graduated from high school, the mainland was "liberated." At that time, colleges in Hong Kong were hard to get into. There weren't many colleges, so the opportunity for higher education was limited. Before liberation, I had tested into a university in Guangdong, so . . . I had to decide if I should go back for my education or stay in Hong Kong to work. . . . That's why I went back to China, to continue my education.

After Mr. Moy graduated from university in China, he was assigned to a job in Shanghai—a work placement that he accepted without question at the time. Looking back at that period in his life, he explained that everyone's goal was to contribute to the country's growth and development.[35] Some of his classmates were assigned to work in cities in northern parts of China; others were assigned elsewhere. He told me he never thought twice about accepting his job placement in Shanghai. It was only later that he wished he had the opportunity to be with his parents and other family members in Hong Kong again:

> After I went to the mainland, my family was in Hong Kong, so I was in China by myself. At the time, I wasn't married, and my parents were healthy, so I wasn't homesick. After I grew up and had a family, then I wanted to be able to see my parents. But at the time, the political situation was such that if you wanted to leave and return to the mainland, you needed official approval. You couldn't just leave on your own. For some reason, I didn't get this approval, and I couldn't go back to Hong Kong. So, I just stayed [in China].

His family situation became even more complicated in the late 1960s during the Cultural Revolution when he, like many other professionals, was sent to perform farm labor in the countryside. In the 1970s, he returned to work and live with his wife and daughters in Shanghai. Throughout this time, he was unable to visit his parents or siblings in Hong Kong.

In the 1980s, around the time Mr. Moy retired, his older daughter married a Chinese man already living and working in the United States, who sponsored her to join him in Boston. At the same time, Mr. Moy's younger daughter moved to Australia to study. The separation from both daughters prompted him and his wife to migrate to the United States:

> [My older daughter] got her green card and then became a citizen, and [at that time] it was easier to apply for parents [to immigrate to the United States than

to apply for them to come as visitors]. It was quick, just a couple of months. She also had a baby, so she needed someone to take care of her daughter. At the time, my wife and I were retired and we had nothing to do, so we came [here] to reunite with our daughter and help her with her workload in the family and take care of her kids.

Unlike many grandparent caregivers who opt to return to China once their grandchildren are old enough to require less care, Mr. Moy and his wife decided to stay in Boston as their grandchildren grew older. They felt settled in their senior housing unit just around the corner from their daughter's house, and Mr. Moy was fortunate enough to find employment that he enjoyed. Once they realized they would be staying in the United States, their thoughts turned to their younger daughter, who was still in Australia, living on her own.

After we immigrated [to the United States] we thought about our daughter's situation in Australia. If she had been married and had a family, then we would have been satisfied, and we would have hoped that she and her family would live a good life in Australia. But after we came to America, she was still not married. So we thought that if she were near us, we could help take care of her. If she had any problems, we could help her so her life would be better. So we suggested to her that after we became citizens, we could sponsor her to join us here. We talked to her about it and said: "You're by yourself and no one is there to take care of you. If you come here we can help you." And through this process she thought about what we said and decided we were right and came over.

Living together with his wife and near his daughters and grandchildren in the United States, Mr. Moy was able to achieve a sense of family unity that he never experienced with his own parents. After he left Hong Kong to attend university in China, he never saw his parents again. Although he could not have anticipated that his decision to further his education in China after 1949 would have led to that outcome, Mr. Moy deeply regretted that separation. Since migrating, he has returned to China several times. En route, he has always stopped in Hong Kong to perform ancestral rites at his parents' graves, a practice particularly meaningful following his almost lifelong separation from them.

A similar desire for family unity motivated Mr. Cheung's migration to the United States. As I have noted, his diasporic family tradition resulted in the "disappearance" of his male ancestors and role models, including a lifelong separation from his grandfather in the United States, his uncle in the Philippines, and his father in Hong Kong. However, it was not this family history that motivated Mr. Cheung's migration to the United States after his retirement in China. Instead, following almost twenty years of separation from his wife and daughters throughout his adult working life in China, he was unwilling to be separated from his wife after she decided to migrate to the United States to take care of their American-born grandchildren.

Like all other working adults in Maoist China, Mr. Cheung was assigned to a job and housing by the Chinese state. However, his *danwei* (work unit), through which all of his food, health care, and other life necessities were provided, was in a location far from the urban area where his wife and daughters lived. As a result, he saw them only once or twice a year, when he was granted leave to visit them. His sense of physical distance from his family was compounded by the lack of communication infrastructure in China during the 1960s and 1970s. Without telephones, he could not call his family, who relied on mail for most communication. His much anticipated annual visits home were also emotionally wrenching, as his young daughters did not recognize either his voice or his face and would initially run away from him in fear. For Mr. Cheung, it was the pain associated with this everyday separation from his wife and daughters throughout his adult life that provided the strongest impetus for his migration to the United States. When his wife decided to move to the United States after her own retirement in 2003 to look after their grandchildren, Mr. Cheung decided to come too, despite not wanting to leave China. He told me, "Back when [my wife and I were young], we were separated for so long, and it was so difficult [C. *gam sanfu*], because we could only see each other once each year. So, we don't want to be separated anymore." The last time we spoke, he remained ambivalent about his migration trajectory, primarily because his younger daughter chose to stay behind in China. He told me:

> I always worry about [C. *gwajyuh*] her because she's not married. Back when I was in Guangzhou, I made soup and good food for her to eat. Now, she's just by herself, and she just eats out most of the time. So, I worry about her and call her sometimes. She tells me that she is eating well.... We don't even have many relatives left in Guangzhou [who could help look after her]. Almost everyone has emigrated and left the country. They're in Canada and America and San Francisco, and a few here in Boston.

While Mr. Cheung's ideal, like Mr. Moy's, was for his entire family to live together in Boston, Mr. Cheung had come to terms with the fact that his daughter would most likely never choose to migrate to the United States. Indeed, it would be to her disadvantage professionally, since she would almost certainly never be able to find a job as well paid and satisfying as her current one in China. At the same time, Mr. Cheung seemed happiest when his daughter was visiting him in Boston, so that he no longer had to worry about her being by herself, with no one to cook or care for her after a busy day at work. In this way, his situation mirrored that of the many other senior migrants I know who left behind aging parents, young grandchildren, siblings, adult children, and other close family in China through their decisions to move to the United States as older adults.

Some of the past difficulties experienced by families split across physical distance—through migration, political fiat, or both—have been mitigated. Certainly, contemporary Chinese families with members abroad are no longer subject to political persecution (and are more likely to be envied). Moreover, with the easing of political restrictions on travel in the PRC and the relatively low cost of international travel compared to the past, many senior migrants are able to travel back to China after coming to the United States, engaging in a transnational lifestyle in which they can continue to interact regularly with parents, children, and siblings in both China and North America (or other worldwide locations). It's true that the costs of traveling back and forth to China are prohibitive for some working-class individuals, who remain largely separated from close family and can afford to make the trip back to China only once a decade—or less often. Yet many of my interviewees traveled back and forth to China regularly—once every year or every other year—until their health or increasingly limited physical mobility made it difficult to withstand the long airplane trip required for travel to Asia. Those who could not travel now have other forms of communication with family members, as even the poorest and least technologically sophisticated migrants found they could make use of wireless and other new communication technologies. Yet for many senior migrants—as with Mrs. Chee, Mr. Moy, and Mr. Cheung—the residual effects of past familial separations continued to haunt them and thus figured strongly in seniors' later-life migration pathways from China to the United States in the twenty-first century.

MIGRATION TO THE UNITED STATES: FAMILY REUNION AS THE REALIZATION OF LIFELONG DESIRES

The diasporic family histories of Cantonese seniors facilitate migration both through the possibility of imagining life abroad—even for older adults like Mr. Cheung, who had not planned on following in the well-worn footsteps of his ancestors—and the actual sponsorship of migrants by parents, siblings, and spouses already living overseas. Many Cantonese seniors are sponsored to come to the United States by parents and siblings, making the migration trajectories of these seniors a decade-long and somewhat uncertain process. At the time of my interviews, sibling sponsorship often took ten or more years of waiting; for seniors who were sponsored by brothers or sisters as they reached retirement age in their fifties, their first entrance to the United States was unlikely to occur before they were in their mid-sixties. As a result, seniors who had parents and siblings abroad ended up being sponsored by their adult children, most often by daughters who had married Cantonese emigrants already living in the United States. Sponsorship by adult children is also common among non-Cantonese-speaking older Chinese migrants whose adult children migrated to the United States as graduate students or as professionals and then asked their retired parents to come take care of American-born children. Yet Cantonese senior migrants' long histories of family-oriented migration trajectories—a history not shared by migrants originating from most other regions of China—means that in addition to joining their adult children and grandchildren, they were also reuniting with sisters, brothers, uncles, aunts, cousins, and parents as part of significant diasporic family networks in North America. These multigenerational family networks, often extending back decades in the United States, created different possibilities for support (and conflict) than is the case for seniors who do not have any other family or friends nearby when they migrate here. They also highlighted the role of diasporic imagination in seniors' decisions to migrate as older adults, completing their lifelong goals of engaging in diasporic practices they had looked forward to since they were young. This was the case for Mr. Lee, the eighty-nine-year old Chinese migrant whose story I told at the start of this book.

Originally from Guangdong Province, Mr. Lee was sponsored to come to the United States by an adult child in the mid-1990s. He also had a long history of family involvement in the United States, including a grandfather who had worked as a laundryman in San Francisco. However, unlike many of my other interviewees who had planned to migrate as children or young adults, following in their fathers' footsteps, Mr. Lee's story was different. After years of social marginalization while working as a laundryman at the turn of the twentieth century in California, his grandfather returned to China and forbade his sons and grandsons from emigrating to the United States. While his grandfather was alive, Mr. Lee never considered going against his wishes. Nevertheless, like my other senior interviewees who grew up in Guangdong's culture of migration, Mr. Lee was aware of a greater world beyond China and was intrigued by that world through the education he had received as a young man at a missionary college. In the end, his curiosity about that world overcame his sense of betrayal of his grandfather's desires. He told me, "[One] reason I wanted to come to America is because in my family's history, two generations didn't come to America. My dad's generation didn't come to America. My generation didn't come to America. My son came to America."

Over the almost hundred-year span between Mr. Lee's grandfather's initial foray to the United States and his adult son's migration, the world had changed substantially. Mr. Lee, who spent many years working as a technical engineer planning China's railroad infrastructure, wanted to learn more about those changes firsthand. As he enumerated his motivations for migrating to the United States in his seventies, Mr. Lee pinpointed his interest in wanting to see the United States for himself as his primary goal:

> In the past 100 years, America has changed a lot. It has changed to a point where the development of science is amazing, the economy is doing well, and it is the most democratic country in the world. These changes, from when I was in school until now, have given me this [positive] image of America. I was in a school that was related to America, and that had a big impact on my views of America. I see America as a free country that is doing very well and has a lot of technological innovations. I wanted to know if [this] was true. I had to experience [America] for myself. I had to see it myself. This was the first real reason [I wanted to immigrate]: I wanted to see America.

As he noted, Mr. Lee's interest in the United States stemmed from his boyhood days in China, making his decision to migrate as a senior the fulfillment of a lifelong desire. Yet because his grandfather had returned to China and also forbidden the migration of Mr. Lee's father's generation, he had no immediate relatives in the United States who could sponsor his migration. It wasn't until some of his adult children migrated to the United States that his own migration became a possibility. Reuniting with his family thus figured into his motivations for retirement migration. At the same time, it was just one of the many factors that he listed for his decision to migrate to the United States in his seventies. He continued:

> [In] China . . . , I had a pretty good life. However, people didn't have freedom. Everything was under the government's control. . . . There is no control by the

government here [in America]. Why shouldn't I come here? I wanted to enjoy a democratic country. I didn't want to have to be controlled by the government. This is the second reason [I wanted to migrate]. The third reason is that after living in China for so long, if I wanted to enjoy life even more, even better, then coming to America was the only good escape. I wanted to come to America and enjoy life. The fourth reason is that I have kids who immigrated here. I wanted to reunite with my kids again. I wanted to enjoy a family reunion. Those were the four reasons.

Family reunion made Mr. Lee's migration in his seventies possible. However, his trajectory was fueled as much by his sense of curiosity to see and live in a world beyond China—a curiosity he had harbored for much of his adult life—as it was to join his adult children, since two of his adult children and the majority of his grandchildren remained in China even after he and his wife migrated to the United States. Like Mr. Lee, many of the other immigrants I interviewed told me that they had multiple reasons for moving to the United States as older adults. Among those articulated reasons, the most common goals I heard were for cultivating personal development, being able to fully retire from work in China, reuniting with family, caregiving for grandchildren, and experiencing freedom—both by living in a democratic society and by having lives financially independent of adult children. Echoing these views, another woman who had initially migrated to take care of her grandchildren told me that she came because she "wanted to see more of the world." When she decided to move to the United States, following in the footsteps of previous generations of migrants in her family, she already knew from those other family members that the United States was a country of freedom (C. *jihyauh*). As we talked, she reinforced her sense of identification with this ideal by adding in English, "I like it!" At the same time, not every senior I met was motivated by similar ideals. Some did not actually want to immigrate to the United States but came—as one woman blurted out—because her "children told her [she] had to" or because they simply did not want to live apart from spouses or other family members who *did* want to migrate, as was the case with Mr. Cheung.

CULTURE OF MIGRATION

Writing about postcolonial migrations, Stuart Hall emphasizes the historical continuity—"the logical culmination of long-standing political and social ties"—that characterizes postcolonial migration flows.[36] While the past relationship between China and the United States has not strictly been a colonial one, it nonetheless has produced significant social and economic ties that continue to fuel seniors' migrant trajectories between the two countries. These ties include long-standing economic interaction and unequal political and power relationships in the global arena. Balanced between the two powers was Hong Kong, an actual colony and the center through which the actors straddling these economic and political relationships helped to perpetuate the Pearl River Delta's pervasive social and cultural imagination of engagement with the world beyond mainland China.

The narratives I present in this chapter make clear that Chinese senior migrants' contemporary trajectories of movement continue to be influenced in important ways by the long-standing Cantonese regional culture of migration. This context fueled seniors' lifelong desires to migrate to the United States in two ways: through providing the familial networks abroad that made seniors' movement practically possible and also through the cultivation of a diasporic imagination fully integrating an awareness of the global into local village life. This awareness led to interaction with the world beyond China that influenced my senior migrant interviewees' aspirations throughout their childhood and younger adulthood. That they maintained this desire to see and experience the world beyond China over many decades of their lives, despite the specific political barriers that made migration to the United States an almost impossible dream during this same time period, sets the later-life migration of Cantonese seniors apart from the growing numbers of senior migrants who hail from other regions of China today and whose migration trajectories as older adults are also influenced with goals for family engagement and interaction.

In the following chapters, I build on this discussion by describing how the Cantonese senior migrants who hoped to fulfill long-standing dreams to reunite with their family members in the United States also hoped to establish a stronger sense of personal fulfillment and social and financial stability in their older age. That the United States paradoxically provides a seemingly ideal location for some Chinese seniors to achieve retired ways of life desired by many members of their generational cohort is the subject of the next two chapters.

3 GENERATIONAL BELONGING IN THE NATION-STATE

Certain moments from my research still stand out to me, even years later. One interview that takes center stage in my mind was with a Cantonese couple in their late sixties who had been in the United States for only a few years when I met them. A social worker had referred the husband to me to interview, but since he spoke more Taishanese than Cantonese, his wife ended up being the main interlocutor for our discussion, which took place in those languages over several hours in the common room of a low-income senior housing estate in Quincy.

Like many of my other Chinese senior migrant interviewees, the couple had a long history of family migration to the United States. Although they had been sponsored to come here by an adult daughter, they were also linked to the United States by previous generations of migrants. Similar to the stories I highlighted in the previous chapter, in which I chronicled the diasporic webs of family life that have tied Southeast China to other global locations over multiple generations, this older couple's migration history was both rooted in an earlier generation of migrants and tied to adult children now in the United States. The husband's father had migrated here before World War II, while the rest of the family stayed behind in China. When one of the couple's adult daughters married a Chinese emigrant husband already living in the United States in the late twentieth century, she sponsored her parents to come to join her. Later, the parents themselves sponsored a second daughter to migrate. At the time of our interview, the couple was just waiting for the third child, their only immediate family left in China, to arrive. It was at this juncture, as the couple expressed their frustration at how long the approval process seemed to be taking to bring their youngest daughter here, that our conversation took an unexpected turn. Why, they asked, was the process taking so long? Wouldn't the U.S. government want their daughter to join them as soon as possible? Surprised, I answered that it was unlikely that "the U.S. government" would have any such desire. Much to my dismay, the woman immediately burst into tears.

It wasn't the first question about why the process to sponsor their daughter was taking so long that led to my inadvertent upset of my interviewee. Long wait periods also characterized the experiences of Chinese migrants I had studied in Hong Kong and are a routine roadblock for would-be immigrants around the globe. What had tripped me up was the second question, around what seemed to me as a naive personification of the U.S. government as a conscious and caring actor with an active role to play in this couple's personal life. The expression of positive feelings about the U.S. government, particularly in relationship to its social welfare resources for seniors, was a viewpoint I had frequently heard voiced by my interviewees. However, I was less familiar with the high expectations this couple held for humane treatment by the U.S. government. As a result, their question crystallized my interest around the origins of this view. It was my own turn to wonder, how they—relative newcomers to the United States who had lived the majority of their adult lives in China and who seemed to be socially and politically marginalized residents of this country—had come to think about the U.S. government in this way.

Over the many years that I conducted interviews and participant observation–based research with Chinese-born recent senior migrants in the greater Boston area, there were many moments when I was able to glimpse emotion central to migrants' experiences, past and present. I have already written about some of these times in other places, including when one of my interviewees began crying while describing her brother's attempts to escape from China to Hong Kong in the 1970s, when he was apprehended and tortured by local PRC authorities.[1] In another case, a widowed woman of eighty had to stop our interview and collect herself as she remembered the forced physical dispersion of her remaining family during the Cultural Revolution. Within days of her husband's death from cancer in the late 1960s, she, like many others of her generation, was sent away to work in the countryside, leaving her young son and mother behind in Guangzhou.[2] As with those cases, my interviewee's tears reflected the culmination of her frustration and worry after many years of family separation and hardship experienced at the hands of the PRC government. Yet unlike those other cases, her emotion centered on a deeply held sense of affinity with the United States—and her expectations for justice through the recognition of her Chinese-born daughter's legal right to join her siblings and parents already living here.

This moment of encounter, and the discussion that resulted from it, is the point of departure for this chapter, in which I focus on one aspect of senior migrants' contemporary engagement in transnational lifeways and global mobility processes. That is, I explore how some Chinese-born seniors have, perhaps unexpectedly, developed strong feelings of emotional affinity with the United States, which are in turn deeply intertwined with their generational experiences as Chinese citizens. As we continued to talk that afternoon and I learned more about this couple's family history, I began to better understand their high expectations for humane treatment by the U.S. government as rooted in the past as much as in the present. These expectations were intimately related to their lifelong experiences as part of a generational cohort of Chinese citizens who were born and came of age just prior to the Communist revolution in China that culminated in the foundation of the PRC in 1949. For this couple, a personal history of past and present hardship in China stood in stark contrast to their hope for positive social and political engagement as U.S. citizens. As a result, the United States was the country on which they pinned their hopes for their children and grandchildren's future lives: they valued the social stability and democratic governance in the United States more than the promise of China's continued economic growth and future prosperity. Starting from this realization, in this chapter, I chart the ways that these migrants' sense of affiliation with the nation—that is, how they felt a sense of national belonging—hinged on structures of feeling and ideological orientations rooted in both their past and current experiences of social membership in China and the United States.

Writing about various forms of membership in nation-states, scholars draw significant attention to what we can think of as disjunctures between formal categories of citizenship and substantive feelings of belonging. Formal categories of citizenship are the kinds of legal categories of membership that result in documentation like passports that provide political and social protections not available to noncitizens. Substantive forms of citizenship refer to deep-seated social and political engagements and familial ties that many individuals who are residents but not always legal citizens of particular states experience. Sociologist Saskia Sassen highlights these disjunctures through forms of citizenship that she calls "authorized" and "recognized."[3] In her view, "authorization" refers to legal categories of membership, whereas "recognition" indexes substantive forms of belonging through which individuals exercise moral claims to membership, which may not be recognized as sufficient for legal authorization by the state.[4] Similarly, anthropologist Susan Coutin highlights how individuals can be both simultaneously "present" and "absent" in a given nation when their legal status does not coincide with their sense of belonging or location of actual residence.[5] As early as 1994, anthropologist Renato Rosaldo coined the term *cultural citizenship* to advocate for the recognition that ethnic minorities' distinctive cultural practices that differ from American mainstream norms are in fact integral to their citizenship claims and experiences. Viewed through the language of Sassen's categories, Rosaldo paints a vivid portrait of how authorized citizenship requires the recognition of ethnic difference.[6]

What these and other accounts of the complexity of membership practices highlight are the multiple forms of affiliation and alignment with state and social values that migrants can experience. Moreover, these forms of affinity may become most visible through the kinds of emotional outbursts like the one I unwittingly provoked that afternoon in Quincy. As geographer Lucy Jackson explains, "Allowing for emotions and feelings in citizenship narratives . . . accounts for more fluid constructs [and means] that social, cultural and political understandings of citizenship alter to become focused more on identity and practice."[7] Yet many scholars writing about citizenship rarely explicitly address these emotions and feelings, even though the roles that emotions play in processes of belonging and affinity with the nation nonetheless seem present just below the surface of their analyses. For example, Susan Coutin focuses on the literal unreality of personal experience that results when individuals are simultaneously present and absent in nation-states.[8] As she notes, citizens may be legally present in the nation-state while living elsewhere by participating in elections by absentee ballot, paying taxes on income earned abroad, or sending remittances that support families and ways of life left behind. Similarly, undocumented migrants who have spent the majority of their lives in one country but are then deported and repatriated to "homes" they have never known struggle to make sense of their removal from a place where they consider themselves to be citizens to new locations where they have no sense of belonging, family, or even legal documentation verifying their citizenship claims. Echoing the language of the fictional genre magical realism, Coutin describes the "incompatible realities that are true simultaneously" for individuals living through these experiences of everyday disjuncture.[9]

Yet the role of emotional attachment to nation-states is well acknowledged by scholars of migration, particularly with reference to displaced groups like diasporas with no recourse to return to longed-for homelands. Similarly, scholars of retirement migration highlight how older, first-generation migrants' emotional orientations may continue to focus on their home country through a strong sense of nostalgia for a past that may no longer exist except in their imaginative worlds. In these accounts, nostalgia serves as a potential obstacle to the formation of emotional ties to new places of residency or draws older migrants back to original homelands after living and working as younger adults in new locations.[10] Less commonly addressed is the role of emotional attachment in creating or constructing new senses of "home" for migrants.[11] One exception is Caroline Oliver's work. Writing about retirement migrants from Britain who settle in Spain, Oliver describes what she calls the "forward-looking" role that emotions like idealism and aspiration play in how older migrants construct new homes and a sense of rootedness in Spain.[12] In the rest of this chapter, I build on Oliver's forward-looking role of emotion building to highlight how nostalgia—that is, a preoccupation with the past—can also be forward-looking, leading to new forms of affinity and attachment to the nation. In this way, nostalgia can play a role in allowing for the development of a sense of belonging in new countries of residence, not just longed-for emigrant homelands. In particular, I explore the ideological ties and emotional affiliations that help to anchor my interviewees in and to the United States, rather than China, as older adults.

My analysis highlights how the PRC's ideological values for social and national advancement remain influential for this cohort of older adults. Yet these principles, including the creation of a stable and equitable society, for which this generation labored throughout their earlier adult lives in China, now seem to have been abandoned by the current Chinese government and are perceived to be more easily experienced in the United States than in China.

SENIOR MIGRANTS' VIEWS OF CHINA: IDEOLOGY AND HARDSHIP OF THE REVOLUTIONARY COHORT

The Chinese seniors I know have been quick to point out that life in contemporary China is a huge improvement over the recent past in terms of access to material goods and China's economic development. They talk with pride about how far the PRC has come over the past few decades and where they hope its current economic growth will lead the country in the future. They express particular satisfaction at China's increased global standing. This praise makes clear that Chinese seniors retain a strong sense of emotional connection to China, even while living in the United States and even after becoming U.S. citizens. This pride is certainly not unique to this generation, yet it takes a distinctive form for them through contrasting China's newly found global ascendance with the economic hardship that characterized most of this cohort's experiences over the course of the twentieth century. At times, hardships were mitigated for those who received remittances from overseas relatives. However, as I explained in the previous chapter, having overseas relatives often created greater political risk and potential economic hardship for family left behind in China, resulting in the kinds of strongly emotional reactions to past experiences that I noted in the first paragraphs of this chapter.

When seniors talked about their premigration past, their narratives reflected the social, political, and economic turmoil through which they lived for the first fifty years of their lives. Although overall my interviewees spanned more than one generation, most of them were in their sixties and seventies during the first decade of the twenty-first century and were born in China in the 1930s and 1940s—years spanning the Japanese occupation of China during World War II and the Chinese civil war that ended with the establishment of the PRC on October 1, 1949. For these individuals, their lives have followed the course of the extreme political and social changes that have marked China's transition from two thousand years of imperial rule to a thoroughly modern nation-state. Although this transition began well before these senior migrants were born, some of the most acute ideological changes have taken place over the course of their lifetimes. The first was the transition from the Nationalist-led Republican government to that of the PRC—referred to as "liberation" by my interviewees. The second occurred in the late 1970s with China's "reform and opening up" (M. *gaigekaifang*) initiated by Deng Xiaoping.

Many of my interviewees were willing to talk about some of the hardships they had lived through, including the disastrous famine following Mao's Great Leap Forward campaign of 1958 to 1961 that resulted in 30 to 40 million deaths among China's rural residents. Initiated as an attempt to fast-forward China's modernization, the Great Leap Forward sought to boost agricultural production through intensive collectivization. Rural residents initially enjoyed the benefits of increased access to food in public canteens and freedom from everyday domestic tasks such as cooking that detracted from their ability to increase agricultural outputs. However, a series of now well-documented political missteps not only deprived rural residents of any of their own produce (which was instead shipped to urban areas) but also rendered those same rural residents powerless to alter the campaign's inevitable outcome: starvation. One senior migrant, a nurse during the early years of the PRC, explained what happened:

> [Everyone] gave fake numbers: if on a farm only six stalks of rice were harvested, farmers would say they cut down ten, so that others would say that they had a good [production] year and praise them and compliment the leaders. But these were all lies, it wasn't the truth. The people who were in charge would do the calculations [for how much food to ship off to urban areas] thinking that there was more than enough to eat. [Everyone believed] that there was no need to worry about starvation, because we had plenty to eat; [officials thought] that there was a lot of food for the farmers to eat. So lots of rice would be cooked [in the public canteens] and when [people] couldn't finish it they would throw it away. [Finally], there was no more rice and the country didn't have enough food. So then cutbacks began [and] people were starving.

Nothing about this account is surprising in relation to the history on record, which documents a system gone awry.[13] Political factionalism resulted in competition among different groups to outdo each other in fulfilling production quotas. Under intense political pressure to demonstrate agricultural success, farmers reported more grain output than they actually produced. Government cadres, willing to believe these reports in order to demonstrate the effectiveness of production in the areas where they were in charge, further inflated production numbers, leading to disastrous outcomes for peasant farmers. Since available food was not initially rationed in a sustainable way, much was wasted—even as some individuals were already starving. Moreover, farmers' entire harvests were claimed by cadres to fulfill their manufactured production claims to send to urban areas, leaving entire rural communities without enough food to survive. For my interviewee, there is no contest between that time and today. As she summed up, "Compared to that time, there's such a big difference now. People's lives are better now: no matter how difficult, it's not that difficult. It's not like before."

Yet nostalgia for the Maoist past by members of these older generations who lived through the Great Leap famine and other periods of extreme hardship, often directly perpetrated by the state, is well documented.[14] Writing about the experiences of older women in rural China, historian Gail Hershatter talks about how women—despite many difficult periods in their lives—often talk positively about their experiences, highlighting how their lives "got better twice."[15] What they describe as the first time their lives "got better" are the concrete improvements they experienced as a result of liberation, when the implementation of economic and social reforms following the establishment of the PRC provided new life opportunities for many women in this and other areas of rural China. These reforms included the redistribution of land away from wealthy land-holding families to all village inhabitants and expanded opportunities for health care, education, and marriage choice for women. Overall, the changes ushered in over the early years of CCP rule brought improvements to the previously impoverished and largely circumscribed roles for rural women, which Hershatter's interviewees still clearly remembered and most certainly influenced the ability of the interviewee I quoted previously to work as a nurse during the early PRC years.

The second time women's lives "got better" was several decades later during the post-Mao era known as "reform and opening up." Following the death of Mao Zedong in 1976 and Deng Xiaoping's rise to power in 1978, this period marked a turning point in the strict political control that had been a hallmark of the Maoist era. The tight restrictions over everyday life situations—where one worked, what kind of work one did, what one was allowed to plant on one's farm, what one could eat, when one could visit one's family—that had been the norm during the Maoist period began to relax and allowed the first significant opportunities for rural families to generate individual income in decades. Hershatter explains, "People are not settling accounts with the collective period anymore.... Many women tell a story of how life got better twice, once in the 1950s and again in the 1980s. In this story, collectivization and decollectivization do not contradict each other; both count as progress."[16]

At the same time, these collective memories of how "life got better twice" coexist with individual memories of the violence and deprivation that accompanied these reforms—particularly collectivization and the implementation of other reforms, including those most intended to "liberate" women.[17] Many of my senior migrants' narratives of their premigration lives in China highlighted both the past hardships they experienced yet still voiced strong support for the PRC government and its laudable revolutionary goals—an ambivalence that pervades other accounts of the Chinese socialist past by members of this revolutionary generation as well.[18]

This duality is clear in the story that Mrs. Wong, eighty years old in 2010, told me about how the establishment of the PRC impoverished her family, which had been moderately prosperous prior to 1949 with residences on both sides of the Chinese–Hong Kong border.[19] Initially from Guangzhou, the family moved to Hong Kong seeking safety from the Japanese in 1936, when Mrs. Wong was a small child. Mrs. Wong's father, who worked in advertising, promoted a friend's pharmaceutical company throughout World War II. Following the war, the director of the company decided to stay in Hong Kong. Mrs. Wong's father, however, elected to return to Guangzhou, where he served as the company's functioning director in his friend's absence. Not long afterward, Mrs. Wong's father was imprisoned for "reeducation," and ownership of the pharmaceutical company was transferred to the CCP. Mrs. Wong explained the devastating effects of her father's imprisonment on her family:

> Before liberation . . . , it was only if you did something wrong that you got locked up. [So, my father's imprisonment] scared my grandma so much that she died. She was really worried. She thought that her son-in-law had committed a crime. She couldn't walk and was blind, and she worried about [my father] so much that she died. At the time my mom was also very worried and didn't know how to deal with [my father's situation]. Then she got sick. We didn't know what was wrong with her at the time. . . . Then she died too. At the time of her death. she was still calling my father's name. She was afraid [for him] because he was in jail.

Following these family tragedies, Mrs. Wong and her younger sisters lived for years in extreme poverty, sometimes subsisting on only a drop or two of soy sauce to flavor their rice at meals and no other food at all.

In our conversations, Mrs. Wong clearly recounted the hardships that she experienced at the hands of the PRC state. Yet despite the virtual destruction of her childhood family following her father's imprisonment, her narrative did not vilify the PRC government. Instead, she emphasized the positive ideals involved in the redistribution of wealth that had motivated the newly established Communist government's action against her father. Although she acknowledged having been scared at the time, she rationalized that fear as stemming from her own ignorance as a young child. She further explained:

> [Now I know that my father's imprisonment was] really not that scary. Why did [he and other businessmen] have to be reeducated? It was so that the Communist Party [could] transfer privately owned, capitalist companies to public [ownership]. Some people didn't know my father was just a representative [of the company and not its real director], but there [were others imprisoned] who actually owned their companies. Once my father understood this policy he accepted it.

Through her rationalization of these harrowing experiences, Mrs. Wong's tale reinforces the pattern of positive views of the past also voiced by Hershatter's interviewees who remember their lives as being significantly improved through the implementation of the same kinds of violent reforms that led to the imprisonment of Mrs. Wong's father. In these cases, seniors did not critique the governmental policies that led to personal hardship, including extreme poverty, malnourishment, and the death of friends and family. Instead, narratives emphasized support for the revolutionary CCP agenda aimed at eliminating class differences and spurring economic development for the country as a whole, since these policies did enable life to get better for many in this generation under Maoist rule. In this way, seniors' accounts of the past highlighted the continuing importance of the ideological values—and, in particular, the state-articulated ideal of egalitarianism—that undergirded their sacrifices and contributions to the Chinese national cause.

My interviewees' stories also emphasized that life improved during the 1970s and focused on how rural families were finally able to make their own decisions about how best to achieve economic success. One of my interviewees, a Taishanese man in his seventies, who had been in the United States for a decade when we talked in 2010, explained the limitations with Maoist era policies preventing innovation and the opportunity to improve his family's agricultural production:

> When I worked on the farm, there were some policies that I came up with [to improve] the farm but [the government wouldn't let me implement these changes]. If you wanted your income to be higher, they wouldn't let you. They said that farmers had to plant rice and wheat; you couldn't think of other ways to make more money. They really restricted us. It was like that even after liberation. If we had been able to plant other crops then we could [have made more money], but they wouldn't let us. I also thought about how [we could make more money if] we could raise fish and sell them.

As a result, he was grateful for the new opportunities for economic development once the Maoist era ended. However, like many of my other interviewees, he also expressed a sense of betrayal by the PRC's current government. After having worked for decades to provide a strong foundation for the Communist state whose ideals they supported, seniors told me they felt abandoned by that same government, which promotes economic growth benefiting many younger Chinese but rarely the members of this older generational cohort. This interviewee continued, "When I was in China, I went through the Communist period, and I've experienced many things. Some people in China work for the government and can depend on it. However, people like us who are farmers—they [the government] don't think about us. If we work, it's as if we worked for nothing. There aren't any benefits for us." For this migrant, contemporary life in China clearly represents a marked improvement on the past. At the same time, his sense of sacrifice and the resultant hardships he endured in support for past CCP policies were acute. His words, "After everything we've been through, the government has never thought about how to treat us better," also encapsulated the concerns of the other senior migrants I interviewed.

SEARCHING FOR A "HUMANE SOCIAL ATMOSPHERE" IN CHINA AND THE UNITED STATES

The sense of abandonment by the current government for this generation of seniors who lived through and largely facilitated China's revolutionary past is particularly strong among migrants from Guangdong's rural areas, who have had fewer benefits than urban dwellers throughout their lives, including, until quite recently, any state-provided pension or old-age support system.[20] Rural residents have never qualified for the social welfare benefits known as the "iron rice bowl" that were available to urban dwellers during the Maoist period and continue to make many urban residents' lives more comfortable and secure than that of rural residents in postreform China. Moreover, as health and welfare benefits that were available to these same rural dwellers through collectivization were dismantled, they suffered disproportionately during the reform period.[21] Yet it's not just through the inability to fully benefit from China's contemporary economic growth that seniors feel upset. My migrant interviewees also complained about other aspects of contemporary Chinese society that compromise seniors' sense of security and quality of life in both rural and urban China, such as perceived widespread corruption, crime in urban areas, pollution, unfair wages, and lack of job security. For members of this generation, who remembered hardships experienced before liberation and worked throughout their lives to contribute to China's growth and development, their critiques focused on the failure of the contemporary state to make good on its promises and, in so doing, highlighted the disjuncture between current CCP practices and the ideological values of Maoist China that shaped these seniors' experiences as younger adults. This sense of betrayal by the PRC state opened up the potential for seniors to recognize the ideological values they prized as younger adults elsewhere. For my interviewees, that recognition took place in the United States.

Writing about labor activism among older industrial workers in North China's rust belt, sociologist Ching Kwan Lee describes how her interviewees' critiques of China's present are deeply intertwined with their experiences of China's socialist past. Laborers talk in largely positive terms about that past—in contrast to the economic and social injustices they experience in China today. Lee identifies three main ways in which workers' remembrances of the socialist past influence their expectations for the present. First, workers are nostalgic for the job security and egalitarianism that characterized their earlier adult years in the Maoist period, noting that they had better "psychological well-being" despite having a lower "material standard of living." Second, they talk positively about their factory work—demonstrating both a sense of pride in having developed particular occupational skills and also a sense of power relative to government cadres. Third, they draw attention to "their contribution and dedication to national development [and] the collective purpose realized in production work." Lee further notes that "in many narratives, these themes are interwoven pieces mentioned in one single breath, as workers depicted in broad strokes the gestalt of an era."[22]

For these workers, similar in age to many Chinese senior migrants now in Boston, factory work was not just hard labor. Instead, they experienced this work, like the work done by my revolutionary generation interviewees who were farmers or nurses or teachers during the early years of Chinese socialism, as part of an important project of national purpose, in which individual contributions were valued as all Chinese citizens worked toward strengthening and modernizing China together. Ideologically, every contribution mattered, and every individual had an equal opportunity to contribute to national development. The ideological quest for egalitarianism that undergirded this generation's sacrifices has now been abandoned. Over the past two decades, as China's gross domestic product has risen exponentially, income inequality has skyrocketed, and the financial security that the older generation so fondly remembers has become increasingly elusive for large numbers of Chinese citizens today, particularly seniors. One of Lee's interviewees explained, "For honest, ordinary, and mediocre people like us, Mao's egalitarianism was much better. My family ate steamed buns, your family also ate steamed buns. The next day was the same steamed buns. My heart felt balanced and relaxed."[23]

Like these workers, my senior migrant interviewees offered an alternative view of China's progress focused on a critique of contemporary excess. One man in his seventies told me, "We didn't used to be very proud of money. Back in the old days, they gave you a place to live, unlike now where you have to buy a place to live. Incomes were small; there was no desire for a luxurious lifestyle.... Now, everyone wants this more luxurious lifestyle.... We never talked about money; it was all about love." Another migrant, in his sixties, emphasized, "The old China was not okay. It has become much more open [which is better than before]. But they say that China's a country that pays attention to social concerns. It's not actually.... After the economic reform, after the '90s, it became a capitalist society. They say that China's a country for the people, but it's not." These concerns echo the nostalgia for a simpler society, oriented around expectations for production rather than consumption. That is, seniors expressed nostalgia for a life in which the ideological values they worked for in the early years of the PRC—collective cooperation, state support of workers, equality, and financial security—are still the hallmarks of daily life rather than the flashy, consumption-oriented lifestyles that characterize Chinese society today.

Lee points out that the power in this "alternative social order" is that it "is not an abstract ideological construct but a lived, historical reality."[24] Moreover, it is part of a historical reality that was groundbreaking for the revolutionary generation whose lives were benefited in concrete material and psychological ways, even as that historical reality was also constructed through the substantial sacrifices they made. Lee also points out that the ideological value placed on work—as part of a production-oriented society in which each individual's role contributed to national development—created a strong sense of direct connection between workers and the state: "When they talked about equality, and security or violence and abuse of power, they referred to the state policy of wages and benefits, rather than the camaraderie of workers with each other."[25] During the Maoist period, households, work, and social activity were all organized around state goals for success; moreover, access to employment, housing, schooling, health care, food, social pastimes, and travel was allocated and controlled through state-based institutions known as work units. As a result, it's not surprising that despite the relative withdrawal from the PRC state from everyday life in China today relative to the past, Chinese seniors today continue to place "the state" at the center of their local worlds.

One of the most frequently expressed ways that my senior migrant interviewees placed "the state" at the center of daily life was through their talk about the rise of social problems in contemporary China. These articulations served as powerful critiques through the stark contrast they provided between today's social ills and what seniors remembered as the more egalitarian and trustworthy nature of Chinese society during the Maoist era. The critiques voiced by my interviewees most frequently centered on a particular Cantonese word, *funghei* (M. *fengqi*), which I loosely translate here as "social atmosphere." Funghei draws attention to a way of conceptualizing society as a concrete entity with a collective morality rather than viewing society as a collection of disparate individuals with competing moral claims. It is also tied to the state through the emphasis placed on how government policies and practices affect the social atmosphere by laying the groundwork for and enforcing collective moral norms. Thus, tied to state governance in ways not necessarily obvious to a non-Chinese observer, "social atmosphere" acts as a force that shapes the collective social interactions among citizens. So when seniors critiqued the social atmosphere in contemporary China, complaining about the wide variety of social ills that detract from their psychological well-being, they were viewing the state as a primary actor in contributing to those ills.[26]

The list of social ills that Chinese seniors identified in contemporary China was substantial, including rising rates of marital infidelity, divorce, mental illness, and corruption. For my interviewees, the prevalence of social ills in China made it a less desirable place to live than the United States where, they said, the "social environment" (C. *sehwui waahnging*; M. *shehui huanjing*) is better. The positive aspects of America's social environment that Chinese-born seniors praised were also substantial. They contrasted America's blue skies with the pollution-clogged air across China to highlight the environmental and health benefits of living in the United States. They cited story after story of the goodwill of strangers who helped them navigate Boston's largely unfamiliar urban environment as evidence of the better relationships of trust among people in the United States. They felt safer overall in Boston, where they perceived the crime rate to be lower than in Guangzhou and other Chinese urban areas. They also praised the well-mannered behavior of Americans, who, in contrast to most Chinese, generally wait in line in an orderly fashion, don't spit on the ground, and greet others, even strangers, by saying "good morning."[27]

For many senior migrants, the contemporary social ills they worried about indexed a concomitant worry about moral decline at the collective level in China.[28] Morality in the PRC today is a pressing topic among many sectors of the population, and citizens' concerns find active expression first and foremost around a basic lack of trust in everyday social relationships. This concern was best expressed by one of my interviewees who set that lack of trust in China in contrast to that in the United States where, he told me, "people are very trustworthy. For example, if you tell someone something, if it's yes then it's yes, if it's no then it's no. If they tell you they'll do it, they will, they won't go against their word." Here, trust is articulated in terms of the social relationships that animate everyday interactions. However, the single largest concern around trust in China has to do with corruption, particularly at the government level and among elites. Unlike the Maoist and preliberation Chinese past, when the particularistic ties activated through social relationships were a means of strengthening "public-oriented morality [M. *gongong daode*]," today in China those particularistic ties are "increasingly oriented towards the accumulation of wealth, power, and status."[29]

Corruption was also a major concern of the factory workers Lee interviewed, particularly as they contrasted their nostalgia for power to counter social injustices during the Maoist period with their relative lack of power in countering social injustices in the PRC today. The same interviewee who explained how her "heart felt balanced and relaxed" in Maoist China when she only had the same steamed buns to eat each day also told Lee how "unbalanced" she feels as a result of corruption today:

> During the Cultural Revolution, my neighbor's family was jailed for ten years for stealing a thousand yuan. On the contrary, today, even if you lined up all officials in the work unit and shot all of them one by one, you would still miss others who are corrupt. . . . I feel unbalanced not because others make more money. If those people get rich by working hard and doing legitimate business, I can only be envious. *But now, workers are outraged because it's all about power.* Tens of thousands of yuan of bribes are all ordinary people's money [emphasis added].[30]

In other words, what these workers and other seniors wanted was the ability to address both real and perceived injustices that occur—either because of individual abuses of power or because of the government's inability to keep pace with and regulate the abuses that have been exacerbated by China's lightning-speed economic development. Controversies over food safety and regulation, chemical storage and pollution, and improperly supervised building sites have all captured public imagination in the PRC over the past decade.[31] Perceived through the lens of collective morality, these common disasters seem to demonstrate that the state has failed not just in its inability to keep up with economic development in terms of institutional regulatory mechanisms but also in its inability to develop a stronger and more positive "social atmosphere" that would prevent individuals from engaging in the abuse of power or other ethically problematic enterprises in the first place.

As anthropologist Ellen Oxfeld explains, moral discourse in China "is frequently about expectations" and focuses on the "evaluation of whether people have met their obligations."[32] For Chinese seniors, many of their expectations remained grounded in their previous experiences. "Liberation did not mean the end of preexisting models of social relations and expectations, and the reform era did not end modes of thinking that had developed during the collective era. Rather, old and new ways of looking at the world and making moral judgments were combined."[33] As a result, seniors' commentaries on China's contemporary moral landscape, although rooted in nostalgic attention to Maoist-era ideologies, reflected the complex and shifting influences of the multiple ideological values that have shaped seniors over the course of their lives. Oxfeld's account also draws attention to the central role of personal and familial obligations (M. *renqing*) in evaluating conceptions of morality in different social and political realms. In this way, she highlights the simultaneous coexistence of multiple understandings of morality as expressed through social obligations, such that reciprocity and accountability continue to be powerful forces in shaping local community relationships even as such values appear to be lacking by the state.[34]

That there is a widely perceived moral vacuum at the state level in the PRC today was clear through seniors' talk that linked the rise of social ills in contemporary China to the breakdown of the government's ability to protect and provide for its citizens.[35] Access to this protection seemed particularly lacking for many Chinese seniors, including my interviewees, whose lives have been rendered financially precarious through uneven state policies around providing pensions for older workers and rural residents. Insecurity was exacerbated by abuses of power, such as when Chinese officials resort to bribery or deny access to necessary resources for seniors who, as Lee's workers attest, also remember the possibility of countering power imbalances like these in the Maoist past.

Situated at this intersection of seniors' nostalgia for Maoist egalitarianism and fairness were my interviewees' vocal concerns about contemporary hurdles of access to medical treatment in China. In particular, seniors expressed outrage at how Chinese doctors over the past couple of decades have routinely refused to treat sick patients who cannot pay (up front) the exorbitant fees reportedly in vogue for even basic services.[36] And while there are now reforms in place in

China meant to address potential corruption in medical practices as well as the stark inequalities in health care provision between urban and rural residents, these reforms were implemented after many of my interviewees had settled in the Boston area and have had uneven success at local levels.[37] For example, in 2002, when many of my interviewees were either already in the United States or thinking about migrating, only 10 percent of China's rural residents had insurance coverage, compared to 95 percent in 2016.[38] These barriers to health care, particularly for rural seniors, stood in sharp contrast to the ease of access they experienced in the United States.

In particular, the U.S. system of Social Security and Medicare for senior citizens, lauded by my interviewees as evidence of the state's generosity and care for its citizens, epitomized the belief that in the United States, seniors can once again benefit from the core ideological values of egalitarianism and fairness that they remembered from their youth and that they felt are lacking for seniors in China today. One interviewee made this clear:

> When my mom was sick, we had to save up money to take care of her. We [barely] had enough money for us to eat, and we had to worry about our mother's health care. . . . In America, seniors don't have to worry about this money issue. . . . In China, seniors don't have to pay to go to parks or to go to the movies. But those aren't big concerns. . . . What's more important is that seniors not have to pay for health care.

Talking about the contrast between Chinese and U.S. health care provision, another migrant told me about her positive impressions of the U.S. system, which is "good to poor people" and "really humane":

> When I came to America, the first good thing [I learned] about America's government was about the health care. Even if you don't have money, you don't have to worry about . . . seeing a doctor. It was different in China. If you didn't have money, then you couldn't go to the doctor. Even if you were only missing one penny, they wouldn't be willing to see you. It was like that. . . . That's why after I came to America I was very thankful to the American government that they cared about us so much.

While many Americans struggle for access to reasonably priced health care and thus might find references to our system as "humane" to be puzzling, it's important to note here that the "humane" practice my interviewee was referring to is simple access to treatment. In other words, the American health system allows for the treatment of illness first and payment later and does not generally turn sick individuals away from emergency services. This practice, what one senior migrant called a "save the dying, help the hurt" attitude, exemplifies for her and others the value on human life that the U.S. government places on its citizens. This claim, focused on the U.S. government's treatment of citizens as "human," echoes the claim made by one of Lee's factory worker interviewees who emphasized that "the [Maoist] regime's commitment to fulfill workers' welfare and livelihood needs" meant that "workers were treated as 'human beings.'"[39]

The praise for what my senior migrant interviewees called the "humane social atmosphere" in the United States goes beyond typical understandings of social membership that use that term to reference the social welfare services available to citizens and legal residents of a nation-state. Instead, this understanding of social membership was intimately related to an emotional sense of affinity to the nation-state rooted in seniors' overwhelming nostalgia for the rhetoric and practice of egalitarian ideology that infused their experiences as younger adults in Maoist China. It was also strongly tied to their disappointment about how the PRC government seems to lack a similar concern for bolstering China's moral and social landscape today. Instead, seniors such as my migrant interviewees saw a failing social safety net that does little to insulate citizens from growing income inequality, lax moral judgment by elites and corrupt officials, and insufficient regulation of China's rapid economic progress—all of which contribute to gross miscarriages of justice for the same citizens that the PRC state professes to protect. Thus, it's not terribly surprising that many Chinese seniors who have migrated to the United States hope to become U.S. citizens despite their continuing strong attachments to China and sense of pride in China's development and economic modernization over the past few decades. In so doing, they and their descendants would have greater opportunities to demonstrate their ideological alignment with core democratic values of freedom and equality and also be able to enjoy the full benefits of what they perceive as the U.S. government's greater commitment to justice for its citizens.

THE DESIRE FOR CITIZENSHIP AND THE PERSISTENT PROBLEM OF ENGLISH

Many seniors I knew had struggled for years to learn English. There was a practical reason they wanted to learn English: to help them deal with the routine obstacles they encountered in everyday life in the United States. Although most seniors I knew had adapted to living here quite well with even a very rudimentary knowledge of English, the sheer number of everyday questions that came up without being able to read or speak in English was formidable. Seniors' ability to navigate a world in which they could not decipher addresses and common names from written information created a host of hurdles in completing seemingly routine tasks, such as confirming doctor appointments, filling prescriptions, managing insurance claims, switching to lower-cost telephone carriers, and registering to vote. Yet the most important reason that seniors struggled, often for years, to learn English was to be able to pass the U.S. citizenship exam.

Almost none of my interviewees had had the opportunity to study English when young. Those who were born in the 1930s and were able to attend university in the early years of the PRC learned Russian as a second language. Most migrants from rural areas had only had a few years of schooling and certainly never had the opportunity to formally study a language other than Chinese. Thus, the primary concern of most interviewees wasn't learning the content covered on the various sections of the citizenship exam—content that they could read about in Chinese and about which they were often enthusiastic to learn. Instead, their main concern was how they could learn enough English to pass the exam, which tested English-language knowledge in a variety of forms, including small talk as well as answering content-based questions in English about American history and politics through both multiple-choice questions and dictation.

For seniors literate in Chinese, just learning the English-language alphabet was a challenge. The extent of this challenge was made clear to me over and over again through my volunteer work teaching seniors ESL. It was also apparent through my interactions with seniors at their citizenship classes (where they struggled to gain basic mastery of common words and expressions) and in informal conversations with them in their residential buildings (when they would ask me for help reading their mail and paying their bills). In almost all cases, seniors blamed their poor memory, along with the natural process of aging, for the difficulties they had in learning English pronunciation and retaining vocabulary. Seniors repeatedly told me that English "went in one ear and out the other" and that learning English is "so hard" when you are old. Many seniors went to multiple English classes, seeking out free classes offered through nonprofit or religious organizations because they had little disposable income. Even when my interviewees did succeed in learning some English, they encountered unexpected difficulties in practicing their new skills. Mrs. Wong, who attended Bunker Hill Community College for several semesters, was almost arrested when a child with whom she had been trying to practice English at a bus stop became alarmed at her persistent attempts at conversation and called the police. Understandably, Mrs. Wong was shocked and ashamed to learn that her innocent interest in trying to practice English was perceived as a tangible threat.

Summing up the difficulty of learning enough English to pass the citizenship exam, one of my interviewees explained:

> You have to answer 100 questions to pass the citizenship test, but it's really hard being able to do that. You have to listen and be able to answer them. . . . How would you know how to understand all those long questions? It's very hard. You say that if you are over sixty-five years old and have lived here for fifteen years then you can use Chinese, but when will it be fifteen years?

For individuals in their late sixties and seventies, fifteen years seemed an unreasonably long time to have to wait for anything.[40] Moreover, for seniors who were hoping to obtain citizenship for themselves because they wanted to sponsor other family members still in China to join them in the United States, waiting fifteen years, by which time they might be gravely ill, incapacitated, or dead, was not a viable option. One woman said, "I want to take classes to see if I can learn enough [English] to take the citizenship test. But my brain is not working well, and I can't remember anything. . . . I just want to become a citizen but it's so hard because I'm so old." When her friend chimed in to note that "it's hard to pass the citizenship test [when] you can't speak English," the first woman added, "That's the one hard thing. Working isn't hard, but learning English is." One couple, retired college-educated professionals, attended English classes in five or six different locations because they were so eager to become citizens. Nevertheless, they had learned very little English overall, pointedly commenting that "immigration officials just don't know how difficult it is to learn a new language, particularly when you're old." Implicit in their commentary was the expectation that immigration officials, as state actors, would be sympathetic to the struggles they were facing and their efforts trying to learn English. In other words, they seemed to believe that if the officials in charge of administering the citizenship test did in fact understand how difficult it is to learn English as an older adult, then they would be more lenient with that policy.

The many obstacles involved with seniors' desire to learn enough English to pass the citizenship exam raise the specter of the indifference to human concerns that can accompany entrenched bureaucratic systems through the hurdles they create to achieving desired outcomes—hurdles that one might think would be reminiscent of the same kind of Chinese bureaucratic apparatuses that facilitate corruption or serve as barriers to accessing health care criticized by seniors today. Yet even as seniors complained about bureaucratic difficulty and insensitivity as they recounted how challenging it could be to pass the U.S. citizenship exam, these concerns did not deter their goals to pass the test. Instead, those goals remained tied to their emotional affinity to their perceptions of the United States as "fair" and "just," along with their aspirations for achieving the benefits of full membership. Indeed, the view that officers administering the citizenship exam should be sympathetic to seniors' struggles and hard work in trying to learn English was compatible with the similar expectations for humane consideration expressed by the woman I quoted at the beginning of the chapter who believed the U.S. government would want her daughter to join her in the United States as soon as possible.

When I asked my interviewees, "Why do you want to become an American citizen?" most seniors told me, in English, "I want to vote." Sometimes they would say, also in English, "I like freedom." For a long time, I was skeptical about these responses, feeling that they were above all else responses of convenience, since "to vote" was the shortest (and therefore easiest to remember in English) among the possible responses to this question. Yet the more I talked with seniors with a variety of life experiences, the more I realized that "wanting to vote" and "liking freedom" reflected the actual feelings that many had in wanting to become U.S. citizens: they desired to be full participants in a social order in which they felt valued. For example, a woman in her seventies who had suffered a stroke in 1991, just after she moved to the United States, explained her feelings of happiness in formally achieving U.S. citizenship:

> I became a citizen in 2000. I was really happy when I became a citizen because I have more rights. I can vote now. So, last time I went and voted for our mayor. I couldn't walk [because of my stroke] so [a social worker] had some cars that drove us there and drove us back from voting. I participate every time there's an election. Because I'm a citizen, I can vote and can be elected. Of course I'm old so I wouldn't be elected. I'm very happy that I get to vote though.

Another senior told me, "I always vote whenever there is an election. Whether it is an election for governor, for senator, for the House of Representatives, or even for the U.S. president, I will always take part in it." My interviewees also explained that poor English-language skills were not an obstacle to being informed about local political concerns. For example, this migrant and his friends successfully navigated the political landscape to make informed decisions by relying on the extensive reporting about political campaigns in the local Chinese-language media.[41] He said,

> Usually I focus on learning the English name of the candidate I think is suitable in advance, so that I can check off that candidate's name when I cast my vote. The candidates all have their own marketing campaigns, so I can identify each one and learn about their goals. It is based on these marketing campaigns that I make my final decision during an election. Besides that, I also have discussions with my friends about politics. . . . Usually our discussions end up with consensus [on a common candidate] we will vote for.

For my interviewees, who felt a strong sense of ideological alignment with what they perceived to be the more "humane social atmosphere" in the United States as compared to China, there were definite benefits to achieving American citizenship. As a result, seniors studied—often in vain—for years with the hope that they would gain strong enough English language skills to pass the citizenship exam and put down permanent roots to secure a better future in the United States for themselves and their adult children and grandchildren still in China.

THE AMERICAN SKY

When I began talking with seniors about their first impressions of the United States, over and again they told me that in the United States, "the sky is so blue!" For my interviewees, many of whom had desired to emigrate here as children or young adults but were able to achieve this lifelong goal only as retirees in postreform China, the blueness of the American sky recalled for them a similarly blue sky in China—one that they remembered from decades ago, when they could only dream of experiencing life abroad. Thus, seniors' talk about America's "blue sky" served as a powerful metaphor indexing relief at finally having arrived, after long and often difficult lives, in the "beautiful country" (M. *meiguo*; C. *meigok*) that fueled their diasporic imaginations harbored since childhood. At the same time, this reference also made clear some of the concrete advantages of living in the United States for these same seniors, who contrasted that clean air with heavily polluted air in China. The fumes that leave a grayish, brownish pall over much of China's urban and rural areas are of course an unfortunate by-product of China's rapid economic development.

Throughout my conversations with seniors, I heard a range of views about what they liked best about being in the United States. To be sure, many of those views reflected the concrete advantages they experienced daily, like clean air. One woman said, "Stuff here is cheap, food is cheap. There are big sales. There's gas and it's warm. There's hot and cold water. In China if it's cold, then you're cold. If you have a job then you have money; if not then you don't." Yet it wasn't only the concrete advantages of living in the United States that Chinese senior migrants held dear. They also wanted to have the right to vote and to make their voices heard in the political realm without fear of repercussion. They wanted to trust in the social relationships they established with others and to trust that the government and the elites who control access to key resources would not abuse their power or act in ways that are morally corrupt. Most important, they wanted the state to make them feel valued as human beings—a value they remembered experiencing as younger adults in Maoist China yet they say has eluded them in today's China.

In the following chapter, I build on this discussion of the ideological and emotional affinity that Chinese seniors in the United States experience by focusing attention on the lifestyle aspirations they had for their "retirement." Although these aspirations remained out of reach for many of my interviewees in China, they found that the United States provided a context of reception that allowed them to achieve the culturally familiar "Chinese" retirement lifestyles they desired.

4 THE MEANING OF "RETIREMENT" FOR CHINESE SENIOR MIGRANTS IN THE UNITED STATES

During summer 2011, as I was interviewing a variety of Cantonese-speaking senior migrants in and around Boston's Chinatown, I met Mr. Wang. He had migrated to Boston from Guangdong Province at the age of sixty just a few months earlier to join his adult daughter and her family, who lived a short commute away from Chinatown. Mr. Wang had been a farmer in rural Taishan and then worked as a migrant construction laborer in nearby Guangzhou, the capital city of Guangdong Province. Despite his brief residency in Boston, his older age, and his inability to speak English, Mr. Wang had recently found a part-time job working in the kitchen of a social service center that provided daily hot lunches to low-income, homebound Chinese seniors in the greater Boston area, for which he was paid a few hundred dollars each month.

Mr. Wang described to me a usual day in his new American life. He woke up early each morning, went for a walk, and then returned home to prepare his grandson's breakfast. Afterward, he took his grandson to school. In the afternoons, after working for at least four hours each day, Mr. Wang walked around different areas of Boston, trying to become familiar with his new city of residence. He often stopped by the grocery store to pick up any needed ingredients for dinner before heading home to spend the evening with his family. Mr. Wang's life was not easy in any conventional sense: he lived with his daughter and her family in a small, crowded apartment on the edge of poverty, unable to communicate with most other Boston residents and separated from the long-term friends and colleagues he had left behind in China. Yet when we talked, he did not seem unhappy with his new lifestyle in the United States.

While it's common for Chinese seniors to migrate to the United States to live with or near their adult children and help care for their American-born grandchildren, it is less common for senior migrants to explain their primary motivation for migration as bluntly as Mr. Wang did when he told me: "Since I am a farmer, my retirement benefits in China are not good. I can get better retirement benefits here by working for a couple of years. Chinese farmers don't have many retirement benefits. . . . I hope that I can have benefits [here] too once I have worked." Focused on the potential benefits he hoped to access through living and working as an older individual, Mr. Wang paid testament to the contemporary landscape of financial insecurity for Chinese senior citizens that stands in contrast to the ideals of collective security for which they worked and sacrificed as younger adults in Maoist China. Like Mr. Wang, many aging individuals in rural areas of Southeast China have no means of supporting themselves other than continuing the agricultural or other kinds of intensive labor that have supported them throughout their lives.

In the previous chapter, I documented that many recent Chinese senior migrants were strongly influenced by the mid-twentieth-century revolutionary ideals of egalitarianism and justice that undergirded their contributions as younger adults to Chinese modernization efforts during the Maoist era. In this chapter, I build on that discussion by turning to the lifestyle aspirations of these seniors who felt left out of China's current economic growth and were critical of the contemporary Chinese state for not "treating them better." In this way, I seek to make sense of Mr. Wang's comments through a discussion of what kinds of goals older Chinese migrants like Mr. Wang had for their "retirement" and how migrating to the United States at the relatively advanced age of sixty or older enabled some Chinese-born individuals to live a retired lifestyle more in line with these goals than if they had remained in China. In particular, I focus on how living in this country provides a level of security that allows them to foresee an end to the intensive labor that they have performed throughout their lives and also to engage with others in a social and leisurely way, living comfortably while also increasing their own and others' well-being.

The situations of the Chinese senior migrants I discuss here fit in with scholarly concerns about how seniors worldwide are navigating the challenges associated with aging in a contemporary global context in which people are simultaneously living longer but receiving fewer state-supported resources providing critical support for their well-being. In North America, one response to these pressures has been the "successful aging" movement, which began "around the 1980s as a medical, public health, commercial, and popular cultural endeavor."[1] Since then, key ideas associated with successful aging—including goals for individual seniors to live independent lives that contribute not only to their own health and well-being but also to the health of the societies in which they live—have spread around the globe.[2] Scholars documenting this movement and its effects offer evidence of seniors who achieve greater well-being yet are also critical of the movement. Criticisms include how the idea of successful aging increases the burden on senior citizens to provide for their own well-being—thereby reinforcing global neoliberal trends contributing to seniors' insecurity in many parts of the world. Scholars also note that the successful aging movement contributes to ageism (that is, negative views about older individuals and the process of growing old) and denies recognition for seniors' growth in how they view themselves and their social roles over the life course. Moreover, these goals are predicated on Eurocentric notions of individual autonomy that stand in contrast to many seniors' desires for social interdependence.[3] To mitigate these concerns, some scholars instead adopt the term *active aging*, through which they seek to examine ideas of senior well-being in its broadest form without reinforcing Westernized conceptions of selfhood.[4]

Unlike countries that have adopted a neoliberal stance toward the demographic pressures associated with their aging populations by cutting back on welfare programs that provide pensions and health care for the elderly, the PRC has instead created new initiatives over the past two decades to increase pensions and medical care access for both urban and rural citizens. Moreover, it has also instituted other resources for retirees, including over seventy thousand "old-age universities" where seniors can be active, socialize, and pursue educational opportunities they may not have had access to as younger adults.[5] Yet because of the enormity of the problem of elder support in China, where seniors currently make up almost 20 percent of the population, the state has passed national legislation mandating that adult children take care of their elderly parents.[6] It has also adopted a similar language as that used by neoliberal regimes worldwide encouraging seniors to be self-reliant for their own well-being as they grow older.[7] This new landscape of aging in China has provided some new social supports for rural seniors like Mr. Wang, but it has also exacerbated existing inequalities among rural and urban Chinese elderly by creating new lifestyle divides between rural seniors and many of their urban counterparts. These contemporary inequalities have their roots in the social welfare system created during the Maoist period, which provided urban Chinese residents with greater social and economic security through access to state-provided housing, food, income, education, and health insurance—security never similarly guaranteed for rural residents.[8] Since the 1990s, urban seniors have had more substantial opportunities to pursue the popular new concept of active aging, which emphasizes their engagement in social networks and opportunities to increase personal well-being and is also influenced by global preoccupations with the successful aging movement.[9] Active aging as promoted by the Chinese government allows seniors to mitigate concerns they may experience about general trends of incomplete state support and changing social norms of family care.[10] By encouraging regular engagement in group social activities and physical exercise, seniors can stay busy, and perhaps healthy, so as to increase both their own well-being and that of the state through their reduced reliance on its welfare.[11]

Despite the state's support for active aging, financially insecure seniors in China do not have many resources at their disposal to improve their lives even as they have grown increasingly aware of the availability of those resources elsewhere. Well-developed circuits of knowledge, available through news media as well as through friends and family abroad, detail ways of aging both within and beyond China that differ significantly from some seniors' own experiences. As a result, even before leaving China, seniors were well aware of alternative models of retirement lifestyles focused around ideals of active aging that were substantially more available to some Chinese residents than others. Like Mr. Wang, they also knew that in the United States, they would have access to paid and voluntary work opportunities, as well as the potential for social welfare support, providing important opportunities for fostering their own well-being. In other words, as fascination with successful forms of aging has increasingly traveled across the globe, knowledge about these ideas has redefined understanding about possibilities for aging well for individuals such as Chinese seniors who have access to transnational migration pathways elsewhere. And while plenty of scholars have explored how elites, particularly in the North American and the European Union context, have made use of transnational networks to attain the retirement lifestyles to which they aspire, few have examined how these aspirational journeys have worked out for financially insecure individuals like my interviewees, for whom aging well as an ideology is influenced as much by culturally Chinese goals of self-cultivation and benevolence toward others as it is by Western goals of self-support and independence.¹² In my analysis, I focus on how the globalization of ideas around the successful aging movement, including contemporary goals for aging well in China, have contributed to Chinese seniors' motivations for migration through the proliferation of new aspirations for retirement as a stage of life oriented around individual and collective well-being.

CONTEMPORARY CONTEXTS OF RETIREMENT IN CHINA AND THE UNITED STATES

Although the idea of retirement has gained more traction in the PRC over the past few decades, it is not an entirely new concept in China. During China's imperial past, scholar officials who had served the imperial court idealized the time when they could withdraw from society to instead focus on quiet pursuits like contemplation of nature and writing poetry.¹³ However, for most Chinese throughout history, individuals had to work over the full course of their lives—as agricultural or other kinds of laborers—to survive.

Only during the past few decades has retirement as a more formally defined life stage become widespread as both an ideal and a possibility for significant numbers of Chinese citizens. With large-scale industrialization of the Chinese labor force during the Maoist era also came formal policies mandating that women and men withdraw from the labor force at the respective ages of fifty (fifty-five for women in professional occupations, such as teachers) and sixty. Through the *danwei* system, individuals living in China's urban areas were assigned to work units through their places of employment, which also provided all housing, food, and health care for workers. Pensions were also allotted by a worker's danwei, allowing at least a modest amount of financial support for all former workers, who were expected to continue to rely on their adult children for additional support if their pensions were not sufficient to support them in old age. In rural areas, in contrast, these mandated retirement ages did not necessarily apply. The intense physical labor required for agricultural production, combined with the absence of work units and any formal pension system, meant that individuals continued to work until they were physically unable to do so and had to fully rely on adult children for their financial support.¹⁴ Yet despite the relative lack of social welfare infrastructures in rural areas as compared to the urban danwei system, seniors still enjoyed relative security during the Maoist period in comparison to today. Collectivization, which assured rural residents community-based access to some basic welfare networks, and the relative immobility of family members, who were locked into their respective urban or rural areas of residency through the hukou system,[15] insulated many rural elderly from complete poverty and minimized economic inequality between rural elderly residents and their urban counterparts.[16]

The legacies of these systems continue to influence the life possibilities of many Chinese citizens today, with China's urban residents (and senior residents in those areas) considerably better off because of work unit benefits like housing, health care, and pensions they may still continue to receive. As inequality between China's urban and rural residents has skyrocketed over the past three decades, so have inequalities among Chinese rural and urban senior citizens.[17] Despite increased economic possibilities for both groups, the legacy of unequal social welfare between urban and rural residents, combined with the dismantling of the collectivist system and the increasing mobility of China's working-age population, has left many rural seniors without a safety net (state or family provided) of any kind. So even as today's Chinese seniors in urban areas may be engaging in lifestyle choices that share some similarities with the retirement lifestyles of American seniors influenced by the successful aging movement—partaking in community-based activities, travel, and so on—seniors in China's rural areas may have none of those same options.[18] Not only are rural Chinese senior citizens much more at risk than their urban counterparts for being impoverished; they may also have no choice but to continue to perform physically demanding agricultural labor well into their final decades of life. This stark outlook for rural elderly is likely a factor in their high suicide rate, which is "three to five times higher than that among the urban elderly."[19] In the PRC today, these divergences in government-mandated political and economic policies for urban and rural residents create significant differences in Chinese seniors' relationship to paid work, which influences their goals and expectations for retirement as both a life stage and a lifestyle.

Despite having a much longer and socially embedded history in the United States, retirement is also not a unitary concept among American senior citizens. Since the 1930s, when growing public concern about the high rates of poverty among American elderly spurred the establishment of the first universal pension system through the creation of Social Security,[20] Americans have been familiar with the idea that older individuals should be able to enjoy a financially secure period to relax or enjoy leisurely pursuits in their later years, supported by each individual's own history of economic productivity and contribution. Over the years, ideas about how to make best use of one's retirement have changed substantially from simply avoiding poverty after withdrawing from the labor force.²¹ Ideals about how to experience a meaningful older age have changed with increasing possibilities of consumption and mobility, as well as access to information about the lives of others; nevertheless, these ideals are also strongly tied to an individual's socioeconomic class positioning, with blue-collar workers more often opting for financial survival and rest and white-collar workers expecting to fulfill long-held desires.²² This now almost century-long acceptance of retirement as a life stage means that there is substantially more social infrastructure to support a range of retirement options for American senior citizens so that they can pursue different kinds of retirement lifestyles. Whether individuals expect to fully withdraw from the labor force or remain at least partially involved in either paid or unpaid work, American seniors have a range of opportunities to reside together with other older individuals, participate in continuing education classes, and engage in other activities developed for (and marketed to) them. This social infrastructure that supports retirement as a meaningful social category and stage of life through which individuals can choose to pursue different lifestyle opportunities would not exist without the economic base on which it rests: Social Security and Medicare.²³

For my Chinese immigrant interviewees, coming as they have from a society in which the concept of retirement is relatively less well developed, American infrastructures of social and economic support for senior citizens were appealing. These support systems were crucial to Chinese seniors' overall economic security in the United States, enabling them to live independently in subsidized senior housing complexes with the tiny incomes they made through low-wage and part-time paid employment or the limited Social Security they received once they formally withdrew from the labor force. Yet for many seniors, the goal of having these benefits was not just about enabling them to finally end their years of backbreaking labor in their seventies. Rather, the financial security these benefits afforded allowed seniors to live a meaningful retired lifestyle that included fulfilling goals of engaging in daily activities that contributed to their own self-development and the well-being of society by helping others in their community. These lifestyle goals have been modeled in recent decades for seniors in China as the PRC government has embraced globally widespread views about successful aging and has encouraged active aging as an ideology among seniors as one way to fill the gap between what seniors need and what the government is willing to provide toward their support. Farquhar and Zhang refer to this popular movement as "self-health." They explain that in the mid-1990s, the "Ministry of Health began to encourage a new era of health propaganda that turned from educating people to use professional care intelligently—an important emphasis in earlier socialist health-care propaganda—to educating them to care for themselves... so as not to become a burden either to their children or to the state." One response to these initiatives has been to cultivate *yangsheng*—a way of living focusing on "nurturing life" through meaningful activities.[24]

Farquhar and Zhang locate the cultural roots of yangsheng in the Confucian philosophical tradition, focusing in particular on the importance of the concept of self-cultivation, which underscores the active role that people take to improve their lives.[25] The active lifestyle that goes along with nurturing life also shares deep connections to the Confucian philosophical concept of *ren* (often translated as "benevolence"), which emphasizes the need to act with compassion in interactions with others as a fundamental expression of humanity.[26] So while not all yangsheng ways of living are altruistic, there is nonetheless a strong connection between yangsheng and the ideals of social contribution espoused by older generations of retirees who were "habituated to providing for others" during the Maoist era and remain strongly influenced by these ideals in their daily life today.[27] Thus, by engaging in the kinds of selfless activities exemplified through helping others, like volunteerism, seniors believed they could ultimately better themselves and also contribute to the well-being of the community as a whole. As Farquhar and Zhang explain, "The whole Confucian tradition, so deeply embedded in everyday language, even today, maintained an expectation that people will actively strive to attain the goodness proper to humans."[28] These views also influenced the Chinese senior migrants I knew in Boston who engaged in volunteerism. They were grateful not only for the personal economic security provided to them through Social Security and other benefits for senior citizens, but also because that economic security enabled them to perform volunteer work and continue to contribute actively to the well-being of society as a whole despite no longer directly participating in the labor force.

From the first days I spent in Chinatown, my interactions with Chinese migrants brought me into contact time and again with seniors who were volunteering their time in different community settings. Some work consisted of small tasks, such as picking up prescription refills for the daytime clients of an adult day health center or singing songs to entertain those same clients. Yet for older migrants taking part in these seemingly routine daily activities, their volunteerism masked the everyday challenges they faced. For example, filling a prescription is difficult when you don't share a language in common with the pharmacist. For these older volunteers who sat with age-mates while they played bingo and accompanied the oldest and frailest immigrants in performing basic tasks, volunteerism was an important form of community engagement. Individuals were happy to help out because volunteer work gave them a sense of purpose, provided a sense of community, got them out of their dingy apartments, and enabled them to achieve at least some small recognition for their selflessness in working with others.

Many of those who were engaged with the larger community through their volunteer work were following a desired path toward a comfortable retirement through which they could find respite from hard labor and instead focus on achieving well-being through leisurely opportunities for learning, socializing, and helping others. In addition to those who were doing a few hours of volunteer work each week, I also met a handful of seniors who were exceptionally committed to contributing to the well-being of their larger community—"compassionate exemplars" whose constant performance of volunteer work was undertaken as a full-time pursuit all day, every day.

In the following sections, I focus on in-depth ethnographic case studies of two Chinese senior migrants, both eighty years old in 2011, as a lens for exploring what retirement as a life stage meant for these two individuals, along with how migrating provided them possibilities for creating meaningful retired lifestyles that resonated with goals for that stage of life widely in circulation in China today. These cases contribute to a better understanding of Chinese senior migrant life in the United States by offering detailed portraits of the daily experiences involved with cultivating well-being for themselves and the larger community of Chinese seniors around them. In both cases, the pursuit of benevolent acts was made possible in large part through the social and economic security available to them in the United States.

"COMFORTABLE" RETIREMENT AS A PLATFORM FOR SELF-CULTIVATION: THE CASE OF MR. LAM

Mr. Lam lived in a state-subsidized senior residential building in Boston's Chinatown that housed almost exclusively Chinese-born individuals. His apartment was typical of other subsidized senior apartments I visited. It was a 300-square-foot space, with a living room, a partitioned kitchen, a bedroom, and a bathroom. Although his bachelor residence was not furnished ornately, it was clean and neat, with bright light from the corner windows. Over several hours during the summer of 2011, Mr. Lam told me about his life. About to turn eighty at the time of our interview, he had migrated to the United States eighteen years earlier through the sponsorship of his adult daughter after working as a construction laborer in rural Guangdong Province. For the first ten years that Mr. Lam lived in the United States, he performed paid labor. He first worked at a restaurant; when that work became too physically demanding, he delivered meals to homebound Chinese elders. For the previous eight years, after retiring from these two jobs, Mr. Lam had lived an "orderly" (C. *hou yauh dihtjeuih*; M. *hen you zhixu*) and comfortable life—the lifestyle he had hoped to achieve when he decided to leave China and move to the United States almost twenty years earlier.

Each morning, Mr. Lam woke up before dawn and went to the neighborhood YMCA to exercise. When he came home, he made breakfast before meeting friends in the community areas of his building or a nearby park where they took a morning walk together. After lunch, provided by delivery from the kitchen in his building, he watched his favorite Chinese shows on satellite TV, napped, and went to the grocery store to buy the food he would cook himself for dinner. Sometimes he played Chinese chess with other residents of the building. Twice each week he met up to *yumcha* with friends—who, like him, had labored in the kitchens of nearby Chinese restaurants after moving to the United States.[29] On weekends, his daughter sometimes came from New Hampshire to visit him. Mr. Lam lived only a few minutes' walk away from two subway lines and one major bus route that led to many other areas of Boston; however, he almost never left Chinatown, even though he was familiar with Boston through his past work delivering Chinese meals to homebound seniors. He sometimes traveled elsewhere, either to China or with Chinese-speaking tour groups to other U.S. destinations.

Throughout our interview, Mr. Lam emphasized that he had achieved his primary goal in migrating to the United States. He lived comfortably off the small Social Security payment he received from having worked and paid taxes for a decade. He noted that his lifestyle now was particularly meaningful in comparison to his options in China at the time he migrated. In China, he had performed backbreaking labor, and as a rural resident, he had no possibility of receiving a pension or other state support once he discontinued that labor. Had he stayed in China, he would not have been able to stop working. He explained:

> I was a construction worker back in China, mainly building houses. I had to work with cement and climb up and down buildings. It was one tough job. It required so much physical energy and took a great toll on my body. . . . I had

to work under the blazing sun . . . every day during the summer. In the winter, I had to suffer the dryness of the weather. It was not pleasant. . . . My daughter, who was married at the time, was already living here in the U.S. before I moved here. When I reached the age of [government-mandated] retirement in China, I called my daughter and complained to her that my construction job was too physically demanding and that my body couldn't take it anymore. After she heard my complaints, she asked me if I wanted to come to here to reunite with her. I told her that I would definitely come if that were ever possible. My daughter started working on my immigration paperwork, and it was approved in about half a year.

For Mr. Lam and many other older rural residents of Guangdong Province, their problem for the future was not only the steady toll that their physical labor took on their bodies and overall health, but also the fact that they had no possibility of ever being able to stop their labor because they had no other means of financial support. Of particular concern was medical care, since the subsidized health care available to residents of China's urban areas was not available to rural dwellers in the 1990s. Mr. Lam explained, "Actually, there was no such thing as retirement back in Taishan. Construction work back then was simply part-time jobs. Our 'boss' just picked people randomly [to do the work] whenever he got a construction project. . . . There was no contract and no retirement."

In contrast, for Mr. Lam, working in the United States seemed like it would be an improvement over continuing construction work in China:

My daughter knew people who worked at a restaurant, and so she passed the word around that her dad just got here and wanted to find some work to do. The people in the restaurant told her right away that I could go and help them out. My daughter told me what they said, and I thought to myself, Why not? The work that I did in China was much more physically demanding and I survived, so I didn't think I would have a problem with this new job.

Nevertheless, the restaurant work was in fact much more strenuous than Mr. Lam had anticipated. He worked at the restaurant for five years, a significant term of employment for an older worker still expected to perform physically taxing labor twelve hours each day without overtime compensation or weekends off.

Once he was allotted a residential unit in Chinatown, Mr. Lam moved from his daughter's house in New Hampshire to Boston, where he was able to find work delivering hot meals to seniors throughout the Boston area. After ten years, he formally withdrew from the labor force and began living the comfortable life that he had hoped for in his older age:

> My working experience was harsh, especially when I was working in the restaurant. When I got off work, I would feel so tired that I would refuse to go anywhere after work. But that changed after I retired. *After all, the reason that I came to the U.S. was not because I needed money for living, but because I just wanted a place where I could live comfortably.* Nowadays I hear that the mainland has improved so much that it is nicer to live there than to live in the U.S. That is just hearsay, and I would argue that there is no way that statement could be true. For example, my medical insurance is entirely covered by the government. This still isn't possible in mainland China. [Emphasis added.]

When Mr. Lam migrated in the early 1990s, his only chance for the comfortable retirement lifestyle he hoped for was in the United States, not in China. Moreover, he noted, it was through the government's generous provision of support for senior citizens that he was able to retire comfortably and realize this goal. That support not only took the form of subsidized housing and medical care, but also the Social Security check he received each month from having been a working taxpayer for a decade in his sixties:

> In terms of living, I feel that there is more security in the U.S. [than in China]. This is even more apparent [to me] since my retirement. I receive from the government a pension fund of about $800 a month. That money has so far been sufficient to meet all my needs for living. . . . This leads to a more general sense of happiness, which in turn reduces the chances of me being sick. This, to me, is very important.

Many of my other interviewees shared Mr. Lam's vision of retirement as a time to leave behind backbreaking labor to focus instead on other pursuits of self-cultivation. Like Mr. Lam, many senior migrants worked (or hoped to work) long enough to qualify for Social Security, thus providing them with a secure income that would not require dependence on adult children for support. Moreover, once formally retired from their labor in the United States, many senior migrants spent long hours in various socially engaged pursuits, including playing music, cards, or mahjong with other Chinese American seniors. These pursuits contributed not only to their own well-being but also to the well-being of others by keeping everyone mentally active. These goals voiced by my senior interviewees echoed those of the retired Beijingers studied by Farquhar and Zhang, who note retirees' ideal "vision is one of a regular life, every day pretty much like every other, peaceful, tidy, comfortable, and sociable."[30] This aspirational lifestyle, while out of reach for many Chinese seniors in China, was accessible in the greater Boston area largely because of the well-developed infrastructure of city, state, and federal senior support.

Yet it's also worth noting that the "comfortable" lives for which my interviewees were grateful were just a fine line away from impoverishment, more aptly termed "comfortable subsistence" made possible through the frugality of seniors. My interviewees knew how to stretch their limited resources by shopping for tiny amounts of food in low-cost Chinatown supermarkets and eating one free meal each day. They also displayed ingenuity in getting by in other ways, as individuals with much needed skills—like cutting hair—provided free or reduced-cost services to other members of their senior communities. The retirement that these low-income senior migrants achieved allowed individuals to trade long days of harsh labor for a comfortable lifestyle near family and friends that they would not have been able to experience had they stayed in China. Even so, most migrants' retired lifestyles were far from the ideal of those middle-class Americans who live in retirement communities with common habits of consumption that my interviewees could have scarcely imagined, and where costs of living far exceed the several hundred dollars per month on which many Chinese seniors survived.

Thus, it's important to recognize the fine line that separates the "good and fortunate lives" of these seniors from a less optimistic lens: one that focuses instead on the stark cinderblock walls and worn and stained carpeting of the low-income housing complexes in which seniors lived. The recreational and entertainment facilities so proudly shown off to me within these housing complexes were rarely larger than one medium-sized room that could just fit a Ping-Pong table and a few bookshelves with an odd assortment of books in the languages of buildings' residents: Chinese, Russian, and English. Many seniors also remained tied to their housing, seemingly trapped together with others and unable to communicate beyond their immediate neighbors. At night, those who lived in Chinatown were awoken by carousing outside: the neighborhood overlaps with Boston's theater district and a college, so there are always tipsy people on the street until early hours of the morning. Similarly, despite significant (and largely successful) efforts to reduce crime in the area, most seniors circulated stories of recent muggings and were afraid to walk on the streets near their apartments after dark.[31]

Nevertheless, this concentration of low-income seniors in Chinatown provided significant opportunities for recent senior migrants who sought to live meaningful lives. For my interviewees, that meaningful lifestyle included not only the individual well-being they experienced through living comfortably but also relied on directly contributing to the well-being of other seniors in the community. For example, Mr. Lam continued to spend several hours each week organizing games and other activities for seniors in his building. And Mr. Wang, who had several more years of paid employment ahead of him before he could formally withdraw from the workforce, also volunteered at one of the Chinatown-area service agencies even after taking on paid work. These are just two examples of how Chinese senior migrants' small contributions contributed to community well-being, yet they were characteristic of the daily acts of compassion that I witnessed throughout my research. In this way, they resonated with the goals for active aging that have been fostered in China by the state and through the pursuit of yangsheng lifestyles. In the next section, I move beyond this portrait of how retirees living comfortably contributed to others' well-being through daily acts of benevolence to the example of individuals for whom living benevolently was a full-time pursuit that defined all of their interactions with others around them.

EXEMPLARS OF COMPASSIONATE BEHAVIOR: THE CASE OF MRS. TAN

When I first got to know Mrs. Tan during the summer of 2011, she was about to turn eighty and had been living in the United States for twelve years. She arrived with her husband and initially settled into their daughter's home near the New Hampshire border to help care for their American-born grandchildren. Following a common trajectory of other migrant grandparent caregivers, once their grandchildren were old enough to attend school, Mrs. Tan and her husband moved to subsidized senior housing in Boston's Chinatown—just steps away from the building that housed Mr. Lam's apartment. Yet Mrs. Tan's ideal of retired life diverged in significant ways from that of Mr. Lam. Rather than spending her days quietly and comfortably socializing with friends and performing occasional volunteer work, Mrs. Tan preferred to spend full days actively helping various members of the Chinatown community. Most days, she worked 9 to 5 contributing to area residents in need of various kinds of assistance—accompaniment to doctors' appointments, advocating for better Chinese-language signage for her building, or encouraging area residents' engagement in activities aimed at benefiting the community as a whole. She had grown up in an urban area in China and worked most of her adult life (except during the Cultural Revolution) as a medical administrator. While her retirement pension in China was not as large as that of urban residents who had worked in larger or more powerful danwei, Mrs. Tan did have a small pension in China as well as a place to live, where she and her husband continued to return once a year to visit their son and his family who had no intention of moving to the United States.

My first inkling of the depth of Mrs. Tan's involvement in her U.S. community came at the conclusion of a meeting for Chinatown seniors where she and I had both been present. She was singled out for my attention by one of the social workers who suggested that if I had questions about the senior community, Mrs. Tan could help answer them. Mrs. Tan beckoned me to sit next to her and without my asking, she got out her personal scrapbook to show me. The moment she opened it, I realized that I was talking with someone unusual. On page after page, Mrs. Tan pointed out the newspaper clippings from the local Chinese news media that she had carefully collected and labeled. Each picture featured her, always standing among a group of people—members of different Chinatown community organizations. Beneath each picture, captions provided evidence of her community activism and involvement. In one photo, she stood with other representatives of local organizations that had raised money for victims of natural disasters in China, Haiti, and New Orleans. In another, she was a member of Chinatown advocates lobbying to institute bilingual ballots and increase voter participation among Chinatown's older, non-English-speaking residents.

Over the next few months, I ran into Mrs. Tan at least twice a week at various community meetings and witnessed firsthand her extraordinary selflessness in volunteering her time to help the community's oldest and infirm residents. I learned that she had taught herself enough English to communicate needs for basic apartment repairs and mediate disputes between her neighbors and her building's English-speaking management. I was party to her "campaign" speech as she sought the support of her (already supportive) neighbors to serve a third two-year term as the building's representative at neighborhood association meetings. I heard time and again from residents of her building how she spent her own time and money to travel to local hospitals to visit ill neighbors without adult children or other close family nearby. Over and over, Chinatown residents described Mrs. Tan as someone who "loved to help others." Her roles included not just taking care of the ill and infirm and mediating disputes between her building's residents and management but also extended to encouraging Chinatown seniors to be politically active and develop self-sustaining support networks.

Mrs. Tan was invariably present at the weekly coffee hour in her housing complex, during which she provided updates about building residents who were in need of help. She also served an educational role, correcting fellow residents' misapprehensions about American policies affecting their lives and schooling them in lessons about responsible citizenship. For example, when she was explaining the status of a fellow resident she had accompanied to the hospital several days before, another neighbor piped up to complain that the U.S. government should do more to take care of them. Mrs. Tan gently corrected her, noting that in fact the government already provides substantial aid to older people and doesn't have the resources to pay for small, everyday expenses like paying for a taxi to the hospital. Nor, Mrs. Tan went on to explain, do service organizations have those resources. She pointed out that service organizations are already severely financially strapped, using as an example recent efforts to help raise enough money to provide free mooncakes for low-income seniors during the Mid-Autumn Festival. Through this example and others like it, Mrs. Tan sought to increase low-income seniors' knowledge about the United States — knowledge many long-term residents were missing because of lack of education, inability to speak English, and decades of living and socializing only within the confines of Boston's Chinatown community.

Many of Mrs. Tan's interactions in the area took on a similarly educational function. In some cases, seniors might not know important information because of their inability to communicate in even rudimentary English. In other cases, Mrs. Tan was aware that with this older population, many of whom were losing cognitive abilities and demonstrating early signs of memory lapse, repetition of important information and careful, detailed explanations about how to navigate seemingly simple situations were key to facilitating understanding. Her impromptu lecture to the weekly coffee group about how to react in emergency situations was a case in point. After first getting her audience's attention by declaring, "Now I've heard lots of people say they don't want to call 911 because they don't speak English," she proceeded to offer two courses of action residents could pursue if they experienced an emergency. One option, she explained, was to dial 911 and repeat the word "Chinese" (in English) over and over to the operator, who would eventually get the idea and put a Chinese interpreter on the line to talk with them. The second course of action was to contact one's children and have them call 911 instead.

Mrs. Tan's roles extended well beyond these issues of individual self-help to larger community social and political concerns. She told me she liked to "urge" (said in English) people to vote. While she was well supported in her political goals by at least one local Chinatown social service organization, she was also singlehandedly responsible for making sure all residents in her building eligible to vote had registered. She also made sure that they were aware of and understood the issues at stake in an upcoming election. At one weekly coffee meeting, she spent time going from person to person, talking to each resident about the upcoming election, and helping the most infirm register to vote by absentee ballot. On voting day, she told me, she always participated in accompanying voters to their polling stations, since some older individuals might not know the way or feel too feeble to walk there without aid.

Mrs. Tan's intense desire to contribute to the well-being of her community was perhaps most evident through her involvement in convincing area residents to participate in a major health study underway in Chinatown while I was conducting fieldwork. Despite seniors' considerable reluctance to participate, Mrs. Tan worked to educate her building's residents about the benefits of the study for all area residents (and in so doing urged them to consider the interests of the community above their own individual reluctance about participating). The study's terms for participation actually precluded Mrs. Tan's participation as a research subject, a fact that seemed to frustrate her and make her entreaties for others' involvement even more passionate. During coffee hour, Mrs. Tan praised those who had already signed up and then worked to convince others in the room to participate by focusing on the benefits involved. Mrs. Tan's explanations were absolutely necessary for the building's residents to consider taking part, because one of the study's most important requirements was having blood drawn, a procedure many Chinese seniors preferred to avoid. After listening to Mrs. Tan's reasoned explanation about the study's benefits, several women in the room exclaimed that they would like to help out but were afraid of having their blood drawn. One particularly vocal woman in the audience shouted out: "I'm sorry [C. *mhouyisi*; M. *bu haoyisi*], but I am scared of having my blood drawn and tested." Mrs. Tan responded by explaining that it was "like losing your hair and growing it back afterwards"—that is, it wouldn't hurt anyone to have blood drawn. When other women expressed alarm that they would learn something negative about their physical condition from the resulting medical analysis, Mrs. Tan reassured everyone that all medical information would be kept confidential. Nonetheless, the women seemed unconvinced, with several of them discussing in graphic detail their experiences of having blood drawn. Mrs. Tan's campaign to increase area involvement nevertheless continued; I saw her give similarly impassioned speeches urging residents' participation in the study and downplaying seniors' concerns about "giving up a little blood" at two other meetings over the following week. Although many remained skeptical about participating, when seniors did sign up for the study, it seemed that Mrs. Tan's personal and persuasive speeches had often convinced them to do so.

Social exemplars have a long history in Chinese culture—not only through Confucian ideals of rulers who "led by example" but also through a Maoist lexicon of model citizens who acted as important vanguards of revolutionary social work and virtuous ideology throughout the Maoist period. These individuals, including women, were community leaders to be obeyed, studied, and emulated by Mrs. Tan's generational cohort.[32] Nonetheless, after watching Mrs. Tan's seemingly endless show of benevolence toward those around her, I wanted to know where her desire to improve others' well-being came from and whether there were limits to her selflessness.

In response to my questions, Mrs. Tan told me that she believed the desire to help others was a personal trait that some people had and others didn't. She said that she had always liked to help others. During the Maoist period, for example, she saved up her ration coupons to give to others. Yet she acknowledged limits to the help that she was willing to give to foster the well-being of others. She explained that when she took friends or neighbors to apply for social welfare benefits or documents needed to receive their benefits, she coached them on *how* to fill out forms, but she would not fill out the forms for them because she didn't want to be held responsible if something was filled out incorrectly. She also told me about a troubling situation with a woman in her building who was exhibiting increased signs of dementia. Mrs. Tan had been going grocery shopping with her each week but recently had needed to remind her to cook and eat the food they had purchased together on those outings. Mrs. Tan was particularly alarmed when, after they had bought some fish together at the market, the woman had no memory of cooking or eating the fish—even denying that she had bought the fish in the first place. When Mrs. Tan persisted and reminded her that they had bought it and cooked it together, the other woman concluded that since she had no memory of eating it, her home health aide must have stolen the fish from her. Mrs. Tan told me she felt sad that this woman blamed an innocent party for something she couldn't remember, yet she offered up this story as a cautionary tale about the limits of her willingness to help others. Perhaps alluding to events in her past—during the Cultural Revolution, when she noted that there was "no way to help others" because anything one tried to do out of generosity could be "twisted around" and attributed to selfish motivations—Mrs. Tan told me that she and her husband had agreed that she would keep helping other people only as long as it didn't cause any trouble (C. *mouh yeh mahfaahn*; M. *meiyou mafan*) for her family.

Mrs. Tan's level of community-based activity was extraordinary for someone with less-than-fluent English-language skills and as a relative newcomer to the area. At the same time, it was also not completely unusual. Mrs. Wong was the same age as Mrs. Tan and had a somewhat similar, if more impoverished, premigration history (including her status as a university-educated native of Guangzhou whose career also had suffered during the Cultural Revolution).[33] Mrs. Wong had focused much of her past decade developing networks and skill sets within the Chinatown senior community to help others, even though she lived in senior housing in a suburban area near her adult son and his family and had to travel two hours each way by bus and subway to and from Chinatown. Nevertheless, she spent every weekday in Chinatown, first exercising at the local YMCA and then volunteering at one of several service organizations, providing administrative support and educational outreach about health and social welfare assistance to Chinese-speaking seniors. Like Mrs. Tan, Mrs. Wong had learned enough English to be able to help with some basic translation services for both Mandarin- and Cantonese-speaking immigrants, thus serving to bridge the gap among needy immigrant groups and overworked service providers who did not have enough hours in the day to answer all their clients' questions. However, Mrs. Wong's good works also extended beyond Chinatown to a suburban senior center, where she organized weekend activities and outings for Mandarin-speaking Chinese seniors residing in Boston's suburban areas who had few opportunities to gather with a greater community of Chinese seniors during the week because of their duties looking after their American-born grandchildren.

Generous individuals like Mrs. Tan and Mrs. Wong—despite their relatively recent arrival to the area—were not new to Boston's Chinatown community. Charlotte Ikels describes a similar phenomenon of "natural helpers" who performed similar kinds of crucial support services for area residents in the late 1970s and early 1980s.[34] Of course, there have been significant changes in Boston's Chinatown over the past three decades, including a substantial growth in the population and a significantly better developed system of social service providers, which were just getting started at the time of Ikels's study. Moreover, Ikels's interviewees, including the natural helpers she wrote about, were not recent immigrants but instead had lived most (if not all) of their lives in the

United States. That said, the needs and concerns of many of the Chinese seniors living in Boston's Chinatown at that time resonated with the experiences of Chinese seniors living in Chinatown during my research. Much of the volunteer work Mrs. Tan performed—including providing basic translation help, visiting ill neighbors, and accompanying infirm individuals to do grocery shopping or visit the doctor—fulfilled the same kinds of needs as those required by Chinese seniors thirty years ago, when, like now, many seniors had little knowledge of English, required help navigating unfamiliar medical and bureaucratic systems, or had no family nearby to help out with caregiving needs.

These structural problems resulting from similarities in the immigrant experience over time are distinctive from needs experienced through the routine processes of aging, as individuals (like the woman suffering from dementia who accused her home health aide of stealing her fish) become increasingly mentally and physically infirm. Yet the combination of both sets of characteristics—the structural impediments for meeting basic needs of a low-income immigrant population *and* the physical and mental decline seniors experience over time—created a unique opportunity for senior migrants' valuable contributions to the Chinatown community. For immigrants like Mrs. Tan, who repeatedly described herself as "happy" and proudly told me that her children routinely praised her life as "active and meaningful" (C. *fungfu*; M. *fengfu*), the retirement lifestyle she led was a direct result of the particular needs of this population. Although Mrs. Tan could have had opportunities to contribute to community well-being in urban China had she chosen to stay there, many of the functions that she performed for the older immigrant population in Boston's Chinatown, including her educational and activist roles, were directly connected to her immigrant context of reception in the United States.

Some aspects of Mrs. Tan's and Mrs. Wong's benevolence toward others in Chinatown were qualitatively different from the activities of those who "clearly value the act of helping."[35] One aspect of that difference was their active engagement in politics, best exemplified by Mrs. Tan's commitment to increasing Chinese seniors' participation as voters and encouraging Chinatown's seniors to contribute to the well-being of community residents as a whole, as she did when she pleaded with them to participate in the community health study. In this way, she contributed to what has been a long history of community-led activism and engagement in advocacy for the rights of Boston's Chinatown residents, often by its senior residents, that has taken increasing prominence with high-profile movements like the one that prevented one of the area's only developable tracts of land from becoming a multistory parking garage that would have reduced area air quality and affordable housing stock.[36]

These new kinds of opportunities for politically motivated volunteer work, supported by community development activists in local Chinatown social service organizations, go beyond goals for active aging encouraged by the Chinese government, which would not permit similarly politicized engagement in China. In this way, Mrs. Tan's and Mrs. Wong's intense volunteerism seems to exceed the potential for increasing seniors' well-being practiced through yangsheng lifestyles in Beijing. By working to improve the well-being of the entire community now and in the future, Mrs. Tan's and Mrs. Wong's compassionate acts reinforce the role of selflessness in their retirement lifestyles and in this way hearken back to the social goals of egalitarianism and justice desired by their generational cohort whose adult lives were shaped by Maoist ideology, as I described in Chapter 3. Yet even for seniors whose compassionate acts were less intensive, their everyday work as volunteers helped to provide a sense of purpose and community involvement that contributed to their own individual well-being as well as to that of others. Such was the case for many of the low-income Chinese seniors I met in and around Boston's Chinatown, who provided a sense of companionship for the elderly, fostered possibilities for seniors' entertainment by singing to them and organizing bingo games, and contributed to successful social service programs by running errands, serving as interpreters, and educating seniors about important social and political concerns. In all these ways, seniors like Mr. Lam, Mr. Wang, Mrs. Tan, and Mrs. Wong—and many others who lived or visited Chinatown on a regular basis—were contributing in important ways to the well-being of others, enabling them to live a meaningful retired lifestyle as older adults in the United States.

RETIRING WELL

Writing about attitudes toward aging in contemporary China, anthropologists explain the changing social landscape in which Chinese elderly have access to "a new lifestyle that emphasizes autonomy and intergenerational independence."[37] Rooted in the stark reality that economic reform in China has led to significant social changes, as well as increasing inequalities among Chinese citizens, these new views about aging also demonstrate the growing social recognition in China of retirement as an important life stage replete with certain kinds of lifestyle aspirations that go along with it. These views, widespread among both rural and urban Chinese, stand in contrast to views on retirement throughout most of China's long history, when only the wealthiest men could afford to withdraw from imperial service. They also provide evidence of the increasing precariousness of seniors' well-being as compared to the Maoist era, when collectivization afforded rural elderly some support and the possibility to be productive members of society, the danwei system provided housing and welfare for urban elderly who had withdrawn from the labor force, and families routinely stayed in place, making care of aged parents easier in both rural and urban locations.

These contemporary aging trends in China are mirrored through many of the everyday activities of Chinese senior migrants in Boston, who routinely meet in group settings to dance, practice tai chi, or engage in less physically active pursuits such as card playing and mahjong.[38] Through these activities, along with the more mentally and physically taxing endeavors provided through paid and unpaid opportunities to work, we can trace a range of social engagement among recent Chinese senior migrants in the United States that mimics the active aging ideology popular in China today. This ideology, which has its basis in global trends related to the successful aging movement but includes the culturally Chinese goal of living a yangsheng lifestyle, foregrounds the importance for these older individuals to remain active, busy, and productive members of society through engaging in compassionate acts. Thus, Chinese seniors in the United States contributed to the overall well-being of their community while also having the opportunity and freedom to pursue additional individual interests, ranging from debating politics with friends, as Mr. Lam did each week, to baking sweet treats for neighbors, as Mrs. Tan had learned to do from watching daily reruns of Julia Child's cooking shows on TV.

For these and other Chinese senior migrants, it was not the idea of retirement itself that had traveled from the United States to China so much as the knowledge and awareness of an American context of reception for retirees that encouraged possibilities for seniors to experience the retirement lifestyles to which they aspire as Chinese older adults but may be elusive for them in China today. Primary among this support is the universal system of social welfare, but additional knowledge about social networks, service organizations, and possibilities for paid and unpaid work also plays a key role. My interviewees learned about the social and economic infrastructure of senior support in the United States from their family members and friends already in the United States and acted on that knowledge when they made decisions to join family members here rather than stay near family still in China. While not all senior migrants who came to the United States chose to stay long term, many of those who did praised the economic advantages of the country's government infrastructures for senior support that allowed them to live comfortably as retirees, achieving individual well-being even as they had additional opportunities to increase the well-being of others around them.

Some Chinese senior migrants' daily activities in the United States mimicked similar lifestyles they could have pursued in China. In other cases, the United States presented better lifestyle options not available in China, where the legacy of the hukou system, taken in combination with contemporary changes in more traditional conceptions of intergenerational relations and senior support, has rendered seniors' lives increasingly precarious. In the next chapter, I build on this discussion of insecurity and contemporary cultural change in China by considering how Chinese-born seniors' adjustment to living in the United States also involved the renegotiation of familiar Chinese systems of value with their Chinese American family members. Just as Chinese seniors' lives in China have been complicated through changing social norms around intergenerational relationships and support, so too do these in-flux value systems affect how seniors interact with their Chinese American families in the United States, where so many Chinese grandparents take care of their grandchildren.

5 NEGOTIATING FAMILY VALUE(S) IN THE UNITED STATES

The financial precariousness that many of China's contemporary senior citizens experience has resulted in changing cultural negotiations around the role of family as a source of support in old age.[1] The situations of Chinese elderly I discuss here reflect similar patterns of precarity in the lifeworlds of aging adults worldwide, who are in comparable positions of having to renegotiate relationships with family around caregiving work more generally.[2] China, like other East Asian countries, has generally depended significantly more on family than on institutional support for their elderly.[3] At the same time, China's rapid development over the past few decades has resulted in new terrains of cultural value that seem to contest traditional conceptions of family support for the elderly in China as the social and cultural discourses around long-standing Confucian ideals of filial duty and family reciprocity are reconfigured in contemporary China.[4] These changing regimes of familial and cultural value in China also influence the intergenerational relationships of recent Chinese senior migrants and their Chinese American family members once Chinese seniors migrate to the United States.[5]

One of the most common social roles for grandparents in China today is caring for their grandchildren.[6] This is also the case for many grandparents worldwide and is particularly true for seniors engaged in global mobility flows—either directly, as they follow adult children to new locations abroad, or indirectly, as they step into the role of primary caregiver for grandchildren left behind by parents who have migrated elsewhere.[7] As Dossa and Coe note, kin work is at the center of transnational migration experiences for many "older men and women [who] sustain their families emotionally and materially over time." Kin work in these contexts includes both paid and unpaid labor, such as caregiving, along with other kinds of work involved with preservation of family identity and memory of past generations.[8] Many of my interviewees provided care for American-born grandchildren in the United States. They had also provided care for Chinese-born grandchildren in China before migrating. One woman in her sixties, who had been in the United States for less than a year when we met in 2009, explained her continuing sense of attachment to the grandchild she left behind in China: "I miss [my son and his family in China] a lot. My grandson always calls and asks me when I'm going back and [tells me] that he misses me. And I tell him I miss him and that I will visit when I have a chance." Other interviewees talked about similarly strong bonds with their grandchildren in both China and the United States. And while leaving behind grandchildren cared for since birth in China made their migration experiences in the United States more challenging, many seniors also found a particular sense of purpose and enjoyment in caring for their American-born grandchildren.

In addition to providing care for American-born grandchildren, senior migrants were also involved with other kinds of kin work, including caregiving for aged parents and infirm spouses or siblings. In some cases, they were also primary caregivers for disabled members of the larger community. This work had significant economic value for senior migrants' Chinese American families—as seniors themselves recognized in their comments to me over and over again. The unpaid child care they performed relieved their adult children of the burden of paying for child care in United States, even as it also freed up income for daily savings enabling families to buy a house, move to a better school district, and so on. Moreover, seniors who worked as paid caregivers outside the home made direct economic contributions to their families' economic lives, supported themselves independently, or—at a minimum—lessened the financial burden they placed on their families. At the same time, the caregiving work that Chinese-born seniors performed had immense sentimental value, as they grew close to their American-born grandchildren, worked together with adult children to promote their grandchildren's future success, and relieved the distress of aged or infirm parents or siblings. In all these ways, Chinese senior migrants' engagement with kin work reinforced patterns that scholars have identified showing how "older adults contribute to family reproduction in contexts where labor markets and states are not sufficient to meet family needs."[9]

As scholars working at the intersection of aging and migration make clear, the various forms of labor that seniors undertake within the context of their transnational families "renders visible the workings of structural forces whose power, in a transnational context, cannot be underestimated." Central to these analyses is the concept of "kin-scription"—that is, "how particular members of the family become conscripted to particular kinds of kin work based on cultural scripts about family roles, which are often based on gender and age."[10] In other words, the fact that Chinese seniors, who are already the primary caregivers of grandchildren in China, would migrate to perform similar functions for their Chinese American families is not a surprise. Equally important, however, is that these cultural scripts are not stagnant. Thus, as Chinese seniors navigate their processes of migration to the United States, they are also involved with creating understandings about their experiences that cannot only be reduced to a simple formula of family obligation. In this way, my discussion here diverges from that of many other scholars focusing on kin-scription as a largely coercive force on the experiences of older adults engaged in transnational regimes of family caregiving. In those accounts, unpaid caregiving work often leads to seniors' loss of autonomy or unrealized desires for their later lives.[11] Instead, here I examine both the ambiguous feelings senior migrants experienced in relationship to their familial interactions but also the ways they found those relationships fulfilling. In so doing, I highlight how Chinese senior migrants engaged with traditional ideas of filial piety both before and after their migration as part of a renegotiation of cultural scripts around intergenerational relationships.

Writing about the cultural processes through which children shifted from economically valuable members of families in nineteenth-century America to "emotionally priceless" but "economically worthless" by the mid-twentieth century, sociologist Viviana Zelizer focuses on the complex interaction between sentimental and economic value in social life. Through her discussion about how children shifted from "objects of utility" to "objects of value," Zelizer demonstrates the importance of paying attention to the ways in which these different forms of value are intertwined rather than "radically incompatible," as cultural values tend to demand. Moreover, through her discussion of the "monetization of sentiment" and the challenges that result when circumstances demand the assignment of monetary value to a life deemed "priceless," Zelizer draws attention to the ways in which sentimental value and economic value are not always in direct relationship with each other and are highly subjective.[12] I make use of Zelizer's insights to explore the complex interaction between economic and sentimental value as products of the caregiving work that Chinese-born senior migrants perform in the United States. Whereas Zelizer documents the cultural processes that lead to changes in children's valuation from economic to sentimental, I foreground Chinese seniors as actors who strategically sought to use their caregiving work to increase their own economic and sentimental valuation and therefore mitigate changing cultural values in contemporary China that have undermined seniors' traditional place of respect and authority in family life.

This exploration of how Chinese senior migrants understood and worked to influence how they were valued by family and society contributes to understanding how these seniors navigated their transition to American life through the intergenerational relationships they cultivated with their Chinese American family members. I argue that the caregiving work they performed in the United States allowed them to renegotiate their sentimental and economic value in the eyes of their family members with the goal of fulfilling their own interests as they continued to grow older. Acutely aware of their precarious social status, senior migrants had to confront a reality in which they might not receive full family support in old age—in neither China, where traditional cultural ideas around senior support are in flux, nor in the United States, where Chinese seniors contend with a complicated set of expectations around senior support influenced by American cultural values. Situated at the intersection of literature on transnational aging and immigrant incorporation in the U.S. context, my discussion doesn't demonstrate that seniors' strategies actually secured future support; many were still far from needing care when I knew them. Instead, it underscores the complicated positionalities of grandparents performing kin work in this immigrant context, where the challenges they encounter were also countered by the joys they derived from relationships with grandchildren and community ties made through paid work and the engagement with others that contributed to the possibility for their well-being in United States.

CAREGIVING AND CHINESE "FAMILY LOVE" IN THE IMMIGRANT CONTEXT

Writing about the increasing engagement of working-age women in global caregiving networks, scholars have documented the emotional strain resulting from familial separation on migrant mothers as well as on the children left behind when parents migrated seeking work opportunities abroad.[13] The situations of Chinese grandparent caregivers who migrate to the United States were not qualitatively different from those in which a child's mother leaves home for work abroad, as grandparents could be the primary caregivers for children over many years—making meals, accompanying children to school and back, even sleeping in the same room with grandchildren when they were young—freeing their adult children for full participation in the workforce and easing the stress associated with balancing career and family life. As a result, grandparents were often integral to and deeply embedded in everyday family life in both China and the United States, demonstrating how the roles individuals play within families are complex and multifaceted.[14] As grandparents performed the everyday work of caring for their grandchildren, they developed intimate ties and strong interrelationships that overlapped with parents' love for and devotion to children. Moreover, grandparents who spent many more hours of the day with grandchildren were particularly aware of how their absence created emotional and other difficulties not just for grandchildren but also for their working adult children.[15]

Most scholarly discussions of intergenerational relationships in immigrant family life in the U.S. context privilege the interactions between first-generation immigrant parents and their second-generation American-born children. Of particular interest is the family's adjustment to U.S. social and cultural norms (including children's educational success) and the conflicts that result between immigrant parents and their children through this adjustment process.[16] Yet scholars writing about intergenerational family relationships in U.S. immigrant family life, like those writing about transnational caregiving networks, confirm the integral roles that grandparents play for many ethnic groups. Immigrant grandparents who migrate with family groups or join family already in the United States provide child care for grandchildren, help with household labor, and play important roles in enabling immigrant families to succeed.[17] Many grandparents, such as those from the Dominican Republic, maintain actively transnational lives helping family in the United States yet without plans to settle permanently here.[18] As Foner and Dreby explain, "Intergenerational relationships in immigrant families help to shape the contours and trajectories of individual lives and also affect involvements outside the family."[19] Thus, better understanding about the role of grandparents in immigrant families' lives is necessary for scholars aiming to develop a stronger understanding of immigrant family success and acculturation.

As with the general literature on immigrant family incorporation to the United States, past interest on Chinese American and immigrant families has focused primarily on intergenerational relationships among immigrant parents and their children.[20] Recent scholarship, however, indicates a growing awareness of increasing numbers of Asian American grandparent caregivers in the United States and attention to the health and well-being of these Asian American elderly.[21] Many of these (primarily quantitative) studies document high rates of depression among Asian American elderly and raise concerns about the potential for stress on this demographic through acculturation and the burden of caring for grandchildren.[22] Central to all these studies' views of Chinese American intergenerational relations is the traditional Chinese cultural value of filial piety—that is, the idea that older generations rely on their adult children for respect and support in old age.

Filial piety as a cultural norm of Chinese family life has garnered substantial scholarly attention for decades because of the intergenerational sense of responsibility and obligation to family that it entails.[23] Yet in the ethnographic literature on aging in contemporary China, there is a clear understanding that this Chinese cultural ideal is not a static concept; although it is still central to ideologies of family life, it is under substantial renegotiation in everyday practice.[24] For example, scholars document changing practices around elder care that might not have been traditionally valued but are increasingly common, such as living separately but near adult children, hiring caregivers, or moving to retirement homes.[25] In each of these cases, adult children may no longer be the primary caregiver for aging adult parents but may still contribute financially to their care and interact regularly with them, creating a wider cultural repertoire for actions socially recognized as conforming to social expectations for filial piety than existed in previous eras.

With only a handful of exceptions, that more flexible understanding of filial piety is absent from scholarly discussions of elderly Asian American life, which nonetheless attribute filial piety as a defining feature of Chinese American cultural values. Debates primarily focus on filial piety as a cause of stress through intergenerational conflict that occurs when Asian American seniors' expectations for care by adult children are not met. In contrast, some scholars posit that seniors' adherence to the cultural ideal of filial piety alleviates the sense of burden they might otherwise experience in caring for their grandchildren.[26] This adherence to a kin-scriptive view of filial piety means that many studies aimed at explicating the experiences of Asian American grandparents do more work to obscure the complex renegotiation of intergenerational relations within these families than to explicate them. In particular, it's worth noting that recent Chinese senior migrants were already actively negotiating the changing landscape of contemporary cultural values with their family members in China before coming to the United States. When they arrive, they bring that sense of negotiation with them. This awareness allows them to draw on cultural tropes about filial piety in strategizing for their own care as they grow old through the language of "value" (versus obligation) of the caregiving services they provide to their family and other community members.

Because Chinese seniors' caregiving work in the United States takes place within the challenges presented by the immigrant family context, seniors must adjust to the new social environments they encounter and also the expectations of their family members—siblings, adult children, sometimes parents—who sponsored their migration. Both groups are aware of different sets of ideas in the United States about personal independence, family life, and education that complicate the intergenerational relationships families develop around caregiving needs. Even so, Chinese-born seniors and their family members remain strongly influenced by traditional Chinese cultural discourses emphasizing the overwhelming importance of family as a deeply seated cultural value of ethnic Chinese—whether in China or abroad. My interviewees refer to this sense of commitment to family as "family love."[27]

"Family love" was implicit in how seniors talked about which set of grandparents would migrate to care for American-born grandchildren and, as part of that process, make sacrifices, including leaving behind other family members in China; dealing with the challenges of living in a new and unfamiliar social, cultural, and linguistic setting; and adjusting to living far away from established networks of friends and colleagues. Often only one set of grandparents was healthy or available to migrate. When both sets of grandparents were available and when families had sufficient economic resources to pay for the cost of bringing grandparents to the United States, both sets of grandparents would come to visit and try out living in Boston for several months. Adult children would ultimately rely on the set of grandparents who seemed better adapted to living in the United States —either because they managed the cultural differences well or because they already had other family members and networks here with whom they wanted to reunite. Similar strategies have been reported by transnational grandparent caregivers for other immigrant ethnic groups in the United States as well.[28]

Even when only one set of grandparents was available to help with caregiving needs, adult children might still have them visit in preparation for their eventual migration. In summer 2012, I met a woman and her husband at a senior community center in Quincy who were about to return to China following a three-month trial visit living with their adult daughter and son-in-law, who hoped to have a child the following year. The older woman explained that she and her husband had considerable difficulty adjusting to living in suburban Quincy because they missed their work, colleagues, and friends back home. Unlike in China, where life was busy and interesting (C. *yihtnaauh*; M. *renao*), in the United States, this couple was alone most days while their daughter and son-in-law were at work. When I asked if, following this trial period, they might decide not to return to the United States in the future, this woman assured me that they (or she, if her husband was not yet retired) would definitely return once the grandchild was born. Although the visit had not taught her to enjoy living in the United States, it had allowed her and her husband to see how hard their daughter worked and how tired she was at night. Drawing on the cultural trope of family love, this woman felt she would have to help ease her daughter's load when her grandchild was born despite the difficulty (and unhappiness) she anticipated in adjusting to living in the United States.

For this would-be grandmother, the justification for migration because of family love underscores the power of kin-scription for older adults as it worked to reinforce traditionally held Chinese cultural ideals of the intergenerational contract. By taking on a difficult although rewarding task for the sake of the family, senior migrants conformed to expectations of a Chinese cultural model of family life, foregrounding the sentimental attachment that binds generations together. This model assumes that seniors will sacrifice for the good of the family despite the fact that their own future security is no longer certain. Nevertheless, the trope of family love also allowed seniors to articulate their motivation to migrate as a choice as they decided which adult children to help, voiced likes and dislikes about the possibility of living abroad, and articulated sacrifices they expected their children to recognize and value. In this way, family love as a concept allowed seniors to create understandings about their experiences both before and after migrating, thereby highlighting the potential for play with traditional kin-scripts that can result in the renegotiation of the cultural values on which they are based.

Trial periods were also important because they allowed seniors and adult children to test out whether they would be able to get along living together in the United States. Seniors talked pragmatically about the difficulties of multiple generations living together under one roof.[29] In doing so, they challenged traditionally held beliefs idealizing that form of living arrangement, even as they continued to reinforce traditional ideas of the importance of family values as a defining feature of Chinese culture that influenced their decisions to live near (but not always with) their adult children in the United States while taking care of their American-born grandchildren.

Although idealized goals of family harmony (ideals that continued to animate seniors' discussions around family love) may have helped seniors to rationalize the challenges they would take on in moving to the United States as older individuals, seniors also made frequent reference to their relative powerlessness and social precariousness within the changing conditions of contemporary Chinese social norms. In this way, they acknowledged the difficulties that occur when members of different generations live together and rely on each other for help. Despite Confucian legacies that continue to perpetuate a Chinese cultural ideal in which elders are deeply respected within the family, seniors' social and familial status in China today has shifted, with younger adults now more in control than the senior generation.[30] While the seeds for this shift were sown during the Maoist era through state-engineered attacks on the family, it is the economic and social changes ushered in during the reform era that have had the most significant effects in weakening elders' social and familial status. As adult children have gained opportunities to earn significant incomes, the senior generation has lost the control of collective family property, along with the ability to command the respect that went along with that control. As adult children have gained access to greater physical mobility, they have moved away from rural locations where family networks traditionally helped care and provide for elders too weak to work in the fields or provide for themselves. Together with the relative lack of social welfare for many seniors in China today (particularly for those living in rural areas, but also for urban residents with only small pensions), many seniors today must rely on the unguaranteed mercy of adult children for support.[31] Thus, as one of my interviewees explained, when seniors and their adult children live together under one roof, it is not necessarily the physical living situation itself that is problematic. Rather, problems result when the two generations do not treat each other with mutual respect:

> People who are older . . . are dependent on their children. In this relationship, if you have respectful children, then they will understand your situation. They won't want too much from you and don't expect you to do what they say. But if you have children who have a different viewpoint, then there are conflicts between the young ones and the older generation. . . . It's not about the living

situation. It's about the relationship between the family members and whether it's equal. Will they listen to you and will you listen to them? ... It used to be that the children listened to the parents, but now the parents listen to the children. Some people are not able to take that, because they're too proud.

My senior migrant interviewees drew heavily on both of these concerns—Chinese cultural values of family love and support and the relative powerlessness of seniors in China today—to explain their postmigration interactions with their adult children and grandchildren in Boston. During one group interview, several senior migrants talked together about the disjuncture between idealized views of family love and the realities of everyday conflict within family life:

> Man 3: Now, we're here and we can still help out and make ourselves useful so that we still have value; that's why we don't really have any problems with our children.
>
> Man 2: That's right. . . . There are some cases with [family relationships], where the principle is I help you, you help me, that's ok. But there are cases where it is purely family love.
>
> Man 4: For Chinese people, family love is very important.
>
> Man 3: Family love is very important. But seeing each other is good, while living together is difficult. It's true! To see each other, to talk with each other, that's really good. But if you live together, that's . . . very difficult.

As seniors debated the pros and cons of living with or near family and how those living arrangements did or did not comply with powerful social and cultural discourses of Chinese family love, they also acknowledged their need to prove their value to their adult children within these complex processes of cultural and social transition. Noting that this value was dependent on their ability "to help out and make [themselves] useful," seniors laid bare the new cultural landscape through which they could no longer rely on traditional ideas of social obligation and respect to ensure their own security and well-being. Without "value," senior migrants' relationships with their adult children in the United States could add to adjustment difficulties and social and economic marginalization in their new country. Seniors' dependency on their adult children was more than just an uncomfortable social situation. Senior migrants were often reliant on adult children for access to food, pocket money, and other daily needs—what Deneva refers to as "kinfare" in her discussion of similar constraints faced by Bulgarian senior migrants who work as caregivers for their grandchildren abroad.³²

Some of my interviewees talked about everyday conflicts that arose when multiple family members lived together in small residential units—conflicts over shared uses of space and objects within those spaces that might at first appear to be relatively insignificant but caused stress for family members engaged in seemingly petty battles over the use and display of everyday furniture and other household objects.³³ However, more of my senior interviewees complained about the daily indignities and sense of servitude that resulted when they were living with adult children. My interviewees made wry jokes about their attempts to try to squirrel away some pocket money for their own needs while shopping for the family. They also described the stress involved with trying to buy good-quality meat and produce to cook delicious meals for their children's family all while being on a tightly controlled family budget: "When old people go out to the market, you will hear them say, 'Oh—what can I get today? This isn't good, that's not good: how can I buy food [to prepare for the family] with just the tiny bit of money my kids have given me?" My interviewees stressed that there was no "free lunch" (C. *baahk sihk baahk jyuh*; M. *bai chi bai zhu*) when seniors lived with their adult children, and that ultimately it was the adult children, not the seniors, who benefited from these arrangements in which seniors often did most (if not all) of the housework, cooking, cleaning, and washing in addition to caring for their grandchildren.

Thus, the same family caregiving work that provided the primary rationale for many seniors to migrate to the United States also left them economically and socially vulnerable. Occupying a murky space somewhere between the commodification of care (since seniors were performing important labor that kept families economically afloat and supported their daily life) and familial duty (as seniors performed the same kinds of caregiving work for grandchildren that they were used to doing in China and rationalized their work through cultural discourses of family love), seniors' caregiving work resulted in fewer economic benefits for them rather than for their extended families. One interviewee in her late seventies wished that she had understood that vulnerability ten years earlier. She told me, "Now, I've only worked three years; I need to work for ten years to get [Social Security]. People told me that when I worked for my daughter I should have filed tax returns; that way I would be able to get retirement [benefits] now. But I didn't know. . . . So it's too late."

Of course, for my interviewees there was no guarantee that their adult children—who, as first-generation immigrants, were also negotiating a new context of changing family values both in China and through their experience as Chinese Americans—would support seniors in their older age. As a result, similar to Deneva's subjects, who experience a loss of autonomy through their acquiescence with kin-scripts, some Chinese-born senior migrants were left in more precarious situations than if they had remained in China, where they were more likely to have networks of coworkers, friends, and neighbors to help them.[34] Nonetheless, seniors found the caregiving work that they performed out of family love to be personally meaningful; moreover, the skills they gained through doing that work were easily applicable to caregiving and other work contexts outside their home, enabling many seniors to find paid work to help support themselves and contribute to their family's income. As a result, seniors were able to use the paid and unpaid caregiving work that they performed both outside the home and for their Chinese American families to prove their value for families. In this way, their experiences were more complex than most kin-scriptive frames of analysis are likely to highlight.[35] As I discuss in the next section, caregiving work, which had both economic and sentimental value, provided Chinese senior migrants with important possibilities for fulfilling their personal goals for their older age by allowing them to demonstrate why they should still be valued by their family members and taken care of once they were no longer economically productive members of family life.

FORGING VALUE THROUGH CAREGIVING: EMOTIONAL, ECONOMIC, AND CULTURAL RETURNS

Studies focusing on Chinese grandparents in North America indicate that caregiving work for grandchildren can be stressful or a meaningful experience. My interviewees' experiences validated both claims. Grandparents' caregiving work included the joy of developing intimate ties with grandchildren and closer emotional bonds with adult children as all family adults worked together to provide the best upbringing possible for the first American-born generation. At the same time, this work also included significant hardships, ranging from regret at having left familiar faces and networks behind in China to daily conflict with adult children. The case of Mrs. Lung, whose caregiving duties for her disabled granddaughter were exceptionally demanding, spoke to both the sense of fulfillment and of challenge that grandparent caregivers in the United States often experience.

When I met Mrs. Lung in 2009, she was sixty-five years old and had migrated to the United States four years before. Like many other Chinese senior migrants, she had already been looking after a grandchild in China before coming to the Boston area. In fact, she had never planned to leave China to live abroad. But after her daughter in the United States gave birth to a disabled child and her daughter's mother-in-law refused to continue to help care for that child, Mrs. Lung and her husband decided to immigrate, leaving behind their other family members, including the grandchild she had cared for there since birth. Mrs. Lung told me:

> In the beginning, I didn't really want to come because I had a grandchild in China. My son had a kid. My son's child and my daughter's child were born in the same year.... At the time, my daughter-in-law said, "Mom, we can take care of our child. But sister's daughter's situation [is too difficult]; you should go and help her." So in the end, we decided to come and immigrated here.

Unlike many other Chinese seniors from Guangzhou who have migrated to Boston following their retirement, Mrs. Lung did not have other friends or family from China in the United States besides the daughter she came to help. In addition to leaving behind her son's family, she left three siblings and her elderly mother, whose care she supported with the small retirement pension she still received from her preretirement employment in China. Moreover, Mrs. Lung had been able to return to China only once since migrating. At that time, her mother was eighty-six years old and seriously ill. When her mother's health improved, Mrs. Lung returned to the United States, where the daily care involved with her granddaughter kept her fully occupied.

Mrs. Lung's granddaughter, her daughter's first child, was born severely disabled. At the time of our interview, Mrs. Lung's granddaughter was twelve years old. She required help with most daily tasks and could not speak, although she had found ways to communicate with her family: " If she's thirsty she can get water to drink herself. If she's hungry she will drag you over to the fridge and get something out.... She can go to the microwave and open the door and let me know to put something there and warm it up for her." Although Mrs. Lung's granddaughter was out of the house part of each day at a school for disabled children, her caregiving needs extended throughout the day and night. Mrs. Lung's duties included sustained intimate care, such as changing her diapers and sleeping in the same room with her granddaughter. As a result, a special bond had developed between grandmother and granddaughter: the child identified her as her primary caregiver and the only household member to whom she would routinely respond. Mrs. Lung told me, with seeming pride at this strong bond, "This granddaughter of mine, the older she gets, the more disobedient she is. She doesn't listen to my daughter. When my daughter holds her hand to go to school, she pushes it away. She has to hold on to *me* and walk out with *me*" [emphasis in original].

Mrs. Lung was also working outside her daughter's home, in Boston's Chinatown, for four hours each day at a job she had obtained as part of a training program for low-income seniors. The work conditions of this job (including light kitchen work, cleaning, and companionship with elderly Chinese immigrants) were not difficult, and the job allowed her both to contribute to the family income and, as she told me, "to pass the time" when her granddaughter was at school and the house would otherwise be empty. She said to me, "Well, if I don't work, my son-in-law has to work; my daughter goes out with her kids' friends' parents; I'm left alone at home and it's very boring. Even if you clean the house, you can't do it for eight hours a day; after an hour or so you will be done. So working here, time passes by easier." Although Mrs. Lung would not have had a job outside the home had she stayed in China, she enjoyed this work. It granted her a sense of freedom from the concerns that she faced with her disabled granddaughter at home and offered her daily interaction with a community of Cantonese-speaking individuals beyond the narrow circle of her immediate family members. Moreover, her small income, just a few hundred dollars each month, contributed to the family economy, covering all additional costs associated with her and her husband's inclusion in their daughter's home life and preventing the need for them to rely on their daughter for pocket money.

Paid work figured prominently in the balancing act that seniors negotiated as they sought to forge a sense of value for themselves within the context of their family lives in the United States. They were aware that within the changing context of contemporary Chinese cultural values, they could not necessarily depend on adult children to help care for them once they became increasing physically and mentally infirm. While some seniors contributed money they earned outside the home directly to their family, others needed the income from outside employment to help support themselves—either because they lived independently from adult children or because, even while living with adult children, they did not want to have to ask for adult children to help pay for their incidental expenses. Working outside the home also had benefits beyond helping them to demonstrate their economic value to children. It enabled them to live more independent lives through giving them access to money, networks, and information about American life beyond their immediate family members; it provided them with meaningful social engagement and aided them in feeling like fully contributing members of society; and it allowed them to earn credits toward Social Security so that they would have access to a small income in their later years. Building stronger community networks through working outside the home may also have helped ease the transition grandparent caregivers experienced as their American-born grandchildren grew up. In most cases, once grandchildren reached middle school and became more independent, seniors either decided to move out from their adult children's homes or were asked to leave.

Even when grandparents stayed in their adult children's homes, the strong affective relationship between grandparents and grandchildren often weakened over time, primarily because of language differences. Over and over again, seniors explained that because they could not speak English and because their grandchildren's Chinese-language skills were often limited, they relied more and more on adult children to translate across generations. Although some college-aged grandchildren had decided to study Chinese, learning Mandarin did not always aid their ability to communicate with Cantonese- or Taishanese-speaking grandparents. Mrs. Wong explained the ongoing disagreements about Chinese-language use that she had with her son and daughter-in-law as her grandson grew up:

> Sometimes I would ask why they wouldn't speak to him in Cantonese, because he understood [Cantonese]. But they only talked to him in English. They responded that after I die, no one [would be around] to talk with him in Cantonese. At the time, I thought that [way of thinking] made sense. . . . Now that [my grandson]'s in college, he decided to study Chinese because he knows that there's a big market [for Chinese] out there. So now I think I was right.

Mrs. Wong's debate with her son and his wife also spoke to another central concern that Chinese grandparent caregivers experienced: conflict with their adult children over their caregiving practices for American-born grandchildren.

Although most conflicts that grandparents reported to me had their roots in generational differences among Chinese seniors and their adult children, these conflicts were exacerbated by the immigrant context through which care for American-born grandchildren took place. For example, one older woman from Taishan contrasted the relative inattention to caring for even quite young children in the rural area she was from to American practices of "intensive parenting." Her friend elaborated, "As soon as the kids back home can walk, you can just put them in an open space. They can take care of themselves and play on their own.

You can just farm on your own. The kids in America are like God's children; you can't just leave them at home or anything like that." Although grandparents from Chinese urban areas like Guangzhou were less likely to find American child-centered caregiving practices as strange as these rural grandmothers did, seniors from urban areas who had previously cared for grandchildren in China still found significant differences between caring for their Chinese-born grandchildren and their American-born grandchildren. One woman told me, "The kids here are different from the ones in China. In China, when you tell them something, they listen to you. Here when you tell them to eat, they just keep playing with their toys. They only care about playing around."

Chinese grandparents and their adult children often had different ideas about the best way to educate American-born grandchildren. Mrs. Wong elaborated:

> We [Chinese] like to point out [children's] bad behavior. But [my grandson's parents] think like Americans and praise him about everything. I don't agree with that practice. . . . Sometimes [my grandson] would have five homework assignments to complete over break, but he didn't do [his work] and just went out to play. [I thought he should work first and play later.] But my daughter-in-law said that [as long as he completed his work], that's fine. . . . The way they educated him was different. They used the American way, and I used a traditional one.

Yet the ability to transmit Chinese cultural values to American-born children— those same values that are in flux as China's vast population negotiates the many social repercussions of China's rapid economic development, widening economic and social divide between urban and rural areas, one-child policy, and increasing global interaction—was an additional factor, over and above emotional ties and economic concerns, that led adult children to sponsor their parents to migrate as caregivers for American-born grandchildren. These cultural values included not just the family focus that seniors identified as family love but also serving as a bridge to Chinese language and culture (including food, classical tales, holiday celebrations, and so on) more generally.[36] One grandfather, Mr. Moy, who took an active role in his grandchildren's education, had stayed particularly close to one granddaughter as she became a teenager and then a young adult. He was delighted with her continued interest in Chinese language and culture and talked with pride about a return visit to China on which he and his wife had taken her, with the specific goal of teaching her about her Chinese heritage. More commonly, however, my interviewees talked with pride about the accomplishments of their grandchildren while also voicing concerns over gradual distancing from them.

The transition from childhood to adulthood of the grandchildren to whom seniors had developed close ties was difficult for many seniors, who often struggled with loneliness that resulted once their caregiving work was no longer of value to the family. Mr. Cheung described his mixed feelings at moving into senior housing with his wife when his daughter and son-in-law moved to a smaller apartment in a new town with a better school district but higher rents, so that they no longer had enough space to house the extended family. Although he and his wife still looked after their grandchildren a few days a week after school, he missed living with them. He told me:

> [Living on our own] is better sometimes; but other times it just feels very lonely. There's only the two of us. Everyone else keeps their doors closed [and] there's very little communication. Also we don't know very much English. We say hello and good morning but we can't really communicate. It just feels very lonely and quiet.

But he also emphasized the benefits that moving away had for his relationship with his wife:

> The environment is very quiet and peaceful. We can eat whatever we want. We can eat whenever we want. Back [when we lived with my daughter] we had to wait until they got off work at 7:00 or 8:00 p.m. [to eat]. [Now] the two of us can eat at 6 p.m. There are positives and negatives.

Mr. Cheung's thoughts echoed the expressions of convenience, freedom, and independence that many seniors voiced about their moves to senior housing, even as they also focused on the difficulty of letting go of the daily routines that they shared when their grandchildren were young.[37]

Thus, caregiving for American-born grandchildren was often a great source of pride and happiness for Chinese seniors, who demonstrated their continued support for Chinese family values through this work by developing intimate and emotionally caring relationships with grandchildren that also eased adult children's economic and emotional burdens. At the same time, this work also allowed seniors to lay claims about their value within the context of their immigrant family life—claims that they hoped would translate into sufficiently strong sentimental ties to ensure that adult children and grandchildren would care for them once they grew old and infirm.

VALUES IN FLUX: CAREGIVING FUTURES FOR CHINESE SENIOR MIGRANTS AND THEIR FAMILIES

In addition to juggling paid work and grandchild caregiving, many Chinese seniors also needed to help take care of their own aged parents. In some cases, parents were in China. In other cases, however, elderly parents were in the United States, but because transnational engagement between Southeast China and the United States meant that family networks often extended across the country—from Boston to New York to Chicago to San Francisco to Los Angeles—adult children did not always live nearby to help out.

One impoverished Taishanese woman in her sixties told me that her siblings negotiated care for her parents, already ninety years old, who lived in Boston. With one sibling in Macau, one in San Francisco, one in New York, and two others in Boston, daily care for their parents was primarily the responsibility of the Boston-based siblings. Because my interviewee was the most recent to have migrated, with less stable job prospects than her siblings had and with adult children still in China, she was perceived as the natural choice to care for their parents. Her mother had put particular pressure on her to provide daily care. She told me:

> One of my sisters lives very close [to my parents] and mostly takes care of them. My brothers are very far away. . . . [My parents] are still pretty healthy. My dad still cooks for my mom. My mom also has a lot of problems with her feet and back. . . . My mother is always telling me I should go take care of them. I go sometimes. She's always telling me to move in with her. . . . She even told my husband he should go back to China, so I could take care of her. I told her that he couldn't do that. . . . Every time I go there to visit she tells me that I should stay with her. . . . When they really can't take care of themselves anymore, then we will see. . . . Now that I've become a citizen, and I don't have to go to the [citizenship] classes anymore, [I have more time to visit than I used to].

For this senior migrant, the family pressure to care for her elderly parents, despite their relatively good health, was extreme. At the same time, what others perceived as a favorable situation—with relatively few family responsibilities in the United States coupled with free time that could be used caring for her parents—was not. Just a few months earlier, she had almost been unable to attend her citizenship swearing-in ceremony because she could not afford the cost of transportation to the city outside Boston where the citizenship ceremony was to be held. Thus, her primary concern was her need to find a job that could provide an income, no matter how small. But once she found a job, she would no longer have any flexibility to care for her parents.

Seniors needing to care for elderly parents also had to contend with the daily work necessary to help aged and infirm individuals and negotiate between elderly parents' more traditional conceptions of filial piety, desiring adult children to be their primary caregivers. In Quincy's senior housing complexes, I met a number of senior migrants who were looking after their parents almost full time. One woman, who had lost her paid job when the supermarket where she worked as a stocker had closed a year earlier, spent every day with her parents. Although she lived elsewhere in the Boston area, she arrived at her parents' apartment at 6:00 a.m. each morning and spent the entire day with them—accompanying them on walks, keeping them physically active, and cooking and cleaning for them. When they napped during the day, she would go to the common room to socialize with other senior residents who lived in the building. This family caregiving was the same work that paid caregivers could also do: shopping, cooking, cleaning, doing wash, giving medications, and accompanying the elderly. As a result, many senior migrants who had otherwise not been able to find paid employment were able to take caregiving jobs, found through informal networks or after training with a social service organization in Chinatown that also helped place senior migrants in paid positions as caregivers. Most seniors I knew who provided paid caregiving services to other Chinese American elderly largely enjoyed their work and felt positive about having a marketable skill and earning money that would help cover their own expenses as they aged. Thus, Chinese migrant caregivers like the seniors I interviewed are contributing in the United States to the renegotiation of more traditional conceptions of filial piety still held among the oldest Chinese Americans—developing what sociologist Pei-Chia Lan calls "networked kinship" with ethnically Chinese elderly whose own adult children may be too busy to provide personalized care themselves.[38]

Part and parcel of the complex familial support system aimed at meeting aged seniors' caregiving needs, younger seniors who were still providing caregiving services to others wondered whether anyone would be available to similarly help them once they reached an age when they would be less mobile and more mentally fragile. Mr. Lee, who had immigrated in his seventies and had just turned ninety when I interviewed him, had already navigated the transition from doing daily paid and volunteer work in Chinatown to staying at home in his senior apartment. Still fit and physically active in late 2009, he nonetheless needed help with cooking and cleaning. He said:

> I'm old now. I'm ninety this year. My kids discussed [what to do] and they pooled together some money and hired someone to cook dinner for me. The senior center can only provide someone to help me cook once a week, and that's Wednesday. So what do I do on the other days? My kids helped me hire someone who's from the same village as me . . . to help me cook dinner at night. It's been half a year already.

Seniors who had yet to navigate that transition weighed the pros and cons of potentially returning to China, where migrants from rural areas knew they still had a significant infrastructure of friends and family to help care for them as they aged. One Taishanese woman, only in her early sixties, was considering returning to China once she was older:

> My sons think that when I'm older then I should go back [to my village in Taishan] because it would be better. Seniors in America mostly live in senior houses. If you don't, then it's not as convenient, because everyone has to go to work and no one can take care of you. If you're in China, all the old people live together in the same village and everyone takes care of each other.

Nevertheless, this view was uncommon among my interviewees, who, after having adjusted to living in the United States as older migrants, planned to stay near family here, where they had access to good medical care and the possibility of buying a funeral plot that would allow them to be buried rather than cremated.[39] One Taishanese man in his seventies who did have access to a family plot in his village nonetheless reinforced how his thinking about eventually returning to his village had changed over the ten years since he had migrated to Boston. When he was newly arrived, he said, "I even joked with my daughter that if I ever got really sick, she should buy me an airplane ticket to get me back quickly to China. I said that I couldn't afford to be buried here." By the time of our interview, however, he no longer had plans to return to China and told me: "I do not think that way anymore; now I want to stay with my family and children here." In this way, his comments signaled a striking contrast to conventional expectations that Chinese seniors will necessarily want to return to China as they grow old—and highlighted instead the possibilities for creating new forms of affinity and belonging through the reconfiguration of seemingly intractable cultural scripts.

FAMILY LOVE

The centrality of caregiving to negotiations of value in family life should come as no surprise. In recent years, anthropologist Arthur Kleinman has been a strong proponent for a politics of recognition around the importance and benefits of care work.[40] Unlike scholars whose views about caregiving often highlight the possibilities for exploitation among caregivers and their employers,[41] or scholars focusing on the kin-scription of older adult caregivers who lose their own autonomy and develop excessive dependence on adult children,[42] Kleinman's focus propels caregiving to the forefront of family life by arguing that our engagement with this deeply affecting and intimate work reinforces fundamental ideals of what it means to be "human."[43] While Kleinman makes clear that caregiving is a deeply moral practice integral to all human relationships, he also draws heavily on his familiarity with Chinese Confucian value systems of self-cultivation to explain how the process of providing care work is meaningful for individuals who, through that work, engage in moral and social practices that make them ever more human.

The Chinese senior migrants I discuss here rationalized their experiences as caregivers for their American-born grandchildren, their infirm parents or spouses, or other elderly Chinese Americans more through a language of pragmatics than of Confucian self-cultivation as they detailed their conscious contributions to family life. Yet if we follow the logic of traditional Chinese cultural values, Chinese seniors in past decades could assume they would be valued by their family members in their own right, whether or not they were active contributors to the economic and sentimental well-being of their households. Seniors' place of respect in family life was buttressed by the Confucian concept of filial piety and a familial caregiving model dictating that adult children were socially obligated to provide support for their elderly parents. This traditional cultural model is still upheld by many seniors who provide care for their aged parents, even as these seniors are simultaneously aware that their own adult children are unlikely to follow this cultural model in caring for them in future years. As a result, today's Chinese seniors have had to find ways to compensate for this future of potential insecurity that has also been exacerbated by the unequal access to social welfare supports for urban and rural seniors in China today that I described in the previous chapter.

Chinese-born senior migrants were able to demonstrate that they were in fact of value to their families through the caregiving work that served as one main rationale for senior migration to the United States. Seniors contributed economic value to family life through the child care they provided to American-born grandchildren, relieving their own adult children from the burden of paying for child care and freeing up income for necessities or family savings. As a bonus, many seniors also performed paid caregiving or other work outside the home—earning money that saved adult children the responsibility of paying for seniors' daily needs and that could help families in tight economic circumstances make ends meet. Yet the value of seniors' caregiving work was not only economic; the money earned and saved through caregiving work also had important social effects. The value that senior migrants accrued through their work was also sentimental, through developing strong ties to their American-born grandchildren and reinforcing ties with adult children (particularly daughters), as seniors' work eased adult children's economic and emotional burdens while also helping to raise the family's first American-born generation. Moreover, seniors' caregiving work had cultural value for families, as migrants passed on not only Chinese-language capability but also the value of family love, which has remained a powerful Chinese cultural ideal despite society's rapid changes and the resulting contested landscape for senior support in China today.

There can be no denying how centrally important senior migrants' caregiving work was to bolstering both the sentimental and economic well-being of their Chinese American family members. At the same time, through their caregiving work, seniors were engaging with the changing cultural landscape of support for Chinese elders in both China and the United States to negotiate new terms for securing support for themselves from their families as they grew older. Having proven their value through economic, emotional, and cultural contributions to their extended families, seniors hoped their adult children and American-born grandchildren would continue to value them and fulfill their own caregiving needs as they continued to grow old. Whether these goals would eventually be fulfilled, Chinese seniors enjoyed other benefits, including joy and community interaction, through their engagement in their kin work.

Throughout this process, seniors' talk of family love, the idiom they most often used to explain their engagement with acts of caregiving within and beyond their immediate families, focused attention on how the idea of a commitment to family values can remain centrally important to Chinese immigrants and their Chinese American family members without concomitantly reifying those cultural ideas into an essentialized view of cultural roles as static and unmalleable—as happens when scholars unreflexively employ the kin-script of filial piety as the reason for Asian American elders' stress or success without paying attention to the nuances of the actual dynamics of intergenerational relations in Chinese American families. Equally important is the recognition of grandparents as actors in these intergenerational family processes; they make important decisions about contributing to family life, not only to strengthen their emotional and cultural bonds with their American-born grandchildren but also to help counteract the precariousness of their financial and social situations as older adults in both China and the United States. That the renegotiation of cultural values associated with intergenerational relationships is changing social norms in China today—as many migrants experienced in China—as well as among the Chinese American families of these migrants once in the United States is one form of affinity experienced by Chinese senior migrants whose participation in these cultural negotiations enables them to strengthen their personal and family relationships, and thus their social engagement, in the United States.

In the following chapter, I continue to focus on how recent Chinese senior migrants negotiated their adjustment to living in the United States as older adults through an in-depth exploration of their homemaking processes in and around Boston's Chinatown. In particular, I focus on how Chinatown and its satellite community in Quincy facilitated senior migrants' well-being as they developed routines and rhythms of daily life that were familiar to them—almost as if they were still aging in place in China.

6   AGING IN PLACE?

Boston's Chinatown serves as an important hub of social and work activity for Boston-area (and New England) resident Chinese seniors, whether they live in Chinatown or elsewhere. Yet the idea of Chinatown as a distinctive urban neighborhood was a seemingly baffling one to many of my recently arrived Cantonese-speaking interviewees—particularly those who lived in Boston's downtown Chinatown but had not experienced living in the United States outside this neighborhood. For them, Chinatown was just "America" like any other residential location they could have chosen. In contrast, interviewees who lived outside Chinatown and had "discovered" it through the introduction of family or friends, talked easily about Chinatown (C. *tongyahngaai*; M. *tangrenjie*) as a distinctive area that provided culturally familiar resources not available elsewhere. At the same time, they lamented Chinatown's shabbiness, dirtiness, and lack of security in comparison to other (what they called "American") urban and suburban areas in and around Boston. Their views were not unfounded: in 2013, Chinatown's environment was so unhealthy because of problems with trash disposal and collection that local leaders established the Cleanup Chinatown Committee to improve the situation.[1] Yet my interviewees' concerns about Chinatown's poor physical environment went further. As one migrant explained:

> I have some bad impressions about Chinatown. For example, the buildings are pretty old. Chinatown is dirty and disorderly. The stores are small and crowded. The stuff on the shelves is not arranged well. They are not like

American stores. There the shelves are neatly arranged, well organized, and clean. Besides, the service in Chinatown stores is not as good as in American stores. American stores treat their customers very well.

Views like these about Chinatown's appearance reflected migrants' surprise and dismay when they discovered that much of Chinatown's physical infrastructure stands in stark contrast to both the modern architecture in other parts of downtown Boston as well as the newly constructed contemporary Chinese urban areas they had visited or lived in before coming to the United States. Time and again, I heard from newer immigrants that Boston's Chinatown would benefit from having more modern building infrastructure. In this way, recent migrants' views seemed to be in contrast to many contemporary community members' concerns that gentrification is destroying Boston's Chinatown and displacing many of its lower-income migrant residents.[2] Yet both groups' views are fundamentally grounded in a similar concern: that Chinatown is home for many individuals who are dependent on the neighborhood's culturally appropriate resources and dense networks of service provision and community interaction for daily life survival and success.

Chinatowns have a long history as contested spaces. They are complex communities that provide networks and resources vital to the survival and acclimation of newly arrived Chinese immigrants. As sites of ethnic diversity and global interconnectedness, they also provide crucial social resources. An essential part of Chinese diasporic life, Chinatowns are found in cities around the world and act (as my interviewees make clear) as a series of globally networked nodes, allowing migrants without much cultural and financial capital to participate in contemporary global mobility processes that would otherwise be closed to them. Yet Chinatowns are also the subject of long-standing stereotypes that essentialize these vibrant and ever-changing urban communities as culturally alien and distinct from mainstream American ways of life—drawing tourists, both Chinese and non-Chinese, to these cultural "oases" of Otherness.[3] Such stereotypes mask the fact that Chinatowns have always been more diverse and globally connected than nonresidents have often assumed.[4] These views also divert attention away from Chinatown "as a real, densely lived and worked place, defined by everyday transactions, practices and interactions, and very much entangled with its surroundings at urban, national and transnational levels."[5] Writing against these stereotypes, scholars over the past two decades have detailed the many social and economic benefits of Chinatowns as ethnic enclaves with long histories as sites of transnational activity that also facilitate social mobility for Chinese immigrants.⁶ In this chapter, I add to this already rich documentation of Chinatowns as important sites for migrant lifeways by focusing on how the physical places of Boston's Chinatown (and its nearby satellite, Quincy) matter for my aging interviewees' processes of "homemaking" in the United States despite the seeming contradiction with their initially negative impressions of the area.

Scholars of migration have paid substantial attention to the ways in which migrants integrate to new areas. Central to these processes is the idea of home and how migrants craft and embrace senses of identification with their often culturally unfamiliar new areas of residency. In Chapter 3, for example, I explored how Chinese senior migrants' sense of affiliation with and belonging to the United States hinged on their perceptions of the country as a location where senior citizens are treated "humanely." As with other studies focused on processes of homemaking for aging migrants, the argument I make in that chapter underscores that we should think of "home" not just as a static place but as a series of familial, social, and political engagements ranging across different locations.⁷ As geographer Russell King writes, "home is a *process*—hence 'homing'—rather than a taken-for-granted place fixed in space [so] people continue to be active and reflexive in their home-making projects well into later life."⁸

Questions of homemaking are particularly salient for aging migrants like my interviewees, since having access to the comforts of home is positively correlated with seniors' physical and emotional well-being as they grow older.⁹ "Home" can figure into senior migrants' trajectories in different ways. Some seniors craft new senses of home in locations separate from their countries of origin or where they have had long-standing ties as adults through work, family, or other interactions.¹⁰ More often, older adults may migrate back to a country of origin as retirees—what scholars call "return migration." In these cases, "homing" processes are more likely to involve reintegrating to ways of life migrants left as younger adults, as they seek a return to culturally familiar contexts in their older age.¹¹ In contrast, aging migrants without the resources to move to new locations or return to their countries of origin may have no choice but to age in place in locations they may not think of as home and where they had never intended to live as older adults.¹² In this latter context, "aging in place" generally takes on a negative connotation—drawing primary attention to the social and economic structures that inhibit mobility and homing processes for aging individuals who migrated to new and foreign environments at some point in their younger adult lives. Viewed in this way, aging in place stands in contrast to the many positive benefits for seniors' physical health and emotional well-being usually associated with nonmigrants who age in place and therefore retain daily access to culturally familiar routines, rhythms, and patterns of social interaction even as they grow increasingly infirm.[13] This divide highlights the differential access to possibilities of well-being as older adults with and without financial resources. It also reinforces attention to the uneven effects of globalization on seniors' lives worldwide, as some benefit from sources of capital facilitating mobility processes while others do not.[14]

Aging in place intersects with migrants' homemaking processes in many ways within the context of their daily experiences of growing older in Boston's Chinatown. Investigating aging seniors' mobility and well-being through this lens provides possibilities for complicating the existing theoretical conventions that link aging in place among aging migrants to geographic immobility—even as the same concept leads to possibilities for independence and seniors' well-being in nonmigrant contexts.

I view Boston's Chinatown and Quincy as retirement communities of sorts, where elderly migrants' interactions with place enable spatial and temporal engagements that produce homing effects. My analysis here centers on gerontologist and social geographer Graham Rowles's ideas of "physical insideness" and "social insideness" to describe how recent Chinese senior migrants developed a set of routines and rhythms of daily life in Boston's Chinatown and Quincy that mimicked patterns of life familiar to them.[15] These daily experiences were supported by key infrastructures that were available to all seniors, whether they lived in these areas or in other parts of the greater Boston metropolitan area. These routines allowed recent Chinese senior migrants to experience life in the United States almost as if they were aging in place in China, creating an unexpected sense of affinity with the physical spaces they inhabited and thereby enhancing their processes of homemaking as they grew older. This spatial affinity meant that Chinese seniors without significant social or financial capital could still experience the benefits of global mobility flows more commonly associated with professional and capital-rich older migrants.

CHINATOWN AND ITS BOUNDARIES

While Boston's downtown Chinatown area is larger than it may at first seem to a tourist wandering through it, it is still relatively compact, packing at least seventy-five organizations into twenty-five blocks of downtown Boston.[16] Within this area, there is access to three subway lines and several major bus routes—all of which lead directly to areas outside Chinatown where many more Chinese seniors live—as well as numerous social services and one major hospital complex. Although one social service organization in particular provides substantial support to the low-income senior demographic (including preparing and delivering over two thousand hot Chinese lunches daily throughout the greater Boston area, running several adult day health centers, and providing access to employment opportunities for low-income seniors), seniors also make use of a variety of other organizations, where they can take English classes, get immigration and legal advice, and access health care, all in Chinese. Many organizations sponsor community lectures—focusing on common concerns around elder health and well-being—that provide important sources of information and also serve as social outings for groups of friends with limited mobility. Social service organizations help with other needs too: translation, recreational trips and activities, legal services, applications for housing and welfare, and information in Chinese about upcoming elections, health initiatives, and neighborhood concerns.

The Chinatown-based social service organizations that provide this rich institutional infrastructure are only several decades old, founded mainly by second-generation Chinese Americans who grew up in Boston's Chinatown after World War II. Well educated and influenced by civil rights concerns in the 1960s and 1970s, these important actors in maintaining Chinatown's viability as a thriving residential community responded directly to community needs by providing services for the low-income, Chinese-speaking residential population, including both long-term immigrants and recent arrivals who came to the United States through family reunion and refugee categories following immigration reform in 1965. These service organizations complemented, but did not replace, Chinatown's original associations that had provided networks of support for Chinese immigrants and residents in the United States since the early twentieth century. These original organizations include *huiguan*, also known as surname associations (that is, groups whose membership is based on a common last name or names), regional associations based on shared location of residence in China (such as the Taishanese Association), and other groups (like the Chinese Consolidated Benevolent Association) that provide business advice and political leadership for the ethnic community.[17] However, unlike the more recently founded social service organizations, most of these long-standing associations may have more restrictive membership practices, even as they also provide certain benefits to their members not available through social service organizations, such as "red envelopes" with small stipends for seniors aged seventy or older at annual Lunar New Year banquets.

Unlike the Chinese immigrants who arrived in the United States through the 1970s, whose primary source of local social and economic support was through the traditional Chinatown associations, recent Chinese senior migrants actively made use of both the newer social service organizations as well as the long-standing associations. While they relied on service organizations for practical advice and help negotiating their personal and financial concerns, they also frequented surname and regional associations, making use of these associations' functions as community centers, providing space for informal gatherings, reading newspapers, playing mahjong, and doing martial arts, exercise, or dance classes. Even less mobile seniors who did not often leave their residential buildings would occasionally attend a special lecture or event held at either a social service center or surname association. One active interviewee in her late sixties who had been in Boston for about two years when I first met her in 2011 described her surprise at all "the different Chinese organizations that are in Chinatown." She elaborated:

> These organizations hold different events, such as holiday celebrations. For people who are unfamiliar with the place, it is a great thing to have [access to all these organizations]. For example, I was stuck [outside] in cold weather and did not know what to do. Someone had told me about the Taishanese Community Center, and so I thought it would be a good idea to go and get a cup of hot tea there. I went and found out that it was a really good place to take refuge during the cold winter season. It was warm, and there were even newspapers for me to read.

At the same time, she also made strategic use of the social service organizations, which had been instrumental in helping her train for and find a job as a home health aide for non-English-speaking Chinese seniors and for locating a subsidized senior apartment in Quincy.

Other spaces in and around Chinatown also provided possibilities for socialization and recreation. These included several dim sum restaurants, where seniors met with friends and lingered, a YMCA where seniors went to exercise each day, and urban parks bordering Chinatown, where seniors took walks, gathered in groups to dance or exercise, or simply sat outside to get some air and watch the hustle and bustle of students, businesspeople, and shoppers all around. Several Chinese-language church ministries, serving thousands of area residents, are also nearby. Taken together with the grocery stores, bakeries, travel agencies, and other specialty shops that market primarily to the local Asian American community, Boston's Chinatown provided the most comprehensive institutional support for Chinese seniors in the greater New England area. The concentration of these resources in an area of only few city blocks made the navigation of that area relatively easy even for individuals experiencing various age-related infirmities or difficulty with everyday mobility.

One reason for the density of these institutional resources for seniors is that Boston's Chinatown has a significant residential community—in contrast to many of the other midsize Chinatowns in the United States that primarily serve as tourist rather than residential locations.[18] Much of the Chinese residential community is housed in subsidized apartment complexes (for families of all ages, as well as for seniors in particular), which were built through city-sponsored urban development programs in the 1960s and 1970s. These complexes have allowed low-income individuals to move to and stay in Boston's Chinatown in housing that is far preferable to the crowded tenement buildings that provide tiny but unsafe living conditions for area residents who do not live in subsidized housing and cannot afford the newly built luxury housing aimed at professionals working in nearby downtown areas. Many older Chinese American residents of Chinatown's subsidized apartment complexes have lived in the United States for many decades; long waiting lists make access to this housing difficult for recent migrants. Thus, most of my interviewees who lived in one of these complexes had been resident in the area for at least ten years.

Chinese American seniors in Quincy also have access to a number of resources that support their needs, although those resources are not always as easy to access as they are in Chinatown. Nevertheless, the infrastructure of organizational support has been growing. Over the past few years, Quincy-based offices for many of Chinatown's social service organizations have been established, as have new organizations and outreach programs specifically targeted to address the needs of Asian American seniors in and around Quincy. Similar to downtown Chinatown, many Chinese seniors live in subsidized senior housing complexes—in some cases, making up almost 50 percent of a building's residents. Less mobile elderly residents relied primarily on outreach services available in their housing complexes for only a few hours each week. Unlike Chinese seniors in Boston's Chinatown who could easily get to Chinese grocery stores, restaurants, and cultural activities and had daily access to subsidized meals, Chinese seniors in Quincy generally needed to take public transportation to access these daily needs. Those who could not take public transportation relied on once-weekly delivered Chinese meals or family help on weekends to get to stores and restaurants. Individuals requiring medical care could qualify for door-to-door public transportation services and translation services when family members were not available to accompany them to doctor appointments. Nevertheless, trying to arrange for these services was challenging for non-English-speaking seniors. Even so, Quincy's substantial Asian American population has created significant opportunities for less mobile Chinese seniors to gain access to important resources necessary for their well-being and also for active seniors to enjoy a sense of familiar daily patterns and activities that they would not otherwise have access to without much longer commutes into downtown Chinatown.

PHYSICAL INSIDENESS: AFFINITY TO PLACE AND THE DEVELOPMENT OF FAMILIAR DAILY ROUTINES

In Chapter 4, I drew attention to the circuits of knowledge about ways of life beyond China that influenced Chinese seniors' decisions about moving to the United States following their retirement in China. One beneficiary of these circuits of information was Mr. Eng, who moved to Boston in 2000 through the sponsorship of his adult daughter. Before he left Guangdong, he had carefully considered the advantages and limitations of living in Boston's Chinatown. He had also thought about moving to New York's Chinatown, where he had many friends, or staying in China, where he still had strong ties, including parents who were alive at the time he chose to migrate. He told me, "I asked many people [in Taishan] about whether I should live in America. They all told me that I would be fine living in the United States. . . . [I also talked to] people who had gone to the United States and returned after two to three years. They were the ones who told me that life in America wasn't that great." Although noting that Boston's Chinatown is "small" and that the market prices for food are higher than in New York, Mr. Eng seemed comfortable with his decision to stay in Boston's Chinatown. He told me:

> After living in Chinatown for a while, I found out that life here was not bad at all. The people here can all speak Taishanese; I would have to be either deaf or mute to have problems. . . . I think life here is pretty convenient. We have a large group of Taishanese people here. We make friends with each other easily. I meet someone at dim sum, and then we run into each other a couple of times after that, and then we become good friends. So I gradually got used to this place, and all my worries were gone.

In this account, Mr. Eng's adjustment to living in Boston hinged on his access to familiar people (other transplanted Taishanese), familiar culture (language and food), and familiar social activities (going to dim sum). Moreover, his lifeways were supported through his ability to navigate the physical environment of Chinatown, where these familiar connections allowed him to develop daily patterns of living that mimicked the kinds of activities he might have pursued had he stayed in China. This sense of familiarity echoes Rowles's concept of physical insideness, a term that explains the sense of affinity and attachment to place experienced by older individuals who have lived for long periods of their lives in a particular location. Over time, they have developed a deep understanding of place that continues to enable their comfortable negotiation of the physical spaces around them, even as they grow frail and experience physical impairments or other significant mobility restrictions as they age.[19]

Scholars set the importance of familiarity of place for older individuals' well-being as they grow older against the concern of how aging in unfamiliar environments can negatively affect seniors' well-being through heightened anxiety about safety and security. These fears revolve around physical concerns, such as navigating stairs, uneven sidewalks, and busy outdoor spaces as physical mobility decreases. Impaired movement increases not only the fear of falling and sustaining serious injury or death but also fear of crime.[20] Given that my interviewees had migrated to Boston as older adults, it would seem natural that they would have similar worries about living in a new and unfamiliar environment. Indeed, they talked frequently about their fears of being mugged, citing cases of friends, neighbors, or family who had had purses, jewelry, or wallets stolen in Chinatown. One interviewee had been attacked at his Chinatown job, leading to his decision to stop working ten years before.

Fears were exacerbated for my interviewees because of their inability to communicate or read signage in English. As a result, routine trips outside the house presented various frightening possibilities, including disorientation, getting lost, or becoming vulnerable to petty criminal attack. Anxiety further increased by venturing beyond Chinatown's borders, causing one long-term Chinatown resident to tell me that "living in Chinatown is like being in jail." Mr. Eng, comfortable with his familiar daily routines, told me that he was so afraid of getting lost that he rarely took public transportation. When he did, he always traveled with a friend to help him find his way. This fear dated from a disorienting experience after he had been in the United States for just a few months:

I was going to watch the fireworks over by the park [just outside Chinatown]. But the weather turned a little chilly, and so I decided to go back home and grab my jacket before they started. I couldn't believe that I got lost on my way back to my apartment! The path was the same as my routine morning walk that I took every day. But I made a mistake on one of the turns and couldn't find my way back from there. After that experience I was too afraid to venture out far again.

This quote demonstrates how easily seniors can become disoriented in even a seemingly familiar environment. At the same time, it indicates the importance of Chinatown's familiar cultural and social environment in enabling Chinese seniors to navigate the physical landscape and establish daily routines—and thus experience a kind of physical insideness despite their moves to this area as young-old (or even old-old) adults. Scholars writing about the importance of aging in place for seniors' well-being implies that long-term residency is crucial for establishing the kinds of ties and familiarity to place that allow seniors to develop emotional affinity and physical awareness that will allow them to remain independent in later life. Yet as Mr. Eng and others can attest, Chinatown's service infrastructure and cultural familiarity seemed to stand in for length of residency in achieving these goals, allowing seniors who had recently engaged in transnational migration processes to establish daily routines that mimicked similarly positive benefits attributed to aging in place for nonmigrant seniors.

These benefits—including the possibility of remaining independent while growing older in a location that still enables interdependence on a larger group of age-mates—were not just available to seniors who lived in Boston's Chinatown. More commonly, seniors resided outside Chinatown, either with or near adult children in suburban areas where there were few other Chinese residents. In these cases, seniors' initial visits to Chinatown were often facilitated by their adult children, who took them there on a weekend for dim sum or to go shopping for Chinese specialty food items. The excitement of Chinese senior migrants' discovery of Chinatown as a culturally familiar location was palpable through my interviewees' vivid memories of their first visit to Chinatown, often just a few days—but sometimes weeks—after having arrived in Boston. Mrs. Tan, at age eighty a resident of Boston's Chinatown, told me that her first visit to Chinatown made her "happy" because for the first time in the United States, she was able to communicate with people around her. She had lots of space to be outside with her grandchildren at her daughter's home in New Hampshire, but it wasn't until her visit to Boston's Chinatown that she had the chance to have a conversation longer than "Hello" and "How are you?" with anyone besides her immediate family. Another interviewee's first trip to Boston's Chinatown coincided with a snowstorm. Thus, her memory of that visit had a magical quality, inseparable from her amazement of the beauty of seeing snow for the first time.

While initial forays into Chinatown were made as part of the weekend tourism that regularly animates Chinatown's gastronomic and other establishments, seniors' initial visits eventually led to more substantial involvement in the Chinatown community, including using institutional resources, working, volunteering, or participating in other kinds of leisure activities. Seniors who initially lived too far to commute to Chinatown daily—in Vermont, New Hampshire, and Rhode Island, for example—often moved to Chinatown (and away from adult children) once they qualified for senior housing there. Other seniors living in and around the Boston area regularly visited Chinatown several times each month, with some making the two-hour, one-way commute by bus and subway twice each day. Echoing concerns voiced by seniors like Mr. Eng who were reluctant to leave Chinatown, my interviewees' first attempts to find their way from other areas to Chinatown on public transportation were similarly tinged with anxious discourse about getting lost. That was even the case for those who lived near public transportation that connected directly to Chinatown, including Quincy, Malden, Cambridge, Brookline, and Newton, among other nearby areas of high Asian residency.[21] While some seniors' main hardship was the long commute from suburban areas, others faced the more daunting problem of not being able to read or remember the English names for the stops they needed. The prospect of missing the Chinatown stop and ending up in an unfamiliar area of the city was terrifying. Seniors shared numerous stories of their initial subway navigation, including their methods for trying to figure out which train to take and how to recognize the right stop. Mitigating these initial fears, almost everyone also had a story about the kindness of strangers who had helped them find their way—aiding them with getting through the turnstile, verifying they had located the correct stop, or explaining how to retrace their steps when they had gone too far. In addition to the language barrier, the cost of taking public transportation was an additional problem for some seniors.

Many of the Chinese seniors who came into Chinatown daily lived in Quincy. The Chinese seniors I met there had most often moved to Quincy with their adult children in previous decades, and they had moved into subsidized senior housing in Quincy to remain close to those families. These long-term residents fell into two categories. One was those who had previously worked in

Chinatown's sweatshops (or occasionally in other capacities, such as restaurant workers) and tended to be socially outgoing and independent. These individuals were comfortable traveling into Boston's Chinatown on the subway a few times a month to get together with old friends and colleagues. Other seniors, who had never worked in Chinatown, tended to be more isolated and never traveled independently to other areas of town (Quincy or Boston) for fear of getting lost. While fewer recent senior migrants tended to live in Quincy than in some other areas (like Malden), those I met who lived in Quincy had heard about its subsidized housing and had applied to live there because of the long waits to get into subsidized housing in Chinatown, because of the ease of transportation to and from Chinatown, and because of the relatively high density of other Chinese seniors living in Quincy's housing complexes.

The more disparate network of service provision in Quincy left nonmobile Chinese seniors seemingly more vulnerable than their counterparts in resource-dense Chinatown. However, living in Quincy nonetheless provided important benefits to both mobile and nonmobile seniors in different ways. For nonmobile seniors, the relative density of Asian (and specifically Chinese) residents in the area meant that many other people had similar kinds of informal networks of neighborly support as those I discussed in Chapter 4. Some community centers and health organizations serving the non-English-speaking Chinese communities also provided outreach support in areas with particularly high numbers of nonmobile seniors. For mobile seniors, the spatial dispersal of residential locations, community centers, and service centers throughout Quincy, all tied to public transportation routes, provided significant opportunities for spontaneous collaboration across the area in planning and holding a variety of social activities. These included exercise and dance groups, musical groups, and Chinese lunch groups. As I frequented two senior centers (one Chinese and one primarily working-class white) and two subsidized senior housing complexes under the same management but at opposite ends of town, I realized that these spatially discrete areas of high Chinese occupancy around Quincy made up an integrated social map. Seniors across the area made daily plans—for example, to attend exercise classes at center A on Monday and Wednesday, but the musical group at residential location Y on Friday. For meals, the same seniors might plan to eat the weekly Chinese lunch at senior center B on Tuesday but at residential location Z on Thursday. In other words, despite the spatial dispersion of these locations of activity, Chinese seniors in Quincy had been able to develop daily routines with a shared foundation in culturally and socially familiar environments. As a result, Chinese senior migrants in Quincy, like those in Boston's downtown Chinatown, had developed the physical insideness necessary for increased well-being and homemaking as they aged in the United States.

SOCIAL INSIDENESS: DAILY RHYTHMS AND PATTERNS OF SOCIAL INTERACTION

Chinese seniors developed a sense of affinity and attachment to Chinatown as a place, enabling them to navigate the area to take advantage of its resources and establish comfortable and familiar daily routines through what Rowles calls "physical insideness." A complementary concept that Rowles developed is "social insideness," defined as a "sense of social affinity" that results from the shared habitation of particular spaces over long periods of time. As individuals develop comfortable rhythms of interaction with each other in the shared spaces in which they live, the locations themselves take on "a social rhythm and ambience that is acknowledged by its occupants" and becomes a "social space." An example of this phenomenon within a family home might include each member of the family having a particular seat at the dinner table—a pattern that, Rowles notes, may become recognized only through the disruption of that pattern, such as when a guest has to be accommodated or when one visits a friend's house and sees different spatial patterns there.[22] Rowles extends his concept to explain not just familiar social rhythms within homes but also to neighborhoods and the patterns of interactions established by residents who live within the same social community. He writes:

> On a larger scale, we may develop similar social affinity with our neighborhood as a result of patterns of interactions with our neighbors and friends. Over the years, neighborhoods develop into social spaces with accepted social norms, expectations, and rules of behavior that are continually reinforced by residents—either formally, through organizations like neighborhood associations, or informally, through characteristic patterns of interactions among neighbors. Such patterns range from suburban over-the-fence or sidewalk conversations to the front stoop and street culture of some crowded inner-city neighborhoods. Individuals are enabled to develop a sense of "belonging" through participation in local culture and through sharing in and nurturing the neighborhood's sense of group identification with place.[23]

Yet that sense of social affinity was often missing when seniors lived together with adult children. Many of my interviewees talked explicitly about how they had failed to develop a sense of social insideness when living in their adult children's homes. One interviewee explained:

> While I was living with my daughter's family, they had their own working schedule. I had to be careful not to wake them up in the morning, and I had to wait for them to get off work until everyone was available at home to eat dinner. Now, living here [in subsidized senior housing] by myself, I don't have those restrictions anymore. I can live according to my own schedule, go out whenever I want, and come back whenever I feel like it. . . . Younger people have their own schedules and ways of life, which are very different from those of the older generation. I feel so much more free now that I don't have to deal with the clash between the two different modes of living.

As this quotation makes clear, one main difference between the lives of adult children and those of seniors was time orientation. Although many seniors worked, their schedules were often part time, resulting in a different daily rhythm from that of their adult children who worked full time. The daily conflicts of rhythm oriented around different work schedules created conflict for some seniors. At the same time, many senior migrants also recognized through their involvement in Chinatown's daily life and routines that they were more likely to feel a sense of social insideness there. For my interviewees, this social insideness had its roots in a shared time orientation of living in accordance with the daily rhythms and needs of senior life, including a slower pace and a sense of heightened anxiety.

For many of my interviewees, a major source of anxiety centered around their adult children's busyness, and thus their potential inability to be available to provide help when seniors might need immediate aid. In these cases, seniors felt that they could depend more reliably on Chinatown's institutional and community infrastructure for emergency help than they could on their family members, particularly their adult children, who were generally preoccupied with their own work and social lives. For seniors like Mrs. Wong, who had a two-hour commute each way from her suburban apartment to Chinatown, moving to Chinatown seemed to offer more assurance for the future than continuing to live in the suburbs. She explained:

> I have already applied to move to housing here [in Chinatown], but I heard that it is difficult [because] people generally have to wait for 10 years. . . . There is only one issue with me moving here, which is that I will be living farther away

from my son, and so he won't be able to come to my immediate assistance if I ever need his help in the future. But there have been many times in the past when my [son and daughter-in-law] were at work when I needed help. Here, I can have greater access to the hospital and the other organizations, and so I will actually get more help by moving into Chinatown.

As Mrs. Wong suggests, it was not just the presence of the resource infrastructure in Chinatown that made it an attractive area to live. Another key factor was a time orientation that ensured key resources would be available whenever they might become necessary, day or night. These areas of dense residency with many other retirees meant that individuals living in and around Chinatown knew they could access help and support when necessary, not just when it fit within their adult children's schedules.

Mr. Lee, for example, was able to get by living on his own in senior housing at the age of ninety after his wife had passed away. He told me:

> My neighbors here have gotten to be some of my closer friends. Sometimes they call me to see how I'm doing, and they help me any way they can. For example, when my computer had problems, I called up my neighbor [who] is a graduate of the Beijing Computer Academy, and he helped me fix these problems. . . . If it had a virus or something he'd help me. Sometimes he'd help me fix the TV. He helps me a lot. [My other neighbor] from next door also helps me with my email. People always send me email. I get to see what the world is like, and I get to see pictures. . . . There's also another neighbor who helps me whenever I need some help. For example, not that long ago [following some eye surgery], I couldn't see anything and [my family] had not hired anyone yet [to help me]. [My neighbor] gave me [his leftover] food, [so that I could eat]. At first I was really scared, especially after my operation, [because] I couldn't see well. . . . This shows the [kinds of] help that neighbors give each other.

In this case, Mr. Lee highlighted his fortune in living among a community of retired individuals with a diverse range of backgrounds and skills. Most important, he explained that because these retired individuals all had similar daily rhythms and understood the precise needs and anxieties of other older individuals, they were ideally situated to provide help at key moments of need. That his neighbor shared food with him when he was hungry spoke not just to his neighbor's selflessness (since most likely he had little food to eat himself), but also indicated a social affinity that arose in this shared space of habitation.

Moreover, Mr. Lee's fear of hunger paled in comparison to his larger overall sense of anxiety at not being able to see. Knowing that his neighbor would help him relieved some of that anxiety. I witnessed a similar example of shared social affinity at one community meeting where most of the attendees were seniors living in the housing complex next to the meeting location. As the meeting was beginning, cries from seniors sitting at the table next to me alerted everyone that a woman had fainted. A woman I recognized—a long-term Chinatown resident and former sweatshop factory worker in Chinatown—took charge of the fainted woman and patted her on the back until she revived. Once up, the woman who had fainted was guided from the meeting back to her building by a neighbor who proclaimed there was no need to call for emergency services. She knew that this woman had fainted because she had not eaten dinner.

In addition to time orientation, my interviewees' sense of social insideness in both Chinatown and Quincy also hinged on other patterns of interactions they experienced, including their familiarity with the ways in which their age-mates gathered daily in shared social spaces. This included sitting on benches to watch the world go by, crowding around impromptu games of Chinese chess in outdoor areas where sidewalks were wide enough to facilitate that activity,[24] or playing cards, mahjong, or other games in the senior common areas of their housing. In both downtown Chinatown and Quincy, relatively consistent groupings of seniors spent time together in the common areas of their residential buildings. Men and women almost always sat apart or pursued different activities, except in one Quincy location where men and women took turns playing Ping-Pong together. Generally, however, men tended to read the newspaper, sometimes chatting with a neighbor, while women played cards, played mahjong, sang together, or socialized. Sometimes women chatted for hours, and sometimes they sat quietly next to each other, just keeping each other company. The residents pursuing these different activities invariably sat at round tables in large, communal rooms that often also doubled as dining tables at mealtimes.

The density with which these shared social spaces were occupied by seniors pursuing activities familiar to them speaks to the fact that, as Mr. Eng explained, Boston's Chinatown is "small." This "smallness," which I heard about over and over from my interviewees, referred not only to Chinatown's compact physical size but also to its relative density of social networks, through which seniors found themselves running into old friends from China or living in the same housing complex with individuals they had hoped never to see again. Because of the dense connections of ties among Cantonese regional migrants, my interviewees had randomly encountered past schoolmates, previous neighbors, and, for one former doctor in China, a patient. Everyone had a story about running into someone they knew from "home" in Boston's Chinatown. Such closely knit and overlapping networks of coworkers, family, and friends invariably included conflict and tension as well as potential solidarity and support. In one Quincy senior housing complex, a woman sat down next to me and complained in a loud voice about another woman standing nearby, whom she labeled a troublemaker. She had known this "troublemaker," she said, for over forty years, since they had both lived in Hong Kong, and had been unhappy to learn that they were living in the same senior residential building in the United States. These forms of tension reinforced the social insideness that Chinese senior migrants in Chinatown experienced, since daily patterns of interaction are not based solely on social harmony but invariably include tensions and conflict as well. In this case, the patterns of conflict encountered among co-ethnics replicated similar kinds of tensions familiar to seniors from their earlier adult lives in China, such as disputes with former coworkers and past neighbors and social divisions resulting from regional differences.

At one weekly coffee hour I attended in Boston's Chinatown, senior residents divided themselves in the following ways. One table had Taishanese speakers (who could also speak Cantonese but not English) who had lived in the United States for thirty years or longer. Most had adult children they had raised in the United States. Many had lived in Guangzhou or Hong Kong before coming to the United States and had worked mostly in sweatshops or restaurants once here. Sometimes members at this table had family who showed up with special treats; at other times, they looked after their young grandchildren. A second table of Taishanese speakers, despite being similarly aged, looked physically older and appeared as if they had just stepped out of the rural Chinese countryside. Unable to speak Cantonese or English, they tended to be quiet in comparison to the more boisterous group of Taishanese speakers at the table next to them. A third table had conversation mostly in Cantonese. One woman at this table was an acquaintance of mine from a different Chinatown location where I had conducted fieldwork several years earlier. By 2011, she suffered from memory loss and told me the same story each week. Another woman at this table also suffered from even more acute memory loss, but there were other Cantonese-speaking women without any signs of mental decline. Some were long-term Chinatown residents, and others had moved to the area within the past five to ten years. Sometimes more tables were occupied: one of men, all recent migrants who spoke Mandarin but not Cantonese or Taishanese, and another of women who liked to sing together in Mandarin as well as other regional dialects. For the most part, there was little interaction among the tables. Sometimes there were confrontations, such as when a group of women began to sing and others thought the singing was too loud. When my acquaintance suffering from memory loss told the same story once too often, another woman loudly scolded her as old and "crazy" (C. *chisin*).

These kinds of regional co-ethnic divisions among seniors who had all originated from Guangdong Province may have been largely pragmatic, resulting from the inability to communicate across regional dialects. Moreover, as Genevieve Leung points out, these divisions indexed meaningful categories of regional identity across different groups.[25] Yet even older Taishanese women who could not speak any Cantonese could usually understand it, and in this way they were integrated into Chinatown cultural contexts and social networks that all used Cantonese as the primary language of communication. The strength of this interconnection and overlap among Cantonese seniors and the organizational infrastructure that served them was viewed as off-putting to seniors who could not speak or understand Cantonese. Mr. Wu, an impoverished man in his mid-sixties who had migrated through sibling sponsorship from Shanghai, most succinctly summed up a sentiment I heard expressed by all non-Cantonese-speaking seniors who lived in or near Boston's Chinatown. Speaking in Mandarin, he told me: "I am not a part of Chinatown. The Cantonese push me out. I try to get along with them, getting into their group, but the Cantonese people do not welcome me. They do not communicate with me."

These regional divisions reflected class differences between those who may have had some education and white-collar work experiences and those who had not. As a result, one of the most salient divisions reflected among co-ethnic seniors was that between former urban and rural residents of China. Commenting on her use of social services in Chinatown, Mrs. Wong explained why she had never visited any surname or regional associations in Chinatown, despite her familiarity with and use of many social service organizations in the area:

> Most of the people at the regional associations are people who come from rural areas, and so the people there tend to be more complicated, and have a slightly inferior culture. I know that the regional associations also provide services to their members, but I am not sure about the quality of the services they provide.

Also, as someone who comes from an urban area, I do not share the same background as the people at the regional association, and so I don't usually associate with the people there. With that said, I do think that I might attend some of their events in the future.

Mrs. Wong's quote reflected the tension inherent in the landscape of organizational infrastructure in Boston's Chinatown. On the one hand, the more traditional Chinatown social organizations had their basis in immigrant networks from an earlier era and relied on regional and family connections as the primary means of determining membership and distributing aid. In contrast, newer social service institutions served a variety of clients, no matter their regional or family background. In other words, Mrs. Wong's comment speaks to the challenge of integrating newer senior migrants into a well-established community of Chinese American seniors for whom Boston's Chinatown was "home." Mrs. Wong's comment also draws attention to a cultural division that contemporary senior migrants bring with them from China: the distinction between rural and urban residents. Mrs. Wong notes that "people who come from rural areas . . . have a slightly inferior culture." Since she instead "comes from an urban area, [she doesn't] usually associate with the people" at the regional association. Similar views from other senior migrants from China's urban areas significantly contributed to my interviewees' assessments of Chinatown's physical environment as less physically appealing than more "American" parts of Boston.

During the past few decades in China, as economic inequality has grown between urban and rural residents of China, so too has the social capital of urban versus rural residency. Contemporary Chinese seniors' experience with this division is complicated by the fact that many urban professionals and their family members were forced to live in rural areas when sent for reeducation in the countryside during the Cultural Revolution (1966–1976). Moreover, today's seniors from rural Guangdong may also have had the opportunity to work as migrant laborers in China's contemporary urban areas as adults before migrating to the United States. Nevertheless, as Mrs. Wong's comment makes clear, the strong cultural differences associated with urban versus rural residents in contemporary China were also mapped on to interactions among co-ethnics in Boston and Quincy. Although some of these interactions seemed positive—through sharing recreational activities like singing, dancing, or playing mahjong—many more had negative overtones. At best, migrants originating from rural areas were referred to as uneducated and uncultured; at worst, rural migrants were blamed for Chinatown's "dirtiness."

Thus, the disappointment in Chinatown's physical environment voiced by recent senior migrants was matched by concerns about negative public behaviors in Chinatown, heightening the tensions among generational and regional groups engaged with different kinds of homemaking processes in Chinatown. My interviewees were ambivalent as to whether undesirable behaviors could be attributed primarily to newer immigrants who had originated from rural areas or to long-term Chinatown residents who should have already learned better "American" manners by virtue of their long-term residency in the United States. Mrs. Wong's comment about these concerns was typical of many that I heard:

> The thing that I dislike about Chinatown the most is that some people in Chinatown display very base public behaviors. These people like to fight over very little things, such as being the first in line. They also spit in public, and they give me angry glares when I point out to them [that they should not spit in public]. I've tried to convey to them the message that their actions have a negative impact on other people's perception of Chinese people, but they don't listen.

According to my interviewees, other "base public behaviors" of Chinatown's Chinese residents included littering, tossing cigarette butts on the ground, talking loudly in public, and generally being disrespectful of others. In talking about these behaviors, immigrants like Mrs. Wong registered a not unfounded concern that "other people" (here meaning non-Chinese) would identify all Chinese people with those undesirable modes of behavior that she witnessed among some of Chinatown's Chinese residents. These concerns as expressed by more recent senior migrants also seemed to offer confirmation of their belief that in general, Chinese people are less "civilized" than Americans and that one primary purpose of their migration was to gain greater exposure to the better social atmosphere in the United States, where seniors hoped not only to cultivate and further develop their own social mores by following the example set by Americans but also to aid their children's and grandchildren's future prospects through their similar exposure.[26]

These criticisms of Chinatown draw attention to some of the challenges associated with homemaking processes for migrants with different cultural, regional, and generational backgrounds, even when the spatial affinity they experienced in Chinatown contributed positively to their experiences of integrating to life in the United States. These concerns were to some extent echoed by the Chinese American seniors I met in Quincy. There, I was told that although life in Boston's downtown Chinatown may seem convenient, that "convenience" is actually deceptive because individuals who stayed in Chinatown were "trapped"—unable to freely move about and interact with a greater diversity of people and places in the Boston area and the United States more generally. Many of the seniors I met in Quincy had migrated in earlier decades as refugees directly from Hong Kong (in the 1960s) or among the earliest waves of migrants from the PRC who were able to mobilize family connections to come to the United States in the 1970s and early 1980s. They appreciated living in Quincy because of what they viewed as the increased possibility of integrating to U.S. life in comparison to living in Boston's Chinatown.

Yet limits to integration to U.S. life also took place in Quincy, where residents struggled with the city's history of racist conflict that characterized interaction among the city's white and nonwhite residents during the rapid growth of Quincy's Asian American population throughout the 1980s and 1990s. This history was being recreated on an everyday basis in one subsidized senior housing complex through the political machinations of one senior citizen, Linda. Linda, an aging white, working-class woman, was the head of the building's resident association. Drawing on support from a small group of other white residents of the building, she unilaterally worked to block communication and service provision for her building's Chinese American residents, even though all services available to Chinese seniors were also available to the building's non-Chinese senior residents. The heart of her battle took place through her control over the use of her building's shared common space. This huge, windowed room on the top floor of the housing complex served as the building's dining hall and had a small library and exercise center partitioned off at the rear. The large space was open to seniors within and outside the building, and it was easily accessible by public transportation and elevator. Thus, it was an ideal spot for the activities that so many of my interviewees enjoyed—dancing, exercising, game playing, and reading. Yet through constant surveillance of the space and how it was used, Linda had managed to prevent almost all of the patterns of social affinity common to Chinese seniors living in other areas from occurring in that space. When she found Chinese women in the library playing mahjong, she complained to the building's management that they were making noise in a space meant to be quiet. When a small group of women gathered to exercise together in front of a TV screen playing Chinese music and dance videos, Linda sat at a table across the room and stared at them. Some activities nonetheless were held in this room. In those cases, the moment an activity was supposed to end, Linda walked around the room and turned off all the air-conditioning units, ensuring that no one would want to linger because of the room's hot temperature and lack of air circulation.

Linda was notorious throughout Quincy's Chinese senior community. Her reputation followed her to every other location frequented by Quincy's Chinese seniors throughout the period of my research. Whether her actions stemmed from her resentment at the large numbers of non-English-speaking residents in her building, her personal desire for power, or the paranoid, racist behavior of an individual sinking into mental decline, we will never know. However, the net result was that as Chinese seniors in and around Quincy organized group activities and created active networks and social ties across different residential and community center locations around town, they all but avoided the common spaces of this building that Linda treated as her own personal fiefdom. Thus, the less mobile residents of this building were denied the same possibilities of social insideness enjoyed both by more mobile residents of their building and by Chinese seniors living in other housing estates in Quincy and Chinatown.

CONTESTED SPACES

I began this chapter by noting that Chinatowns have always been contested spaces. While much of that contestation can be traced to long-standing, negative stereotypes of Chinatowns by nonresidents, contestation can also be traced to the divergent "homing" practices among different generational and regional groups of migrants who depend on Boston's Chinatown as a physical place crucial to their American lifeways. At the same time, even as it seems to trap some migrants into fewer possibilities of daily mobility beyond its boundaries, it also contributes to increased possibilities of global mobility for Chinese seniors who otherwise have little financial or social capital to participate in retirement migration pathways available to others.

Boston's Chinatown is just one Chinatown among many around the world. For my interviewees, these seemingly discrete places—like the dispersed sites of Chinese senior social activity in Quincy—served as a series of globally networked nodes that provided additional possibilities for travel in the United States and abroad. All of my interviewees, even those with tiny incomes and little to no English-language ability, had traveled to other Chinatowns in North America (or elsewhere, like Sydney, Australia). Most often these trips were to visit friends or relatives, but sometimes seniors went as tourists on group trips organized by Chinatown-related organizations. These visits provided my interviewees with important points of reference to evaluate their quality of life in Boston's Chinatown. Most interviewees compared their Chinatown favorably to the other Chinatowns they had visited. New York's Chinatown was thought to be too crowded, with worse air pollution than Boston's, and Chicago's Chinatown was seen as lacking in social services for seniors. Mr. Lam, who had lived in the United States for almost twenty years at the time of our interview, had visited many different Chinatowns. He said:

> I think they are all pretty similar. I like the one in Vancouver the most. The people there all seemed to be enjoying life. The Chinatown in New York is simply too busy. The one in San Francisco is the biggest, I think. Actually, it is better than the one in Boston [because there are] recreational places for Chinese people only. For example, there are no movie theaters that play movies in Chinese here in Boston. But there are some in San Francisco. I have never watched any movies here. I was offered free movie tickets once, but I turned them down because I couldn't have understood the movie [in English]. So, my activities here are restricted to going to dim sum or taking a walk with my friends.

Even with the limitations to seniors' recreational possibilities in comparison to San Francisco—a limitation that second- and third-generation Chinese Americans working on behalf of Boston Chinatown senior residents' needs are trying to remedy—the networks available through Boston's Chinatown made it possible for my Chinese senior interviewees to engage in new forms of international mobility processes while also achieving desired lifestyles by growing old and living active lives in a seemingly familiar place and meaningful space. This familiarity reinforced Chinese senior migrants' sense of belonging in the United States, even when these same migrants remained critical of Chinatown's environment and the people around them there.

In the final chapter of this book, I return to the issue of co-ethnic community divisions begun in this chapter and expand on that discussion by situating the lives of my Cantonese-speaking recent senior migrant interviewees within a larger Chinese American senior diaspora living in and around Boston. Through charting migrants' daily practice of ballroom and other forms of Chinese dancing in and around Boston, I examine how these forms of cultural performance were crucial for the further development of community ties that facilitated seniors' navigation of the challenges that accompanied their experiences on the social and economic margins of American life. In so doing, I build on the discussions of the global flows of ideas, lifestyles, and cultural practices discussed in previous chapters, which together highlight the many forms of affinity that Chinese senior migrants in the United States experience between their so-called Chinese and American ways of life.

7 MY CHINESE HEART

During summer 2011, as I focused on learning about how recently arrived Chinese senior migrants from different areas of Boston interacted with the resources available in Boston-area Chinatowns, I was introduced to a group of Chinese American seniors who met up to five times weekly to ballroom dance. Speaking Cantonese, Mandarin, Taishanese, Shanghainese, and Vietnamese, many of these dancers had lived in the United States for many years and represented a diverse sampling of national, regional, and class backgrounds that are characteristic of Chinese diasporic groups around the globe. They had developed well-planned circuits for traveling to different community locations in the greater Boston area four to five times weekly. For two full hours in the afternoon, dressed in stunning clothes and sparkling shoes, they gathered together at these locations to dance to the complex musical rhythms of rumbas, tangos, and waltzes. Twice each week, the ballroom took place in Boston's downtown Chinatown. It was at this location that I met Ho Long—a regular not only at this ballroom location but also at others in Quincy, Boston's South End, and Cambridge—whose background and journey to the United States shared many similarities with the majority of my other interviewees. Below, I translate from the Cantonese his thoughts about why dancing was so important to him, taken from a video interview collected by an independent photojournalist that same summer:

> My name is Ho Long. I am 78 years old. I come from mainland China. Through dancing, I can make friends and relax together with everyone. Also, if there's

anything that I'm unhappy about, it's easy to work through those problems while dancing. Dancing solves everything.[1]

Like Ho Long, many of my Chinese-born senior migrant interviewees participated in a range of performative cultural activities in Boston and Quincy. For some, these cultural practices included ballroom dancing. For others, they included doing tai chi, singing, performing Cantonese opera, and playing traditional Chinese musical instruments. Participants spanned a range of potential Chinese migrant experiences in the United States, making for an extremely diverse community of Chinese Americans with histories linked to differing national origins and political affiliations throughout East and Southeast Asia in addition to regional, dialect, and class distinctions within mainland China. These individuals included Cantonese-speaking seniors who emigrated in the early 1980s—at least a decade earlier than my interviewees and as soon as the post–Mao reform-era policies allowed them to leave China; Taishanese-speaking seniors who came to the United States while the exclusion laws were still in force (or just after they were lifted) and have lived here ever since; Cantonese-speaking women who emigrated from Hong Kong in the 1970s and worked in garment factories in Boston's Chinatown before retiring to Quincy; Cantonese-speaking Vietnamese Chinese seniors who came as refugees following the Vietnam War; English- and Cantonese-speaking retired white-collar workers who came to the United States as Chinese refugees via Hong Kong in the 1960s; Mandarin-speaking seniors from both Taiwan and mainland China; and still others. Less common trajectories included ethnically Chinese seniors who migrated through family reunion policies from other Southeast Asian locations, such as Macau and Malaysia, or who came from Latin America. In other words, the seniors participating in these performative cultural activities, while all ethnically Chinese, had vastly different regional and national backgrounds, even spanning oppositional political and ideological orientations. Many didn't speak the same language. Their wide variety of life experiences is indicative of "the deep and significant ruptures and discontinuities that exist within any community and are subject to the continuous 'play' of history, culture, and power."[2]

These significant variations in life experiences among diasporic Chinese seniors serve as the starting point to examine how, despite these differences, community interaction nevertheless took place that helped to mitigate some of the many challenges senior migrants experienced in the United States as low-income individuals with little knowledge of English or the cultural and bureaucratic structures they needed to navigate to obtain medical care, housing, and other life necessities. As the literature on diasporic identity makes clear, sharing a similar ethnic background is not sufficient to ensure that meaningful interaction takes place across diasporic difference. Instead, scholars theorize how community identification across diasporic difference solidifies through the imaginative possibilities of recognizing shared experience across that difference.[3] Here, I explore a slightly different but related question: how recent Chinese senior migrants' involvement in performative cultural activities contributed to their social embeddedness within a larger community of co-ethnics living in the greater Boston area despite the overwhelming diversity of these age-mates' life experiences. This question is tied to the recognition that community support is a crucial factor in seniors' well-being as they age in new locations. For example, as I discussed in Chapter 6, Chinese seniors' social embeddedness within the ethnically familiar environments of Boston's Chinatown and its satellite community in Quincy fostered senior migrants' "homing" processes, allowing them to age as if in place and thereby contributing to their well-being as they grew older. Anthropologist Monika Palmberger similarly points out that aging Turks living in Austria, who also embody a range of life experiences, rely on a multiplicity of religious and political associations throughout the Austrian Turkish community to find different potential sources of affiliation that support their well-being.[4] Yet the social engagement that I observed through seniors' participation in performative cultural activities in and around the Boston area demonstrates a richness of community interaction that goes well beyond involvement with preexisting institutional structures of ethnic community support. In this way, my ethnography foregrounds the importance of focusing on a variety of ways that community interaction is constituted and experienced across diasporic difference in order to understand how interaction with co-ethnics is tied to senior migrants' well-being in different ways in different contexts.

Focusing on how well-being hinges on mundane but crucial forms of daily or weekly interaction with others, I describe seniors' participation in two kinds of cultural performances: ballroom dancing and a form of synchronized group dancing commonly practiced by senior citizens in China today, labeled "congregational" dancing by anthropologist Claudia Huang.[5] My approach, foregrounding the richness of community interaction among diasporic age-mates in practice, differs from that of many scholars of the Chinese diaspora, who treat identity as an abstract phenomenon or one that is mobilized for specific political ends.⁶ Instead, I highlight that daily performance in these dance forms provided seniors with different ways of imagining and engaging with Chineseness—and of contributing to a richness of community interaction—because seniors' long lives (that is, their temporal positioning) created opportunities for imagining commonalities of experience across both time and space. As one Chinese American senior noted, "We all come from different parts of China, from Beijing to Shanghai to Guangzhou. We all speak different languages. At ballroom you don't need words, you just need dance."⁷

THE CULTURAL PRODUCTION OF CHINESENESS

The exact definition of *diaspora* and, with it, the appropriateness of its use in relationship to different populations of displaced individuals dispersed across the globe, has been a major subject of intellectual debate over the past few decades.⁸ That debate, however, has without hesitation rarely carried over to the Chinese context, which instead has identified the concept of diaspora as central to processes of Chinese migration more generally.⁹ For example, historian Adam McKeown advocates for treating studies of Chinese migration with what he calls "a diasporic perspective that can direct the analysis of geographically dispersed institutions, identities, links, and flows."¹⁰ Following this approach, I explained in Chapter 2 how the later-life migration trajectories of many Chinese senior migrants in the greater Boston area are embedded within the long history of Chinese dispersal overseas. This is particularly the case for the Cantonese-speaking seniors who grew up in the Pearl River Delta's culture of migration and had planned to migrate to the United States as younger adults but were unable to do so. Yet the lives of other Chinese American seniors in Boston also reflected the long history of dispersal from Southeast China. Some had complicated familial migratory trajectories resulting from the long-standing economic connections between their Southeast Chinese homelands and Southeast Asian countries, particularly Malaysia and the Philippines. Others' routes resulted from the decades of social and political upheaval that accompanied the transition from imperial to Republican rule followed by the Pacific War as numerous individuals fled China's Guangdong Province for Hong Kong, Burma, Vietnam, and other seemingly more stable locations beginning in the late nineteenth century through the middle of the twentieth century. Many Chinese American seniors' pathways were bound up with the political divides that split Chinese citizens once the PRC was established in 1949, as those with Nationalist connections to Chiang Kai-shek's government or business endeavors to protect left the mainland for Taiwan and Hong Kong, and from those locations, continued on to the United States.

Diversity of life experiences is a commonality shared as well by members of the Chinese diaspora in other parts of the world. Anthropologist Lok Siu writes, "Chinese belonging is shot through with difference and disjuncture. Differences in immigration cohort, class, nationality, racial mixture, and gender all result in divergent experiences of what it means to be Chinese in the diaspora."[11] Taking into account the extreme diversity of Chinese diasporic experiences of dislocation, (re)settlement, and engagement with communities often far removed from mainland China, scholars have focused particular attention on the idea of "Chineseness" and debated how "Chinese" identity depends (or not) on one's positioning relative to mainland China, traditionally viewed as the center of Chinese cultural life.[12] Ien Ang, for example, discusses the power inherent in defining a category like "Chineseness" and wonders how "Chineseness is made to mean in different contexts." Ang writes, "In other words, how and why is it that the category of Chineseness acquires its persistence and solidity? And with what political and cultural effects?"[13] While the very messiness of the category means there will never be full consensus on how to define "Chineseness," it remains useful as a theoretical concept in drawing attention to the vast array of life experiences that "being Chinese" encompasses. It is also important because it highlights the continued pull of mainland China as a critical influence on the lived experiences of individuals even many generations removed from living in territorial China.

Yet for the Chinese seniors I knew in Boston—the majority of whom had left China late in life—the fact of their Chinese identity had never been in question. That is, no matter how much they also had strong senses of affinity with American lifeways, as I have documented in myriad ways throughout this book, they retained strong pride in being Chinese. As reflected in the lyrics of one of the most popular songs that Chinese seniors sang together at many different community localities all around Boston, "My Chinese Heart" (M. *wode zhongguo xin*), seniors continued to feel that fundamentally they were Chinese above all, even when they outwardly expressed views that indicated disagreement with contemporary PRC policy and society.[14] In the words of one of my interviewees, "[When] we sing 'My Chinese Heart,' it reminds us of China. We are all Chinese people and we all have a Chinese heart. China's history, its geography, it's always in our mind; we remember the Yellow River. It should be like that." As a result, what I explore in this chapter is not whether and how senior migrants expressed their Chineseness. Instead, I focus on how seniors from a range of Chinese life experiences nevertheless formed a sense of diasporic Chinese community. That the development of that community does not necessarily depend on previous networks or consistent ties across space and time is a point made by historian Adam McKeown. In particular, he notes that through everyday interactions and social encounters, individuals can come to recognize similarities of experience they might not have previously suspected and thereby lay the foundations for the development of new cultural forms of Chineseness.[15] This insight serves as a useful starting point for understanding how Chinese senior migrants' engagement in practices of cultural production as they danced together in Boston and Quincy may have contributed to overcoming their vastly divergent life experiences to develop a sense of community with other Chinese American seniors—some friends, others strangers, sometimes sharing a language, at other times not.

Cultural production has been central to processes of community identification for many diasporic groups. For example, writing about the role that music plays for members of the Syrian Jewish diaspora, ethnomusicologist Kay Kaufman Shelemay provides rich evidence of how music is instrumental in creating group memory and identity over time. She notes, "Music, particularly song, provides a medium that binds together disparate strands of experience, serving as a malleable form of cultural expression able to transcend the vagaries of time and space." She details the specific ways in which music and its performance through ritual song have worked to provide memory of the group's past otherwise absent from written historical records and create a continuing sense of cultural community even after centuries of dispersal from their original homeland. Key to Shelemay's analysis is the idea that for members of the Syrian diaspora, songs should be understood through a heterotopic lens—that is, songs act as "sites for various constructions of present and past, containing simultaneous commemoration of both individuals and collectivities."[16] Thus, the performance of song is a process of individualized self-expression within a ritualized and community-centered context that facilitates remembrance and identity for both the individual performers and the group as a whole. Overall, Shelemay's work provides two important insights that are also relevant to a discussion of cultural performance and identity among other diasporic groups: (1) cultural performances are heterotopic—that is, they function as complex sites that should be interpreted in relation to experiences of both the past and the present, and (2) cultural performances can simultaneously create different yet interconnected meanings for individual performers and groups as a whole.

The situation invoked through the diasporic history of the Syrian Jews that Shelemay discussed has important differences from that of the Chinese senior migrants whose experiences form the core of this book. For example, my interviewees were all first-generation migrants, many of whom continued to travel back to China for regular visits as long as their health allowed, meaning that their sense of connection to China was relatively continuous rather than separated by vast expanses of time and space. Nor was there a need to rely on aural or visual cultural production to sustain a community historical record for this group. Nonetheless, that singing together provided an important role for Chinese-born senior migrants' continuing cultural expression was clear. Seniors sang together at just about every location I visited and often told me things like: "Everyone likes to sing" and "Singing makes people happy." As one interviewee summed up, "They sing these songs because they are from a different era they shared together when they were younger, and they can remember those times when they sing that song."[17] In only one case did I hear a complaint about group singing. It came from a retired professor who commented on the potential divisiveness of singing popular songs from the Maoist era, like "The East Is Red." For him, these songs could not be divorced from their inherently political content. Thus, the nostalgia for times past expressed through singing songs like this one entailed the foregrounding of ideological views that would not be equally supported by all community members—and, in so doing, prevented the potential for heterotopic interaction. In contrast, the music accompanying seniors' ballroom and other dancing activities, while also Chinese in origin, usually included lyrics with less openly ideological content, thus facilitating all Chinese American seniors' community engagement.

In addition to music, dance helps members of the Chinese diaspora maintain a sense of connection to Chinese cultural heritage and serves as a political act through which migrants can publicly demonstrate their Chinese cultural identity for all to see.[18] The power of Chinese dance as a symbolic expression of Chineseness has most often been related to the display of archetypal cultural forms that are universally recognized as part of China's ancient and long-standing cultural tradition. Writing about the performance of Chinese dance by Chinese Americans in the U.S. Midwest, Wilcox documents the central role of the dragon as the symbolic frame deployed by one dance troupe to "invoke common ancestry and 'Chinese culture' [as d]ancers and audience were asked to sing in unison at the end of the . . . production, 'We're *all* descendants of the dragon' [emphasis in original]." The "Chineseness" asserted through performative acts like these thus essentializes "Chinese culture" into a fixed script that is easily recognizable in concrete forms as traditionally "Chinese," particularly to individuals who are not themselves ethnically Chinese.[19] In contrast, the "Chineseness" that was performed through the Chinese seniors' dance groups in Boston and Quincy appeared qualitatively different from these symbolic cultural performances that serve as essentializing Chinese identity markers—with or without intentional political effects—in other settings. Both forms of dance practiced by seniors that I discuss here (ballroom and congregational dancing) had concrete connections to China's past and have served as important aspects of social life in China over the past one hundred years. At the same time, participating in these two forms of dance allowed contemporary participants to reconnect with different visions for China's future path to modernization over the past century. In other words, seniors' engagement in dance was not about reliving the past but about engaging with both the past and present simultaneously. As I explain in more detail, both dance forms present possibilities for engaging with multiple forms of and orientations to Chineseness that today's older generations have experienced. At the same time, both forms of dance also evoke a Chineseness that reflects the modernized PRC's contemporary power in the contemporary global order.

BALLROOM AND CONGREGATIONAL DANCING IN THE CHINESE PAST AND PRESENT

Given the different histories represented by ballroom and congregational dancing in China, perhaps it's not surprising that these two forms of dance appealed to and attracted different members of the diaspora in and around Boston. Recent senior migrants from mainland China were active participants in both groups; however, the ballrooms tended to draw participants from a wider variety of regional backgrounds (including seniors originally from Shanghai, Taiwan, Vietnam, and Hong Kong). Both forms of dance—ballroom and congregational dancing—are an integral part of seniors' lives in the PRC today, part of what Farquhar and Zhang identify as the yangsheng lifestyle that I also discussed in Chapter 4.[20] Echoing Ho Long's sentiments, my other interviewees also focused on the health benefits—mental and physical—of both forms of dancing. In these ways, their words, which I record in more detail in this chapter, also confirmed evidence provided by Canadian gerontologist Daniel Lai, whose quantitative data track a positive correlation between

Chinese Canadian seniors' engagement in "culture related activities" that reinforce their ethnic identity and "healthy aging."[21]

Ballroom dance was popularized in Republican-era China, particularly in urban areas like Shanghai before World War II.[22] China was in political transition, with both Communist and Nationalist groups in competition for political control of the country. At the time, it was unclear which group would gain ultimate control, and so each presented radically different potential paths for China's future modernization. In Shanghai, ballroom dancing was popular in elite circles under the Nationalist government and facilitated interaction with diplomats and other foreigners. From there, it spread throughout China, taking slightly different forms in different regional areas, including the Communist stronghold in Yan'an, where ballroom dancing was reportedly popular with even Mao Zedong.[23] Of course, the Communists eventually overthrew the Nationalists and established the PRC in 1949. However, the decades prior to that time were exciting periods of cultural experimentation and interaction, fueled by a cosmopolitan orientation as the Nationalist government encouraged modernizing practices that combined aspects of Chinese and Western ways of life. One marker of this internationalist worldview is represented by the increasing numbers of Chinese students sent abroad to be educated in the United States during this period—many of whom returned to China and were influential in politics and business circles through the 1950s in the PRC and even longer in Taiwan and Hong Kong.[24] During the early years of the PRC, this internationalist orientation continued through the integration of Western-style cultural forms to the revolutionary "culture of the masses" promoted by Chairman Mao.[25] Ballroom dancing and ballet, two forms of cultural production already popularized in the Soviet Union, were viewed as desirable alternatives to Western European capitalist forms of cultural production.

Some of the ballroom dancers I met in Boston's Chinatown remembered learning to dance as youth in Republican-era China; others learned in Taiwan or Hong Kong, which took over as sites practicing cosmopolitan-oriented modes of modernization after 1949. According to my interviewees, despite its later negative association with foreign domination after 1949, ballroom dancing continued as a recreational activity in some areas of the PRC at least into the 1950s throughout the period that China and the Soviet Union enjoyed strong political cooperation.[26] During the reform period, following Mao's death in 1976, ballroom dancing was reintroduced by the PRC state (via its continued popularity in Eastern Europe) as a group activity and form of exercise to replace mass calisthenics. Ballroom dancing remains a hugely popular form of daily exercise among senior citizens in China today. It is also familiar to younger adults by its inclusion as a competitive sport, Dancesport, in the 2010 Asian Games in Guangzhou, where Chinese dancers won all ten gold medals.

At contemporary Chinese American ballrooms, the performance of ballroom dancing represented a kind of visual link to China's pre-Communist past. Glitzy, showy, and encouraging individual expression and prowess on the dance floor, the dancers' performances seemed to highlight an ideological connection to a past in which economic, political, and social visions for creating a modern China were deeply interconnected with the international realm beyond the boundaries of mainland China. Today, the resurgence of ballroom dancing in the PRC serves as a reflection of contemporary China's integral engagement with the "global"—and modernization long aspired to and finally achieved.

Group congregational dancing, in contrast, seems to be the quintessential expression of the collectivist ethos that prevailed throughout China from the 1950s to the 1970s. Seniors in China today gather in large groups, often in public parks or other outdoor areas, to practice this form of dance together to benefit from the social interaction and physical exercise. Relying on heavily synchronized, rhythmic movements that require no particular training or expertise to master, group dancing is seen by many today as being too egalitarian in form and content, echoing Maoist ideological principles that guided China's projects of modernization throughout the first three decades of the PRC.[27] This form of dance, when viewed alongside ballroom dancing, seems to represent a competing past political vision for achieving future global predominance and modernity in China. This past ideological vision, with its strongly collectivist orientation, ultimately failed in the PRC, and yet, as I discussed throughout Chapter 3, it continues to resonate strongly today with many contemporary Chinese seniors, who are uneasy with the growing economic inequality and the concomitant social emphasis on individualistic and materialistic desire in China today. Other contemporary criticisms of this group dancing by seniors in China today—including noise in common areas and inconvenient disruption of public spaces by large groups of seniors—are unified around a central concern that this type of dancing is "old-fashioned" and a remnant of the collectivist past.[28]

At the same time, it would be a mistake to interpret participants' engagement in these dance forms as evidence of a singular nostalgic orientation to either China's Nationalist or Communist past. Despite contemporary criticisms that portray senior performers of group dancing as old-fashioned champions of

China's collectivist past, anthropologist Claudia Huang instead documents how seniors' engagement with this dance form is so popular precisely because it fosters both the coexistence of individualized engagement with contemporary consumer culture and collective identity.[29] In a similar way, ballroom dancing does not just showcase individualized prowess; it also requires carefully synchronized movement together with a partner or partners. In other words, both forms of dance serve as ways to balance individualized expression and group identity, and in this way, they reinforce the role of heterotopic cultural production in creating and maintaining diasporic identity.

By adopting Shelemay's heterotopic lens for analyzing Chinese seniors' engagement in these two forms of dance performance as simultaneously evoking both the past and the present, we can begin to see how seniors' temporal positioning allows for the development of a shared imaginative worldview focused on China's contemporary modernization and growing power on a global stage that contributes to diasporic identification for this diverse group of Chinese American seniors. These two forms of dancing evoke different Chinese social and political pasts—pasts with significant ideological twists and turns that have largely shaped the adult life experiences and later-life migration trajectories of today's Chinese senior migrants. Yet despite the different ideological orientations of those pasts, all shared a common goal of modernizing China and strengthening its power on the global stage. Thus, these two forms of dance, which are also popular with seniors in China today, resonated with different members of the Chinese American diaspora in Boston and Quincy by appealing to all Chinese seniors' contemporary desire for the development of a strong, modern China—evoking seniors' "Chinese hearts" as full of pride for their Chinese ethnicity. This participation was not about reliving the past as it was about living in the present. That is, it was about finding possibilities for familiar cultural interactions and community engagement that could help to relieve the stress experienced by many Chinese-born seniors who had lived long, eventful lives often defined by hardship who, in the latter decades of their lives, also struggled again in a new location as low-income, marginalized Americans, often with little English-speaking ability. Those limitations were visually apparent through the worn edges of seniors' sparkly, high-heeled shoes, along with the frayed edges of their skirts and collars at ballrooms in Quincy and Chinatown.

In other words, seniors' community interaction across diasporic difference depended in large part on the possibility of integrating a variety of personal experiences of ways of being Chinese within a larger context of group belonging, which was possible through the opportunities for mutual interaction provided when seniors danced together in group settings that were culturally familiar and oriented around a shared imaginative worldview. At the same time, Chinese American seniors' dancing also highlighted goals of staying healthy and developing social community among a group of similarly positioned individuals who were all dealing with natural processes of aging.

"SWEATING AND CHATTING": BALLROOM DANCING IN QUINCY AND BOSTON

It was a Thursday afternoon in the middle of summer. Sitting outside the front door of a residential senior housing complex in Quincy, I saw familiar faces as the Chinese ballroom dancers arrived for this afternoon's event. They came both individually and in pairs, mostly of women but occasionally of spouses. Many had walked the short distance (across two parking lots and a busy street) from the nearby subway stop. Others arrived in cars. Although the weather was hot and humid, the men looked dapper, dressed in neatly pressed button-down shirts, pleated slacks, and leather shoes. The women were carefully made up, wearing colorful skirts or long dresses and carrying bags that contained the sparkly, high-heeled shoes they would change into before dancing.

Once inside the building, the dancers rode the elevator to the top floor, a large and versatile common space that served as both a cafeteria and a recreational area for the seniors who lived in this building. Often this space was largely empty, its underutilization symptomatic of the tense atmosphere between the building's white and Chinese inhabitants.[30] Yet on Thursday afternoons, the space was full of boisterous dancers moving across the floor. Some were well practiced; others were novices at complicated ballroom steps. Would-be dancers sat and chatted at the round tables positioned along three sides of the large rectangular room. The majority of the senior dancers were Chinese, although their backgrounds and immigration stories were tremendously varied: they came from Hong Kong, Shanghai, Taiwan, Guangdong, and Vietnam; many had lived in Boston for decades; others had been in the area for only a few years. They traveled from all around the greater Boston area for their two hours of dancing, which they approached with a level of seriousness bordering on professionalism. They made an impressive spectacle, admired even by the same white residents of this building who generally resented the presence of so many Chinese seniors where they live.[31]

The members of this ballroom group were different from the building's regular

Chinese senior residents, many of whom originated from rural Guangdong and Hong Kong and had lived in the Boston area for many decades. Although anyone who wanted could join the dancers, who happily welcomed new additions to their group, the majority of the building's Chinese residents chose not to participate. Instead, like the white senior residents of this building, they looked on from the sidelines. As older individuals from rural areas in China, they were less likely than individuals from urban areas to have had access to this form of entertainment as young adults. Many of the dancers explained that their interest in dancing dated from their teenage years in China or Hong Kong, when ballroom dancing seemed fun and glamorous and because it provided the only socially sanctioned way to get close to members of the opposite sex. In the 1980s, as political repression eased during the reform period, ballroom dancing enjoyed a resurgence of popularity in China, particularly among seniors, who practice this and many other forms of group recreation in a variety of indoor and outdoor locations across China's urban areas.

In Quincy, Chinese seniors who enjoyed watching the spectacle from the sidelines—while looking after grandchildren or just taking the opportunity to get out of their rooms and have something to do—viewed the dancers with both particular interest and distaste. On the one hand, the Chinese onlookers were captivated by the exciting spectacle created by the dancers—gliding, spinning, and moving in pairs all around the room, flowing through waltzes, tangos, and rumbas. On the other hand, like the white spectators who sat along the sidelines, they commented on the women's fancy clothing as inappropriately revealing for women in their sixties and seventies. And unlike the white spectators, they also said it's disgusting (C. *yuhksyun*) for old men and old women to be so close together, touching and making sexy dance moves in public. For these viewers, this style of dancing reeked of vulgarity and promiscuity, echoing criticisms lodged against ballroom dancing in early twentieth-century China—including Hong Kong and Taiwan. Yet the skill and stamina needed to dance well were clearly valued by all ballroom participants. Ballroom participants themselves viewed dancing as an integral and particularly meaningful part of their daily lives, and they oriented their schedules to accommodate traveling to dance locations around the greater Boston metropolitan area as many days each week as possible.

The ballroom dancers explained their motivations for dancing in both simple and more complex terms. At the most basic level, they danced because it made them happy, although the seriousness with which they treated their turns on the dance floor might not have made their delight obvious to an outside observer.

While some of the dancers talked about learning how to dance as youth in China or Hong Kong, others talked about just watching dancers when they were young, wishing they could also learn to ballroom dance and glide elegantly across the dance floor. For these dancers, who made up the majority of the ballroom groups in both Chinatown and Quincy, much of their time at the ballroom was still spent admiring the more accomplished dancers in the room. This was the case with one woman in her late sixties, who told me that although she had dreamed of ballroom dancing most of her life, she had begun learning to dance only over the past few years. She had first watched dancers when she was a young girl in Hong Kong, and she thought they looked lovely. Her husband, however, was never interested in dancing, and it was only relatively late in life that she finally had the free time and opportunity to learn. Once her children were grown and she was able to retire from her work in the United States, she began taking lessons and joined the ballroom group several years before I met her at the Chinatown ballroom. All dressed up, like the other women who were dancing there, she sat and chatted with me or with other women between dances, waiting for the opportunity to get back on to the dance floor. As she pointed out one couple on the dance floor—a husband and wife who had lived in the United States for several decades and never danced with anyone but each other at either the Boston Chinatown or Quincy ballroom locations—she mused that it would be ideal to be a couple and dance, since one would have substantially more opportunity to practice. At the same time, she agreed that her ideal was far from the norm for most dancers, since the majority of them came to the ballroom to dance individually, without their spouses, who were otherwise occupied with other daily pursuits, not in Boston, or deceased.

The dancers I met were all proud of their dancing. Like this woman, many had invested substantial time and money in learning to dance. In so doing, they were fulfilling a desire they had had since they were young or picking back up an art form they enjoyed participating in as young adults in the early 1950s—a more optimistic time in China's twentieth-century history than the difficult years of political machinations, famine, and chaos that dominated much of the Maoist period and colored everyday Chinese life from the late 1950s through the mid-1970s. These individuals also approached their dancing with seriousness, using the setting of the ballroom to admire and learn from more accomplished dancers, as well as to continuously practice and refine the steps that they had been working hard to learn in the private classes they also took during the week with different dance instructors in Chinatown and Quincy. Generally the atmosphere at the ballroom was cooperative, with dancers of all backgrounds helping each other to master steps they found challenging. Regular attendees encouraged newcomers to join in. And because sometimes there were fewer men than women or the men present were simply more accomplished dancers, female dancers practiced by dancing with other women at their level rather than missing the opportunity to dance at all. Neophytes also stood on the sidelines, dancing together through difficult steps, taking a break from the dance floor but still enjoying the social setting and the exercise. From time to time there were complaints about the music selection, favoring some steps and rhythms over others. But for the most part, both the selection of music and the running of the group seemed to be largely democratic, with each participant contributing one dollar each week to cover the cost of using the large community room. Individuals also took turns being in charge of the musical selections. Overwhelmingly, selections favored Chinese songs, particularly those of Taiwanese pop star Teresa Tang, who was "probably the most famous Chinese singer in the world when she died" in 1995.[32]

The dancers were also proud of the exercise that they got while dancing. Indeed, two hours of ballroom dancing can be an intense workout, requiring not just stamina but also physical dexterity. Dancers who attended even one ballroom a week got a good workout that left them sweating. The dancers who attended several ballrooms, dancing as often as possible throughout the week, were able to keep fit and healthy while also engaging in a fun activity with friends. Time and again, when I asked the dancers why they danced, they told me, "I mainly do this for exercise." One man in his late seventies, a regular at both the Chinatown and the Quincy ballrooms who arrived in the United States from Guangdong via Hong Kong in the early 1980s, explained that the level of physical activity involved with dancing was too intense for many seniors—both Chinese and American—and noted that in addition to dancing for exercise almost every afternoon, he also swam regularly at the YMCA. Another regular at the ballrooms, a man in his early seventies from Shanghai who learned to ballroom dance as a youth in China, confirmed that he attributed his good physical health to his regular dancing, which he picked up again after moving to Boston a decade before I met him. He said, "I am hardly ever sick. I keep moving. If you are unhappy all the time, then it's easy to get sick. I do not take any medicines. I do not have diabetes, no high blood pressure. Dancing makes me happy. I look younger than my age. When there is a chance to dance, I go dance." As this man's words made clear, dancing fulfilled his need to stay physically active, enabling him to stay healthy and also feel and look younger than he was. At the same time, his comment alluded to the fact that the health benefits derived from intensive ballroom dancing were not only physical. The benefits were also mental, providing a daily structure and purpose for getting out of the house and meeting and socializing with other Chinese seniors. In this way, this senior's account of why he goes dancing recalls Palmberger's argument about the importance of aging Turkish migrants' daily interactions with ethnic associations in Vienna as a means of creating the social ties that contribute to their social embeddedness.[33]

Both Chinatown's and Quincy's ballrooms took place in rooms capacious enough to accommodate many pairs of dancers at once. As a result, these were the most popular ballroom locations, attracting dancers from varied and diverse regional and ideological backgrounds. (In contrast, another ballroom took place in a much smaller physical space that could accommodate only a handful of dancers, without even enough room for sitting on the sidelines. This ballroom tended to be frequented by a much less diverse group of Chinese American seniors and was largely eschewed by the dancers from Chinatown and Quincy.) But in Chinatown and Quincy, at any given time throughout the two-hour event, as many individuals sat on the sidelines as danced. Sitting out dances was necessary to catch one's breath and rest between dances. It was also a way to chat with friends, catch up on gossip, or watch and learn from the most accomplished dancers on the floor. Indeed, in addition to getting exercise, or "sweating," as many seniors referred to the workout they got while dancing, many members of the ballroom groups told me they attended the weekly event for the opportunity it provided to socialize—what they called "chatting." One man told me, "I make friends through dancing." Another explained, "I come here to dance. I meet most people through dancing. Sometimes before dancing, my friends and I go to have breakfast together. Sometimes we go out to have a cup of coffee after dancing. After we finish our coffee, everyone goes home." As was common with most dancers, he had been introduced to the group by a friend already familiar with the ballroom, thus broadening his network beyond a closely knit circle of contacts.

It was clear that individuals had formed friendships and ties across the different migrant groups. Regulars greeted each other in a friendly manner, commented on the dancing prowess of others at the ballroom, and often danced with partners with whom they might not be able to converse. However, I most often observed that groups of chatters tended to be relatively consistent at each ballroom every week, often comprising individuals sharing similar backgrounds or migration histories: a group of women who all spoke Mandarin and had arrived in Boston to take care of grandchildren several years earlier; a group of Cantonese-speaking men who migrated in the 1980s and currently lived in the same town; a group of Vietnamese Chinese refugees who were residents of the same senior center; and a group of Cantonese-speaking women from Hong Kong who had worked in factories or restaurants in Chinatown throughout most of their adult years.

At Quincy's ballroom, these divisions were sharper than at the ballroom in Chinatown, perhaps because Quincy's ballroom attracted a number of participants living in suburban areas around Boston's South Shore, as well as individuals for whom driving was a more convenient form of transportation than riding public transportation. These two groups (those living well outside Boston's urban areas and those who owned cars) tended to be seniors who had already lived many decades in the United States, having migrated either as refugees (escaped from mainland China through Hong Kong in the 1950s or 1960s or from Vietnam as ethnic Chinese who were displaced following the Vietnam War) or economic migrants joining family members in the United States during the 1970s or 1980s. These groups, whose life experiences diverged substantially from those of the seniors who migrated to the United States after 1990, generally spoke Cantonese—in contrast to the variety of languages spoken by the full range of ballroom participants, which also included Mandarin as well as Vietnamese, Shanghainese, Taishanese, and sometimes English.

But while chatting depended on the ability to communicate well with others, whether in Cantonese, Mandarin, Vietnamese, or English, dancing did not, resulting in possible dance pairings across the diaspora: a Vietnamese Chinese man and a woman from Nanjing; a man from Shanghai and a woman from Guangdong; a Hong Kong woman and Chinese American man; a woman from Taiwan and a man from Guangzhou. As documented in Jennifer Carpenter's photography exhibit, *Generation Dance*, this process of coming together and performing physically challenging dances was valued by all members of the ballroom, whether they had grown up in the PRC, Hong Kong, Taiwan, or elsewhere.[34] All participants had memories of ballroom dancing from earlier stages of their lives. All derived extensive pleasure from the social engagement and daily exercise with similarly aged Chinese American individuals whose individual migration trajectories had nonetheless landed them in Boston at various times over the past several decades. In these spaces, I never heard individuals make disparaging comments about other Chinese seniors with backgrounds different from their own, which was a frequent occurrence in many of my formal interviews (and also occasionally openly expressed in other community settings). Instead, critiques were voiced only by nondancers—both white and Chinese—such as those present at the Quincy ballroom who sat on the sidelines, fascinated by the spectacle yet disapproving of the dancers' physical closeness and fancy dress. Moreover, individuals from different backgrounds had all come to recognize each other as they "chatted and sweated" over weeks, months, and years. Participants routinely discussed not just those few particularly exemplary dancers who impressed everyone but also many others they had gotten to know over time through their repeated encounters on the dance floor and its sidelines.

In other words, the ballroom provided a level playing field through which a rich diversity of Chinese senior migrants could come together and interact meaningfully with others in the diasporic community. That community was based on a shared love of "sweating and chatting," along with a deep-seated appreciation of ballroom dancing as a culturally familiar form of exercise and movement with roots, for many of the dancers, in youthful desires to experience more glamorous, modern, or fun ways of being Chinese—forms of Chineseness of which they could all be proud through China's contemporary rise in the global arena. In this way, the interactions that took place at ballroom mirror the possibilities for "the creation of a common [Chinese diasporic] sentiment and cultural heritage that exists above and beyond political loyalties and personal experience."[35]

MOVING ALL TOGETHER: GROUP DANCING AND EXERCISE

At a community-based senior center just a few blocks away from the Quincy ballroom location, Chinese seniors had a daily menu of activity options that covered not just a range of potential interests but also different levels of physical exertion and dexterity. Every weekday morning there were several hours of active bodily movement through group exercise, including tai chi and congregational dancing. Like ballroom dancing, these group-based activities focused on maintaining individual physical fitness and dexterity, keeping seniors mobile and active. But unlike ballroom dancing, with its potential for highlighting individual prowess on the dance floor, these group activities were anything but showy and depended instead on everyone following a series of repetitive cues in unison, through the direction of a live instructor or through imitating moves demonstrated on the large TV positioned at the front of the room. Alternatively, if seniors were not interested in participating in the group exercises, they could sit alone or with others at the many tables set up on one side of the large recreational space to play cards or chat. At all times, there were also people playing (and waiting to play) Ping-Pong, a vigorous activity as practiced by these seniors who invariably worked up a significant sweat through the exertion required to maintain the fast and skillful volleys that animated all games. On some days, seniors also had the option of attending cooking classes or ESL classes. On other days, representatives of health care or service organizations came to offer talks on medical care, home health care, or living wills. At these times, all the large and small group activities would cease, as individuals filled the seats at the center's tables and listened attentively to these guest presentations.

The group activities pursued by Chinese seniors at this location were similar to the group activities that I encountered in other locations—community centers, residential buildings, social service organizations, surname associations, and so on—in Boston's Chinatown and Quincy. They are also similar to the many different senior activities available in China, practiced most often in parks but also in other public areas where seniors are likely to congregate, socialize, and work to keep themselves fit and healthy.[36] The near-constant focus on keeping physically active, in both mind and body, largely through consistent and repetitive group activities, was shared across every location where I spent time with Chinese seniors. When seniors did not have access to group activities, they would find ways to exercise individually: swimming, walking in the park, or, as one woman explained, even washing her clothes by hand so that she could continue to exercise her hand muscles even as her overall physical mobility declined. Another senior, at eighty-eight years old among the oldest of the active individuals I knew, explained that when inclement weather prevented him from taking a daily walk outside, he would walk in a circuit through his small apartment one hundred times, making sure that he had sufficiently exercised his legs and body. Like the ballroom dancers who took pride in the physical fitness they maintained through sweating while dancing, the seniors engaged in other forms of physical exercise enjoyed telling me about the health benefits they received from participating in these activities.

Echoing the ballroom dancers, many seniors explained that the benefits they reaped were as strongly linked to mental as physical health. In particular, they singled out the repetitive and coordinated group exercises like congregational dancing and tai chi as especially beneficial, explaining that as people age and their memories grow weaker, it is important to find ways to continue to exercise their memories. Remembering dance moves—how to do the steps and in what sequence—was frequently cited as good training for the mind and in helping to keep one's memory sharp. Moreover, many seniors enjoyed their group opportunities of moving sequentially together, both because it required more concentration than moving alone and because of new physical challenges presented in the process. At times, these shared experiences of syncopated physical movement also translated into other forms of collective cohesion through mirth or shared sympathetic understanding, as the groups' participants experienced not only physical motion in common but also limitations to that movement. This was the case during one beginning-level tai chi lesson, in which the atmosphere was one primarily of concentration, punctuated by occasional bursts of laughter as everyone focused their mental energy on emulating the seemingly simple physical movements that the instructor modeled. Yet the collective experience was one of challenge, since the moves were anything but simple and resulted in collective amusement when group efforts to remain synchronized instead deteriorated into mild chaos. In another case, the entire room erupted into laughter when the tai chi master demonstrated an impossibly challenging set of new moves, ending with (in one variation) a push that would knock down an enemy or (in another variation) a high kick—a move entirely beyond the range of any of the seniors' physical dexterity. Almost immediately, the master backpedaled on the kick, saying that he did not want anyone in the room to lose balance, fall, or get injured by trying that move, or, at least, no one should try to kick as high as he had just done. The overall effect was one of solidarity and delight rather than dismay, as everyone contemplated the impossibility of the move given their physical limitations and the momentary lapse that led the tai chi master to get carried away and forget his audience.

While the health benefits of group exercises touted by seniors focused on the concrete physical and mental processes that were improved through engaging in these group activities, seniors also benefited from the social opportunities presented in spaces where group activities were organized. One member of the senior center in Quincy explained that although seniors may say that their primary reason for coming to the senior center was to engage in group exercise, they may actually come because they are lonely. The group activities at the center fulfilled a need to be with others, particularly since the seniors who frequented this community center in Quincy were more likely to live in dispersed locations in comparison to the denser networks of peers where seniors lived in Boston's

Chinatown. As one man explained, highlighting the importance of this group social engagement for seniors who could have achieved similar exercise routines in dispersed locations or on their own, "Of course, they can actually exercise anywhere . . ." Even congregational dancing can easily be practiced at home, in front of the TV following instructional videos. Yet by meeting together regularly to exercise as a group, seniors had the opportunity to share information, discuss changes in their family lives, and meet new friends. The possibilities of this togetherness afforded through mutual engagement with familiar Chinese cultural activities were highlighted through the example of the lone, non-Chinese white senior who came regularly to the community center. While she fully participated in the physical aspects of the group activities alongside Chinese-born seniors, she was excluded from their conversations beforehand or afterward. She attended the classes every day, but no one knew her name or where she lived. Language barriers between Chinese and English meant that they had never talked with her.

The sense of group solidarity in the Quincy senior center, as individuals joined together in group activities, masked the challenges presented by oral communication among senior migrants with significantly varied backgrounds. The gulfs in life experience loomed just as large for the members of this community center as they did for the ballroom dancers, despite the fact that the synchronized group movement required by congregational dancing and other popular activities, which often involved everyone at the center at any given time, often worked to obscure those differences. The common use of Cantonese by the center's staff also masked the fact that some seniors at the center neither spoke nor understood it.

Similar to the kinds of communication-related challenges I experienced at all locations where I spent time throughout my fieldwork, the shared common spoken language of Cantonese hid the fact that Chinese American seniors had substantial difficulty communicating across regional dialects. In contrast to the ballroom group, where Mandarin (and sometimes other local dialects in addition to Cantonese) was commonly spoken, Cantonese remained the general language of operation at the Quincy community center location—reflecting the fact that upwardly mobile Chinese American immigrants from Boston's Chinatown began moving in large numbers to suburban Quincy in the early 1980s. Yet the migration histories of these seniors still varied substantially. One woman in her early seventies from rural Taishan had migrated to the United States twelve years earlier through family sponsorship and currently lived in a subsidized senior apartment in a distant area of Quincy, accessible only by a combination of bus and subway. Although she did not speak Cantonese, she did speak Mandarin, since she and her husband, a former government official, had lived for many years outside Guangdong Province. One man, a former factory manager from Hubei who could neither speak nor understand Cantonese, had migrated three years before I met him and lived with his grown daughter and her husband not far from the center. He spent most days caring for his two preschool-aged grandchildren, whom he sometimes brought with him to the senior center where he loved to play Ping-Pong. Another couple, retired professionals who had come to the United States as refugees in the early sixties, lived nearby in their own home, where they had raised their three Chinese American children, now grown and working in white-collar jobs. Group diversity thus extended well beyond region of origin to educational background, work experiences, and class status in both China and the United States. Yet as with the ballroom dancers, these differences seemed to fade away in these spaces of community recreation in which everyone was largely involved in similar pursuits of congregational dance, tai chi, and other physical activities. Regional differences, language differences, educational differences, and class differences—none of those differences seemed important as individuals came together in (at least attempted) synchronized group movement, and as those on the sidelines seemed to welcome (at least occasional) social interactions with others from different backgrounds.

This community interaction reflects what historian Adam McKeown has written about the formation of diasporic connections through everyday interactions among Chinese migrants—through which previously unfamiliar individuals "find they speak a similar language, eat similar food, have ancestors from nearby villages, and can read each other's body language." These shared activities ultimately lead to the realization of shared commonalities and trust in each other "in which differences in personal experience can be overcome."[37] Likewise, while dancing and exercising together in Quincy's senior community centers, Chinese seniors formed strong social bonds among diverse members of the Chinese diasporic community, aiding their well-being as they aged in Boston.

THE CHINESE DIASPORIC COMMUNITY

Anthropologists writing about the PRC have drawn significant attention to the importance of synchronized, physical activity in contributing to the creation of a collective social body in China.[38] Through Chinese seniors' engagement in collective group activities, including ballroom dancing and group dancing and exercise in the greater Boston area, the physical activity and performative qualities inherent in those dance forms undoubtedly facilitated the development of strong social bonds across difference. These physical activities could be practiced together despite seniors' fluency in different Chinese dialects that might otherwise prevent them from being able to speak to one another directly (although sometimes seniors did serve as interpreters for each other). Moreover, the social interactions that took place over repeated days, weeks, and years in these spaces—gossiping and chatting on the sidelines as individuals rested between dances or observed physical movements they hoped to master—promoted community interaction in organic ways that differed significantly from the more organized forms of co-ethnic institutional support that I highlighted in the previous chapter. The inclusion fostered in these spaces of Chinese gathering and activity did not completely mask the differences of regional, class, and education background of these migrants. However, those differences were significantly minimized through the practice of these group activities and the creation of a shared sense of common experience and understanding in which migrants' cares faded away. These cares often centered around their loneliness as individuals sometimes living far away from all family and friends; around fears about growing infirm—whether those fears meant an inability to participate in active daily life or concerns about who would take care of them once they could no longer look after themselves; and around having enough money to eat and pay rent.

However, it has been my goal with this chapter to suggest that the diasporic community constituted through Chinese seniors' engagement with these two forms of dance and exercise in Boston was more than just a product of the physical and social interaction they experienced in these spaces. Instead, I argued that their sense of community hinged on their shared temporal positioning as *seniors*, for whom age mattered because it created additional possibilities of imagining commonalities across differences of past life experiences. In particular, age was the key to understanding the shared conceptions of Chineseness experienced by seniors through ballroom and congregational dancing, even though engaging in these forms of dance was not primarily about asserting Chinese identity for these senior migrants. Rather, both forms of dance allowed for heterotopic possibilities of engagement with different forms of Chineseness reflected in different Chinese ideological pasts. This included the presocialist past that sparkled with the excitement of an internationally oriented future reflected in ballroom dancing as well as the collectivist ethos that structured the majority of seniors' younger adult lives in the PRC. Even so, seniors' dancing reflected their immediate needs in the present: to stay healthy and develop social ties that would help them navigate their marginalization and forge community across the Chinese American diaspora.

In other words, through dance, senior migrants were able to become socially embedded in a Chinese diasporic community in ways that might have eluded younger members of that same diaspora. Their temporal positioning formed the background for shared experiences of engaging in familiar forms of cultural production that allowed for a variety of ways of expressing Chineseness through complex interaction with different Chinese ideological pasts. It also explained the practical desire to keep healthy and fit through exercise, made more interesting through these shared forms of activity that fulfilled diasporic seniors' social needs. Most important, it contributed to seniors' community interactions through a shared recognition of seniors' pride in being ethnically Chinese. After what for many seniors has been a lifelong experience of hardship and displacement, with many unexpected trajectories across space and ideology, China's rise as a powerful contemporary global actor is particularly poignant, fulfilling long-held hopes for China's modernization harbored since their youth.

Thus, pride in being Chinese was central to the experiences of Chinese senior migrants in the United States, where recent Chinese-born senior migrants have nevertheless found significant ways to root themselves as Chinese in physical locations well beyond the borders of territorial China. At the same time, as I have demonstrated over these pages, the renegotiations of Chinese cultural ways of being that have taken place through these processes—through senior migrants' engagement with family, neighborhood, and community—have also created important possibilities for seniors' affinity to the United States as their primary place of belonging.

8   RECONFIGURING RETIREMENT

Over the past decade, as the numbers of Chinese-born seniors migrating to the United States as retirees has grown, their demographic makeup has shifted in important ways from the individuals I focused on in this study. As a group, Chinese senior migrants are now much more likely to be educated Mandarin speakers from urban areas in China well north of Guangdong Province. The reasons for this demographic shift have their roots in some of the same factors that mattered for Cantonese seniors' retirement pathways to the United States in previous decades. Similar social, political, and economic factors are at play for contemporary migrants; it's just that it's taken time for the pathways that were initially available primarily to Cantonese seniors to now be available to seniors from other regions of China as well. In particular, Chinese seniors from all regions of China may come to provide child care to their American-born grandchildren, born to adult children who came to the United States in the late twentieth and early twenty-first centuries to pursue graduate-level education or work in white-collar, professional occupations. Thus, family reunion is the key to these seniors' migration trajectories, particularly as members of the more recent generation of senior migrants from China are likely to have had only one child. When that one child settles in the United States to live and have children, it is more likely that aging parents will follow, even if those parents are less likely to have strong networks of other relatives or peers in the United States when they first arrive, as was the case for many of my interviewees.[1] And while my Cantonese-speaking senior migrant interviewees were the first to benefit from the more relaxed exit policies initiated in post-Mao, reform-era China as they used family networks to relocate abroad, those same policies make it possible for all Chinese seniors to leave China today.

Yet as I finish writing this book, the future political landscape for migrants and their families in the United States seems to be particularly precarious, with the country sitting at a crossroads of policy paths regarding how potential migrants are selected and allowed legal entrance. A primary focus of debate is the reevaluation of family reunion categories as a significant means of admission—the only way that most senior migrants can gain legal entrance to the United States. This ethnography, with its focus on one particular group of senior migrants, provides an important perspective to better understand what's at stake as these policy decisions are debated.

The possibilities for affinity with American lifeways experienced by my interviewees take a particular form because of the Southeast Chinese regional culture of migration that framed my interviewees' aspirations from their very earliest years. Of course, there were numerous individuals, particularly students, from other regions of China who also went abroad in the late nineteenth and early twentieth centuries.[2] The cosmopolitanism of early twentieth-century Shanghai and other Republican-era urban Chinese areas meant that there were always many Chinese citizens involved in international circuits of politics, education, trade, and travel. Yet for Chinese residents of the Pearl River Delta region of Guangdong Province, going abroad was a routine fact of life. Many rural areas were as deeply intertwined with international migration networks as major urban areas. As a result, my interviewees' deep-seated feelings of connection since childhood to the United States —which they hoped throughout their lives to see for themselves—make for a qualitatively different experience from that of their generational age-mates from other regions of China. Moreover, Cantonese seniors' engagement with global mobility flows was aided by family and peer networks that had already preceded them abroad—just as their participation in global mobility flows as low-income, older adults has been facilitated by their connections to Chinatowns worldwide.[3] These particular forms of social capital that enabled my interviewees' global trajectories are now increasingly able to help support senior migrants from other Chinese locations as they forge new retirement pathways to the United States.

Since it was residents from Southeast China who first emigrated around the world, migrants from that region initially benefited the most from networks of ethnic support, including familiar language-based resources, in the new areas to which they moved. As these networks changed in the United States from Taishanese speaking to Cantonese speaking over the twentieth century, Chinatowns in many areas continued to provide networks of reception that aided lower-income immigrants' economic survival in the country through access to employment in restaurants or, for women, in garment factories. Many midsized Chinatowns in the United States were razed during urban redevelopment in the 1950s and 1960s, but those that retained a solid residential core, like Boston's Chinatown, developed infrastructure that still benefits recent Chinese senior migrants. Recent migrants now have access not only to traditional regional and surname associations but also to many social service organizations founded by second- and third-generation Asian Americans fighting against social and economic injustices experienced by Asian American populations. In Boston, these latter organizations are becoming ever more accessible to all migrants, despite the complaints I heard from some senior migrants who told me that they felt excluded from the services in Boston's Chinatown because of their inability to speak Cantonese. Conversely, it's also the case that some healthy Chinese seniors residing in suburban locations around Boston, who could make use of Chinatown's many resources, do not do so. Reasons vary but include an inability to access public transportation, lack of time because of caregiving or other work duties, availability of alternative spaces for socializing, or simple disinterest in the area, echoing the criticisms of other new immigrants who found Chinatown to be dirty and a far cry from the modern, urban spaces they had left behind in China. Yet many seniors come to Chinatown on a regular basis to take part in vital pursuits like employment, educational opportunities, and possibilities for socializing with friends, confirming the neighborhood's importance not only for Cantonese-speaking but all other Chinese senior migrants as well.

Throughout this book, I have documented the ways that my interviewees shared a common marginalized social and political position in the United States. As low-income, non-English-speaking ethnically Asian individuals residing in and around Boston, many of my interviewees tended to live in enclave areas, largely separated from the non-Asian American mainstream—which my interviewees referred to, in distinction to themselves, as "Americans" (C. *meihgwok yahn*). They worked in blue-collar jobs or other temporary positions, more often in cleaning, caregiving, and food distribution services than in any other kind of employment. Their physically intensive labor required long or inconsistent hours, for which paid compensation was usually minimal. When recent senior migrants lived with their Chinese American family, many had experienced a lack of freedom of daily schedule and had to negotiate for power with their adult children, even as they performed vital social and economic roles by caring for grandchildren and others. For these reasons, seniors who were able to move into subsidized housing, where they could live together with their senior peers—albeit in minimalist and sometimes even squalid conditions—often expressed greater comfort with their living arrangement. Yet because subsidized housing is limited, particularly in and around Chinatown where seniors have the best access to Chinese-language support services, many migrants lived in areas with fewer forms of ethnic support. Thus, as they aged, many found that their worlds became smaller as they feared venturing farther from home, had fewer opportunities to interact socially with their diasporic age-mates, and experienced the mental or physical deterioration that is a natural part of growing older.

Some of these challenges resonate with those of other low-wage younger adult migrants in many world areas, not just the United States. Many migrants' pathways to developed world areas include motivations for economic survival best explained by segmented labor theory and the diversification of family risk— as discussed by sociologists whose studies of migrant populations fall within the framework of the new economics of labor migration.[4] These adult migrants experience similarly marginalized social and economic situations, including physically demanding work and dependence on ethnic social networks for everyday survival. Yet seniors' navigation of those challenges draws attention to the distinctive aspects of migration processes for individuals whose stage of life at the time of their migration creates a particular set of concerns over and above those of individuals who migrate as younger adults to new world areas. As a result, as I have argued throughout this book, seniors' age—that is, their temporal positioning as migrants—creates new possibilities for exploring forms of interaction, collaboration, and affinity to places, people, and ideas that might otherwise seem unexpected. It's from these unexpected interfaces that we learn how my interviewees achieved a sense of well-being despite the potential obstacles they faced every day—lessons that can apply to other groups of senior migrants as well.

When viewed through a temporal lens, it is clear that the structural factors contributing to the conditions of marginality for my interviewees matter as well for other senior migrants, even when they may have significant demographic differences from the group I examined here. In particular, cultural distance from mainstream American ways of life, conflict with family stemming from tensions around caregiving and support, and potential isolation from meaningful social interactions with ethnic age-mates are challenges faced by all Chinese-born senior migrants, not just those from the Pearl River Delta area. Moreover, goals for financial and social stability and nostalgia for past ways of life, including the desire to be treated humanely as older adults, were shared by all Chinese senior migrants I encountered. Even with the increasing opportunities for senior support in China today, the motivations for migration that I discuss in Chapters 3 and 4—centering around Chinese seniors' ideological affinity with perceived values and comfortable retirement lifestyles in the United States—resonate with generational concerns shared by Chinese seniors from all over China, not just the Pearl River Delta region. Other shared desires included the flexibility to live near but not with adult children and grandchildren and to undertake interesting pursuits as older adults, including ballroom dancing, educational opportunities, and travel abroad. That the ability to achieve these desired ways of life in North America—and not just in China—is more widespread than just among my relatively healthy and active Cantonese-speaking interviewees is confirmed by other recent studies. Mui and Shibusawa find that alongside challenges faced by their Mandarin-speaking interviewees in New York, seniors were nonetheless resilient in adapting to life in the United States.[5] More recently, gerontologist Daniel Lai has documented the active engagement of Chinese Canadian seniors contributing to the Canadian public good in important ways, and a team of researchers from Georgia Tech confirm that Mandarin-speaking grandparents who moved to be near their Chinese American adult children and grandchildren are happy living in Atlanta.[6]

A variety of conditions matter for Chinese-born seniors' abilities to create desired retirement lifestyles in the United States. One important factor includes access to structural supports at the local, state, and national levels that aid all senior migrants. At the local level, that includes the networks of health care and other Chinese-language and culturally appropriate support service infrastructures for seniors in Boston's Chinatown and Quincy. At the state level, Massachusetts has significant subsidized housing available for low-income seniors. Even when they are not able to live in Chinatown itself, senior migrants can apply for subsidized housing in many suburban areas around Boston, often near where their adult children live. And senior migrants who find opportunities for paid employment after migrating not only have small salaries to support themselves—providing much-desired freedom from relying on adult children for financial help—but also achieve additional security by receiving a small monthly income from Social Security over the final years of their lives. While often just a few hundred dollars each month, this income combined with Medicare benefits provides seniors the ability to achieve a basic level of social stability not always accessible in China today but desired in particular because of seniors' generational experiences of social and political upheaval throughout twentieth-century China, during which they sacrificed as younger adults for an egalitarian ideological cause promising them security as they aged.

Yet the time period during which they migrated to the United States was crucial for seniors' abilities to access these important structural supports. In particular, 1990, the year of the earliest arrival among my sample population, marks an important transition as compared to the Chinese seniors who left China before that time. On the one hand, by 1990, seniors arriving in Boston (and the rest of the United States more generally) entered a different context of reception from that encountered by previous migrants. While racism was still a factor affecting their adjustment, it was less immediately present in many seniors' lives in comparison to the stories that I heard from low-income Chinese Americans similar in age to my interviewees who had migrated as younger adults in the 1960s and 1970s, before the establishment of many social service organizations providing advocacy and support for Asian American community development, rights, and organizing. On the other hand, individuals in this earlier group were also economically disadvantaged in relation to current senior migrants. By having worked throughout their adult lives in the United States, instead of for the minimum period to qualify for Social Security in their sixties and seventies, they did not always qualify as "low income" for the purposes of access to subsidized housing, a key social support for contemporary senior migrants. At the same time, they (like many older working-class Americans today) did not have enough retirement savings to live well as older adults and faced daily uncertainty to make ends meet. Yet because they left China before its postreform economic boom, they also lost out on opportunities to make money in the radically changed financial environment of postreform China, making them doubly disadvantaged economically—in both the United States and China—in relationship to more recent migrants. As a result, the senior migrants who moved to the United States beginning around 1990, like most other migrants throughout the world, were generally coming from better-off economic situations rather than from the most impoverished conditions, even if their pensions in China were too small to live off of and they could not always rely on their adult children for financial support. They were also less likely to be migrating out of desperation for economic support and instead were more likely to be migrating in response to desires for self-fulfillment and in order to be active contributors to their family and community well-being.

Life in the PRC is changing so rapidly that seniors living there today already have better access to forms of old-age support, including pensions and medical care, than did those who came to the United States beginning around 1990. This is just one of many ways that seniors in China are facing very different possibilities and supports from those historically available—mirroring the situations of aging populations worldwide, where everyone is navigating a changed landscape around the possibilities for achieving well-being in older age. For seniors in China today, the idea of retirement as a life stage is a relatively new idea. The political, social, and economic changes that have taken place over the past few decades there that have contributed to this outcome, and its concomitant focus on active aging, take a particular form but dovetail with demographic trends spotlighting the need for attention to the problem of promoting well-being for older adults worldwide. In many countries, that discussion has been framed around how to promote successful aging as populations age and the number of seniors relative to younger citizens continues to increase, aided in large part through advances in medicine and technology.[7] These concerns about senior support resonate as well in China, where the transition to substantially longer average life spans has been particularly compressed over just a few decades. Challenges to senior support have been further compounded by the long-term demographic and social effects of the one-child policy and the dismantling of Maoist-era systems of collectivization that served to provide a basic safety net to seniors through the 1970s. These significant changes in Chinese social and family life over the past few decades, in combination with residual (and increasing) inequalities in economic opportunities and health care access between urban and rural areas, mean that many Chinese seniors experience social and financial precariousness also faced by many aging individuals worldwide.

At the same time, on a global level, insecurity for seniors is generally linked to neoliberalism, as many states have cut back on pensions and other forms of support for their growing populations of older citizens over the past two decades.[8] China has taken a different tactic and instead has actively promoted the development of new and more comprehensive forms of elder support to promote healthy aging over this same time. Faced with one of the fastest-growing aging populations in the world, China in 2015 already had over 200 million senior citizens—more than in all European Union countries combined. By 2040, the ratio of the working-age to retired population in China might be as low as 2:1.[9]

To deal with this impending crisis of senior support, the PRC government has initiated new pension and medical policies to address income inequality among urban and rural residents and to help all aging citizens gain access to needed medical care and support.

My interviewees were aware of these initiatives and commented on them, yet they still believed their lives in the United States were likely to be much more economically stable than if they had remained in China. They also believed that their overall ability to live a comfortable retired lifestyle was more possible in the United States, where they were close to multiple generations of family who had left China before them and achieved well-being through community engagement and interaction with diasporic age-mates who embodied a wide range of life experiences and migrant trajectories. It's certainly possible that the many state initiatives underway in the PRC today to provide stronger support for aging citizens, combined with the longer wait periods to enter the United States now in comparison to those of a couple of decades ago, may reduce the number of Chinese-born seniors who decide to move permanently to the United States in future years. However, many grandparents will still come at least as temporary visitors to spend time with family, particularly since younger seniors originating from China's urban areas today are likely to have only one child. Whether they decide to stay permanently in the United States will depend on a variety of factors but may ultimately hinge on whether recent groups of Mandarin-speaking seniors now moving to suburban areas develop senses of affinity with the people and places in their new locations of residence, where overall, there are fewer possibilities of interaction and support among age-mates than I documented in this ethnography. Most likely is that these seniors will engage in what some scholars of aging and migration call pendular migration—a form of transnationalism through which seniors move back and forth between their original location of residence and the new locations where their adult children (in this case, child) and grandchildren live.[10]

The demographic shifts that have accompanied Chinese senior migrants' increasing presence in the United States over the past ten years mean that Chinese American seniors today are more likely to be retired professionals or from well-off families in comparison to my interviewees. Nevertheless, as they are also older individuals who are unlikely to speak English, they come through the sponsorship of adult children already living here. This is in contrast to sponsorship by siblings or parents as the culmination of lifelong dreams to live in the United States, as was the case for many of my interviewees. Yet in both cases, rejoining family abroad, even as other family members stay behind in China, is the mode through which seniors' moves take place, thus making their engagement in global mobility processes dependent on the family preference categories that have dominated legal possibilities of entrance to the United States since 1965—and which are increasingly under debate because of concerns that migrants who come through family sponsorship do not actively contribute to the country's economic growth. Of course, it's true that the family relationships that unfold following seniors' moves don't always work out as intended—and therefore comprise one important reason that some seniors choose to return to China.[11] But for my interviewees—that is, the seniors who decided at some point in their journey to stay permanently in the United States—their new engagement in the country as residents and citizens provides compelling evidence of how their presence contributes to the economic and social well-being of local communities. This is particularly apparent through the labor they provide as paid and unpaid caregivers for members of their family and other elderly and infirm individuals—a population that will only increase in coming years as the demographic trend toward aging populations continues to intensify in the United States and elsewhere. As I have documented here, many senior migrants achieve their own goals of well-being even as they provide crucial help to other Chinese American seniors navigating the challenge of taking care of themselves as they grow old, often alone. This engagement demonstrates that (even) low-income seniors can reshape their lives through alternative imaginings of retirement as a stage of life that presents new opportunities for achieving desired goals associated with promoting well-being. Overall, what stands out is that a multitude of factors matter in seniors' engagement in migratory trajectories as older adults. These factors include seniors' interactions with globally circulating ideas like active aging, as well as their hopes of reuniting with family members abroad, achieving lifelong dreams, and interacting meaningfully with other age-mates.

The situations of Chinese-born senior migrants described here may not seem to conform to the preconceived notions of retirement that many of us hold. This disjuncture was something that I also encountered as I listened to my interviewees' stories, replete with the significant hardships one would expect with struggling to navigate ways of being and belonging in the world in new locations different from those where my interviewees had lived for the first sixty or seventy years of their lives. Some worked long hours of often physically demanding labor. Many experienced anxiety, loneliness, and frustration in communication. All had taken on significant new challenges, requiring time and effort to establish networks of support and social interaction, which were not guaranteed to be successful. Yet these individuals cannot be said to have been duped by a global neoliberal framework that has robbed them of the support they had expected to achieve as older adults. Instead, they demonstrated marked resilience in overcoming barriers to their well-being, including the structural disadvantages they experienced in China as members of a generational cohort largely excluded from the benefits of China's contemporary economic growth and success. My interviewees acted strategically to achieve the retirement lifestyles they desired by making use of well-worn migrant pathways to leave China and in this way engaged in migration processes more often associated with well-off individuals from the West who retire to sunbelt locations. They also used the social roles familiar as part of their Chinese ways of life to benefit their adjustment to and engagement with family and co-ethnic age-mates in the United States. These roles aided seniors' abilities to promote their well-being through cultivating interdependence with their new American families and communities in ways that complemented the independence that they could experience with the help of the social and economic supports available to them in the United States.

Among the most significant critiques of the globalization processes associated with aging and well-being are the insecurities associated with aging in a contemporary world where goals for seniors' well-being are modeled on a worldview reliant on Western conceptions of personhood foregrounding personal independence above all other concerns. Lamb writes that instead of the purported "freedom" experienced through aging well individually, many seniors in the world in both the past and today prefer interdependence to independence.[12] For many seniors worldwide, the interdependence that they may most often desire is to grow old surrounded by family. However, as the experiences of my interviewees show, family may not be always be present even when multiple generations reside in the same country because of social transformations that devalue elder care in comparison to the past, because adult children and grandchildren are busy working, or because family members are already deceased, have migrated domestically, or were never born.

The seniors whose stories form the core of this ethnography did not migrate to the United States as older adults because they needed to be cared for but because moving here was a strategy that provided access to ways of life as retirees that provided security, interdependence, and the opportunity to experience something new all at the same time. That they were able to achieve these goals may seem counterintuitive, particularly within the context of increasingly alarming statistics about the inability of many older Americans to retire at all. Although levels of poverty among elderly in the United States are similar to those of many other developed nations, disparities of wealth have been growing among all members of the U.S. population, including seniors, who are working past age sixty-five in ever increasing numbers by both desire and necessity.[13] This situation also applies to the seniors featured in this book. Yet despite these Chinese-born seniors' engagement with global social processes that have lead to dehumanizing outcomes for many older adults, their stories also suggest other possibilities. The surprise revealed through their stories is that my interviewees are happy in the United States and are doing well here. Of course, many Chinese American seniors could substantially benefit from additional forms of advocacy and support. Not all are engaged in the significant opportunities for meaningful community interaction experienced by my interviewees. Moreover, seniors' family relationships in the United States (and even with family left behind in China) do not always work out as they had hoped or expected when they decided to migrate in the latter decades of their lives. As I have shown, seniors clearly face significant daily challenges and unexpected disappointments in the United States. But overall, the picture their stories paint is a clear view that is forward looking, about placing roots—for themselves and their grandchildren—in new locations in ways that indicate a permanent presence and not just a reluctant or temporary one. In other words, even low-income seniors on the social and economic margins of their own societies can participate in "homing" processes that increase not only their own well-being but also the well-being of others around them in new locations of residency.[14]

In this way, the stories told by these Chinese senior migrants are humanizing ones, championing the experiential ambiguities inherent in migration trajectories overall. These stories also demonstrate the negotiation of multiple ways of being and belonging alongside the strategic navigation of power structures largely assumed to be disempowering. As the numbers of aging individuals around the world continue to increase over coming decades, the possibility for positive outcomes for seniors who decide to take part in opportunities for global mobility need to be recognized alongside the potential disadvantages seniors may experience through participation in migratory lifeways as older adults. This does not mean, as our current debates pitting nationalism against immigration in the United States and around the world today suggest, that seniors' engagement in migratory trajectories and new possibilities for retirement in different global locations will be well received by the areas in which they settle. Yet as long as seniors continue to search for ways to achieve economic security, social stability, and comfortable and engaging lifestyles as life spans continue to grow ever longer, they will continue to forge new pathways contributing to the globalization of retirement.

NOTES

CHAPTER 1

1. That book is *Uneasy Reunions: Immigration, Citizenship, and Family Life in Post-1997 Hong Kong* (Palo Alto, CA: Stanford University Press, 2008).
2. I thank the Blakemore Foundation for supporting me for a full year of Cantonese language study at the Yale-in-China Program at the Chinese University of Hong Kong from 2000–2001. Because I could already speak and read Mandarin Chinese, which I studied in college and also in Taiwan from 1991–1993, I was able to complete most of the two-year Cantonese curriculum during that one academic year. Since 2001, Cantonese has been my primary field language, although sometimes I also conduct research in Mandarin Chinese and, of course, English.
3. CORI (Criminal Offender Record Information) provides a record of any court appearances made in the state of Massachusetts. It's routine to have a CORI check when doing volunteer or paid work with youth or other vulnerable populations in the state.
4. Zong and Batalova 2017.
5. Terrazas and Batalova 2010.
6. Poston and Wong 2016.
7. Poston and Wong 2016.
8. Kuhn 2008.
9. Xiang 2015.
10. Zong and Batalova 2017.
11. Zong and Batalova 2017. Other popular destinations are Canada, 939,000; South Korea, 751,000; Japan, 652,000; Australia, 547,000; and Singapore, 511,000. Zong and Batalova 2017. In 2010, the United States was ranked as the fourth largest country of residence in the world for overseas Chinese; this includes second-, third-, and fourth-generation ethnically Chinese individuals. The United States is the only non-Asian country among the top five. Poston and Wong 2016.
12. Skeldon and Wang 1994; Wang 1980, 2002. See also Yang 2000 and Ong 1999.
13. Newendorp 2008, 2011; Freeman 2011; Chu 2010; Pieke et al. 2004.; Fong 2011.
14. Zhang 2009.
15. Lamb 2007, 2009; Sun 2014a, 2014b, 2016a, 2016b, 2018.
16. See, for example, Faier 2009; Jackson 2013; Ossman 2013; Mahdavhi 2016.
17. See, for example, U.S. Chamber of Commerce 2016.
18. See, for example, Watson 1975; Myerhoff 1978.

19. See, for example, M. Hsu 2000, 2015; Chang 2015.

20. Although Mr. Lee first shared these details with me as a student in my volunteer ESL class, I include them here because he subsequently repeated them in recorded interviews that I conducted with him during the fall of 2009.

21. For a detailed discussion of this desire and its contribution to Mr. Lee's migration goals, see Chapter 2.

22. In Massachusetts, almost 45 percent of Chinese Americans aged sixty-five to seventy-four and 55 percent of those over seventy-five are low income. Lo 2006.

23. See also Mui and Shibusawa 2008.

24. Throughout the text, I reference particular Chinese words using Cantonese and Mandarin romanization systems rather than Chinese characters. "C" refers to Cantonese and "M" to Mandarin. For Cantonese, I rely on the Yale system; for Mandarin, I use *pinyin*.

25. Ngai 2004.

26. Ngai 2004.

27. Ngai 2004; Lee 2004, 2015.

28. Hsu 2015; Sassen 2006. See, for example, Kibria 2003.

29. Ong 1999.

30. Nee and De Bary 2014; Wong 1988; Kwong 1987.

31. Ikels 1983.

32. See, for example, Lan 2002; Yoon 2005; Mui and Kang 2006; Wong, Yoo, and Stewart 2006; Mui and Shibusawa 2008; Chow 2010; Lai 2010; Xie and Xia 2011.

33. Guo 2000.

34. See, for example, Kim 2016; Thang, Sone, and Toyota 2012.

35. Tatlow 2015a, 2015b.

36. Zhang 2009.

37. Zhang 2009.

38. Tatlow 2015a, 2015b. See also Zhang 2004; Shen, Li, and Tanui 2012.

39. Zhang 2009; Lou 2015.

40. Lamb et al. 2017.

41. See, for example, Sokolovsky 2009.

42. See, for example, Lamb 2009.

43. Yarris 2017.

44. Yarris 2017. See also Parreñas 2001a, 2001b.

45. Yarris 2017, 19–25.

46. Sampaio, King, and Walsh 2018.

47. Horn and Schweppe 2017; Walsh and Nare 2016.

48. Horn and Schweppe 2017; Walsh and Nare 2016. See also Benson 2014.

49. See, for example, Chi, Chappell, and Lubben 2001.

50. Sun 2014a, 2014b, 2016a , 2016b. See also Xiang, Yeoh, and Toyota 2013.

51. See, for example, Oliver 2008; Haas 2013; Ono 2015; Toyota and Thang 2013.

52. Nare, Walsh, and Baldassar 2017.

53. Zong and Batalova 2017.

54. Following San Francisco, New York, Los Angeles, and Chicago. To 2008; Newendorp 2017a ; chinatownatlas.org.

55. *Chinatown Masterplan* 2010. See also Newendorp 2017a.

56. See, for example, Fong 1994.

57. Chung 2000.

58. Quincy's Asian residents are 67 percent Chinese with Cantonese predominating, 13 percent Asian Indian, and 11 percent Vietnamese. Additional groups represented are Filipino, Korean, Thai, and Japanese. Manning with Connelly 2013.

59. Newendorp 2017b.

60. Lee 2015, 376.

61. Glick Schiller, Basch, and Blanc-Szanton 1992; Levitt 2001.

62. See, for example, Levitt 2009.

63. See, for example, Hall 1991; Siu 2005; Ho 2019.

64. See, for example, Hsu 2000; Teng 2013; Chang 2015.

65. See also McKeown 1999.

66. Here I make a distinction between overseas Chinese as migrants—that is, recently removed from China—and as diasporic populations, which may include individuals many generations removed from living in China. Identification as "Chinese" is much more complicated among the diaspora, which I discuss in Chapter 7. Wang 1980, 2002; Kuhn 2008, 4–5, 49–50. See also Siu 2005 and Ho 2019.

67. Tu 1994; Louie 2004.

68. McKeown 2008.

69. Nyiri 2010, 49–60.

70. Nyiri 2010, 49–60; Fong 2011, 198–199.

71. Xiang 2015, 14. See also Ho 2019, 5.

72. See, for example, Hess 2016.

CHAPTER 2

1. Chi, Chappell, and Lubben 2001; Lamb 2009.

2. Horn and Schweppe 2016, 2. See also Walsh and Nare 2016, 7.

3. See, for example, Chi et al. 2001.

4. See Kuhn 2008; Chu 2010.

5. Kuhn 2008, 36–38. See also, for example, Hsu 2000; Johnson 2002; Ong and Nonini 1997.

6. Kuhn 2008. See also Louie 2004.

7. See also Hsu 2000; Kuhn 2008.

8. Leung 2011, 205.

9. Focusing just on statistics from Taishan County, historically the main sending area of Cantonese migrants to the United States, Hsu (2000) notes that "between 1978 and 1985, an average of 8,118 people left Taishan each year—about 138,000 in all. In 1980 alone, 16.2 percent of the county's population departed for other countries" (183–184).

10. Kuhn 2008, 51.

11. Kuhn 2008, 141.
12. Kuhn 2008, 51. See also McKeown 1999.
13. Sinn 2013, 2014.
14. For a detailed history of the Hong Kong–China border from 1949 onward and its repercussions on family life, see Newendorp 2008, chap. 2.
15. I have previously written about Mr. Cheung's story in Newendorp 2011. Some of the quotes in this chapter for Mr. Cheung and for other senior migrants discussed below, including Mrs. Chee, Mr. Moy, and Mr. Lee, use the wording I adopted in writing that essay. These names, as with all interviewees throughout the text, are pseudonyms.
16. Hsu 2000; Louie 2004; Kuhn 2008.
17. Hsu 2000. See also Shen, Li, and Tanui 2012.
18. Hsu (2000) notes that in 1986, out of 950,000 residents of Taishan County, "460,000 . . . were related to someone overseas" (184).
19. See, for example, Watson 1975.
20. Coe 2012, 920.
21. Students and merchants were not included in this policy, nor were Chinese born in the United States to migrants who had been legally resident before the exclusion laws were passed or who were legally resident through their status as students or merchants. See Chang 1991 and Lee 2010 for more details.
22. Hsu 2000.
23. Kuhn 2008.
24. Ong 1999
25. Szonyi 2005; Ong 1999. See also Cohen 1976.
26. Hsu 2000.
27. Szonyi 2005.
28. Chin 2000; Lee 2013.
29. Watson 1986.
30. Shen et al. 2012.
31. Shen et al. 2012. See also Hsu 2000.
32. Shen et al. 2012.
33. Johnson 2002.
34. Johnson 2002. See also Oxfeld 2001; Shen et al. 2012.
35. See Chapter 3 for a more detailed discussion of the history of this time period, including the role of worker contribution.
36. Hall 1991; Chu 2010, 33.

CHAPTER 3

1. Newendorp 2011.
2. Newendorp 2011.
3. Sassen 2006, 290–298.
4. Sassen 2006, 290–298.
5. Coutin 2007.
6. Rosaldo 1994.

7. Jackson 2015, 818.
8. Coutin 2007.
9. Coutin 2007, 5.
10. King 2016, 243.
11. See also Walsh and Nare 2016.
12. Oliver 2016.
13. See, for example, Bernstein 1977.
14. Guobin Yang (2003) has also written about the nostalgia of China's zhiqing generation—that is, the generation of youth who came of age during the Cultural Revolution and would have been about forty in 1990. My interviewees are older by at least twenty years.
15. Hershatter 2011.
16. Hershatter 2011, 268.
17. Hershatter 2011.
18. See, for example, Lee 2007.
19. See Chapter 2 for a more thorough discussion of the movement of Cantonese families back and forth over the Hong Kong border prior to 1949.
20. See, for example, Liu and Sun 2016.
21. Whyte 2010. See also Zhang 2009.
22. Lee 2007, 144.
23. Lee 2007, 145.
24. Lee 2007, 156.
25. Lee 2007, 156–157.
26. See also Kleinman et al. 2011.
27. See also Fong 2011.
28. See also Yan and Bear 2009 and Yan 2011.
29. Osburg 2013, 184–185.
30. Lee 2007, 145.
31. See, for example, Osburg 2013.
32. Oxfeld 2010, 27–28.
33. Oxfeld 2010, 31.
34. Oxfeld 2010, 31.
35. See also Zhang and Ong 2008.
36. See also Fong 2011, 166–170.
37. Brown, de Brauw, and Du 2009; Hong and He 2013; Liu with Vortherms and Hong 2017.
38. Liu et al. 2017.
39. Lee 2007, 145.
40. The exam could be taken with the help of a Chinese translator only if seniors were able to get a doctor's note stating mental health issues that prevented them from being able to take the test in English, or if they were age fifty or older and had lived in the United States as a legal resident with a green card for at least twenty years. Since most of my interviewees had immigrated at age sixty or older, they would have to wait until they were at least eighty.

41. See also Zhou and Cai 2002.

CHAPTER 4

1. Lamb 2017, xi.
2. See, for example, Lamb 2017; Walker 2015; Lulle and King 2016.
3. Lamb et al. 2017, 8–12.
4. Walker 2015, 18–20.
5. S.D. 2018.
6. Lou 2015.
7. Lou 2015; Zhang 2009.
8. See also Whyte 2010.
9. Zhang 2009; Farquhar and Zhang 2012; Lou 2015.
10. This subject is the topic of Chapter 5.
11. Zhang 2009; Farquhar and Zhang 2012; Lou 2015.
12. Lulle and King 2016.
13. Zhang 2009.
14. Zhang 2009. See also Davis-Friedmann 1991.
15. The hukou system, also known as the household residency system, designated all PRC citizens as either urban or rural residents, tied to their mother's place of residence. Because food and other benefits, like education and health care, were available only through one's hukou place of residence, individuals could not easily move from one area to another. Despite creating a two-tiered system of unequal benefits for urban and rural residents, this system did help protect China's older rural residents, whose adult children continued to live nearby because they could not freely move away to other urban areas, as has become the norm today.
16. Zhang 2009.
17. Zhang 2009.
18. Zhang 2009. See also Farquhar and Zhang 2012.
19. China has "the third highest suicide rate in the world" (Wei et al. 2018, 2 of 10), with those over sixty-five completing suicide at a rate that is "four to five times higher than the general population" (Dong et al. 2015: 121). It's worth noting that this higher-than-average rate carries over to the diasporic Chinese population. In the United States, the suicide rate among "Chinese American older women is higher when compared with the general population" (Dong et al. 2015: 121; see also Lim et al. 2011).
20. Social Security was not the first pension in the United States, but it was the first to provide widespread support. Relatively modest at first, it grew throughout the 1970s to include not just primary workers but also their dependent family members and disabled individuals. Social Security has also increased in the amount of support provided, been modified to increase with the cost of living, and been supplemented with Medicare, which provides health care coverage for all citizens sixty-five and over. https://www.ssa.gov/history/briefhistory3.html..
21. Retirement today is also complicated because, unlike in the past, it is not just a discrete life stage. Instead, scholars talk about life stages, and the process of retirement

as staggered or blended as older adults move in and out of periods of paid and unpaid work. Moreover, some seniors continue to engage in paid labor not because of financial necessity but because of camaraderie with coworkers and the sense of purpose they derive from working (Lynch 2012), similar reasons voiced by Chinese seniors.

22. Lynch 2012.

23. Not everyone over sixty-five is eligible for Medicare. To be eligible, seniors must be eligible for Social Security or have a spouse who is.

24. Farquhar and Zhang 2012, 16, 129.

25. Farquhar and Zhang 2012, 13.

26. See Yu 2010; Yu, Tao, and Ivanhoe 2010.

27. Farquhar and Zhang 2012, 189.

28. Farquhar and Zhang 2012, 13–14.

29. *Yumcha* is a Cantonese word that literally means "to drink tea" but in actuality involves spending hours chatting and snacking on dim sum treats in a restaurant with others.

30. Farquhar and Zhang 2012, 159.

31. See Chapter 6 for an extensive discussion of Boston's Chinatown.

32. Hershatter 2011, 89–95.

33. Mrs. Wong is featured in more detail in Chapters 2 and 3.

34. Ikels 1983, 216.

35. Ikels 1983, 216.

36. Leong 2010.

37. Zhang 2009, 205; Farquhar and Zhang 2012; Lou 2015.

38. I discuss seniors' involvement in some of these cultural group activities in detail in Chapter 7.

CHAPTER 5

1. This chapter has been adapted from an article originally published in 2016 in *Ageing International*: "Negotiating Family 'Value': Caregiving and Conflict among Chinese-Born Senior Migrants and Their Families in the U.S." It is reprinted here with permission of Springer. doi:10.1007/s12126-016-9269-z.

2. Parreñas 2005; Lamb 2009; Dossa and Coe 2017; Yarris 2017.

3. See, for example, Davis-Friedmann 1991 and Ikels 2004.

4. Zhang 2009.

5. Chinese grandparent caregivers in Canada also talk about their intergenerational family relationships in this way using the Mandarin term: *ge dai qing*. See Zhou 2017, 49.

6. Zhang 2009.

7. See, for example, Parreñas 2005; Yarris 2017.

8. Dossa and Coe 2017, 2.

9. Dossa and Coe 2017, 4.

10. Dossa and Coe 2017, 9, 12.

11. See, for example, Deneva 2017; Zhou 2017.

12. Zelizer 1985, 3, 5, 11, 15; See also Fong 2004 and Lan 2002.

13. See, for example, Parreñas 2001a, 2001b, 2005; Constable 1999, 2007; Yarris 2017.

14. See also Rodriguez-Galan 2013; Dossa and Coe 2017.

15. Da 2003.

16. Foner and Dreby 2011, 550.

17. Treas 2008.

18. Gilbertson 2009.

19. Foner and Dreby 2011, 546.

20. See, for example, Zhou 2009.

21. See, for example, Yoon 2005; Xie and Xia 2011; Mui and Kang 2006; Mui and Shibusawa 2009; Chow 2010.

22. See, for example, Yoon 2005 and Xie and Xia 2011; Mui and Kang 2006; Mui and Shibusawa 2008.

23. See, for example, Ikels 2004.

24. See, for example, Yan 2003 and Zhang 2009.

25. Ikels 1996, 2004; Feng et al. 2011

26. Lai 2010. See also Da 2003.

27. Chinese grandparent caregivers in Canada also talk about their intergenerational family relationships in this way using the Mandarin gloss: *ge dai qing*. See Zhou 2017, 49.

28. Treas 2008.

29. See Zhou 2017.

30. See, for example, Yan 2003; Ikels 2004; Zhang 2009.

31. Yan 2003; Zhang 2009.

32. Deneva 2017.

33. See also Newendorp 2008, chap. 4.

34. Deneva 2017.

35. One exception is Yarris (2017), who emphasizes how Nicaraguan grandmothers left to care for grandchildren whose parents have emigrated abroad find meaning alongside the challenge and economic precarity they experience in their caregiving roles as they contribute to the overall well-being of their transnational families. Of course, unlike my interviewees, who were also navigating transitions to living in the United States as older adults, Nicaraguan grandmothers continued to interact with networks and forms of support in their home communities.

36. See Da 2003.

37. Newendorp 2014. See also Chapter 6.

38. Lan 2002.

39. For the cultural importance of burial in China, see Watson and Rawski (1990). Burial is increasingly rare in contemporary China, where officially only cremation is now allowed (Ikels 2004). See also Zhou (2017, 58), whose Canadian Chinese senior interviewees likewise "indicate their preference to die or be buried in the homeland."

40. Kleinman 2009.

41. See, for example, Hochschild 2003; Constable 2007.

42. Dossa and Coe 2017.

43. Kleinman 2009.

CHAPTER 6

1. For more information about this initiative, see https://aaca-boston.org/cleanup-chinatown/.

2. See, for example, https://cpaboston.org/en/programs/chinatown-stabilization-campaign and https://www.northeastern.edu/thescope/2018/02/09/faced-housing-crisis-chinatown-residents-note-absence-media-coverage/.

3. The essentializing idea that Chinatowns are unchanging and potentially undesirable residential locations has to some extent been reinforced through the changing settlement patterns among an increasingly diverse and growing Asian immigrant population in the United States, who more commonly choose to bypass traditional urban enclaves for more spacious and upscale residential locations (see, for example, Fong 1994). Mirroring these changes, a new paradigm has emerged with the concept of "ethnoburbs" (Li 1998, 2009). Tracking the movement of many Chinese Americans, including immigrants who have arrived in the latter decades of the twentieth century, away from urban Chinese centers into suburban areas where they interact with a diverse and multicultural population of immigrants and other citizens, Li (1998, 2009) argues that these new social and economic communities are fundamentally different from traditional urban ethnic enclaves and satellite Chinatowns.

4. See, for example, Anderson 1987, Hsu 2000, Lui 2003, Zhou 1992, 2009.

5. Anderson et al. 2019, 2–3.

6. See, for example, Hsu 2000; Lui 2003; Wong 1982; Zhou 1992, 2009.

7. See Walsh and Nare 2016.

8. King 2016, 40.

9. See, for example, Shenk et al. 2004.

10. Oliver 2016; Walsh and Nare 2016.

11. Sun 2016; Walsh 2016. See also Xiang, Yeoh, and Toyota 2013.

12. King 2016.

13. Rowles 1993. See also Kong, Yeoh, and Teo 1996; Shenk, Kuwahara, and Zablotsky 2004.

14. Sokolovsky 2009.

15. Rowles 1993. See also Shenk et al. 2004.

16. Liu and Geron 2008.

17. See Wong (1982) for a much more detailed discussion of the various community roles and responsibilities fulfilled by these associations although in New York, not Boston. He also documents a similar rise of social service organizations, both complementing and replacing associations' roles, as also took place in Boston's Chinatown.

18. Tsui 2009, 2014.

19. Rowles 1993. See also Kong et al. 1996; Shenk et al. 2004; Rowles and Bernard 2013.

20. Phillips 2013.

21. While Quincy has the largest number of Chinese American residents outside of Boston, Malden, Cambridge, Newton, and Brookline also have significant Chinese American populations. The populations of these five suburban areas, all of which connect to Boston's Chinatown via direct subway lines, account for about 40,000 ethnically Chinese residents, as compared to 26,000 in all of Boston and about 4,500 in Chinatown proper. http://www.umb.edu/iaas/census/2010/10_cities_towns_largest_population_of_asian_americans_in_ma.

22. Rowles 1993.

23. Rowles 1993.

24. I thank Tunney Lee for pointing out to me the relationship between aspects of Chinatown's built environment, like sidewalk width, and the different recreational activities carried out in public spaces.

25. Leung 2015.

26. See a full discussion on this topic in Chapter 3.

CHAPTER 7

1. https://vimeo.com/21629168, from *Generation Dance*, Jennifer Carpenter's exhibit. Here, I use Ho Long's actual name, rather than a pseudonym, as he used it in this public video recording.

2. Espiritu 2010, 611.

3. Hall 1991; Parreñas 2001a. See also Lowe 1996.

4. Palmberger 2017.

5. Huang 2016.

6. See, for example, Tu 1994; Ang 1998; Kuehn, Louie, and Pomfret 2013.

7. The quotation is from Carpenter's exhibit: http://generationdance.weebly.com/about.html.

8. See, for example, Clifford 1994; Cohen 1997; Ang 2003.

9. See, for example, Eng and Davidson 2008 and Hoe 2013. Numerous scholars document the extensive history of Chinese dispersal overseas. For Poston and Wong (2016), that history begins over two thousand years ago, during the Qin dynasty (221–207 B.C.E.), when Chinese emigrated to Japan and the Philippines. More commonly, accounts of the substantial movement of Chinese overseas date that movement at least to the fifteenth century, as individuals left Southeast China in particular for other world areas, including Southeast Asia, the Pacific Islands, Australia, Europe, and the Americas (Kuhn 2008). In recent decades, efforts have shifted from tracing past patterns of movement to situating these historical processes of Chinese dispersal within interpretative frameworks that make clear their embeddedness in global power hierarchies, including colonialism, industrialization, and restrictive immigration policies as applied particularly in North America and Australia to Chinese and other Asian migrant populations throughout the peak of Southeast China emigration from the 1850s to the 1920s.

10. McKeown 1999, 307.

11. Siu 2005, 197.

12. Siu's (2005, 197) examination of diasporic citizenship complicates this view by focusing on the pull of Taiwan as a Chinese homeland for Panamanian Chinese. Yet territorial China still remains central to conceptions of belonging; the China-Taiwan conflict cannot be separated from negotiations of diasporic Chinese identity, leading to debates "about who they are, where their allegiances lie, and where they belong" among Panamanian Chinese. See also Tu (1994) and Ang (1998, 2003).

13. Ang 1998, 226, 227.

14. Written in 1982 to protest how Japanese history textbooks were portraying the Second Sino-Japanese War, "My Chinese Heart" champions a lifelong affinity with China and its traditional natural and cultural symbols, including the Yellow River and the Great Wall of China (Gorfinkel 2017). For full lyrics in English, see http://blog.chinadaily.com.cn/thread-676932-1-1.html.

15. McKeown 1999, 330.

16. Shelemay 1998, 213, 10.

17. See also Hershatter 2011.

18. The role of Chinese dance in identity formation is well documented See, for example, Chang and Frederiksen 2016; Wilcox 2011; Schein 2000; Wong 2013.

19. Wilcox 2011, 321; Wong 2013, 133.

20. Farquhar and Zhang 2012.

21. Lai 2012, 113.

22. Field 2010; Chang and Frederiksen 2016, 36–38.

23. Liu 2004.

24. Hsu 2016.

25. Liu 2004, 88.

26. See Chang and Frederiksen 2016, 39.

27. Huang 2016.

28. Huang 2016.

29. Huang 2016.

30. See the discussion at the end of Chapter 6 about the political dynamics controlling this space.

31. Approximately 50 percent of this building's residents in 2012, all seniors, were ethnically Chinese.

32. Hsu 2015.

33. Palmberger 2017, 237.

34. http://generationdance.weebly.com/photography.html.

35. McKeown 1999, 330.

36. Zhang 2009; Farquhar and Zhang 2012.

37. McKeown 1999, 330.

38. See Brownell 1995.

CHAPTER 8

1. See, for example, Zhou 2017 and Ke 2019.

2. Hsu 2015, 2016.

3. See also Ong and Nonini 1997.
4. Massey, Durand, and Malone 2003; Castells and Miller 2009.
5. Mui and Shibusawa 2008.
6. Lai and Andruske 2014; Guo et al. 2016.
7. Lamb et al. 2017.
8. Polivka and Luo 2013.
9. Asian Development Bank 2017.
10. Horn and Schweppe 2016, 2.
11. See also Zhou 2017.
12. See, for example, Lamb et al. 2017.
13. Coder, Rainwater, and Smeeding 2001.
14. King 2016.

REFERENCES

Anderson, Kay J. 1987. "The Idea of Chinatown: The Power of Place and Institutional Practice in the Making of a Racial Category." *Annals of the Association of American Geographers* 77 (4): 580–598.

Anderson, Kay, Ien Ang, Andrea Del Bono, Donald McNeill, and Alexandra Wong. 2019. *Chinatown Unbound: Trans-Asian Urbanism in the Age of China*. London: Rowman and Littlefield.

Ang, Ien. 1998. "Can One Say No to Chineseness? Pushing the Limits of the Diasporic Paradigm." *Boundary 2* 25 (3): 223–242.

Ang, Ien. 2003. "Together in Difference: Beyond Diaspora, into Hybridity." *Asian Studies Review* 27 (2): 141–154.

Asian Development Bank. 2017. "Population and Aging in Asia: The Growing Elderly Population." January 18.

Benson, M., and Nick Osbaldiston. 2014. *Understanding Lifestyle Migration: Theoretical Approaches to Migration and the Quest for a Better Life*. Basingstoke, UK: Palgrave Macmillan.

Bernstein, Thomas. 1977. *Up to the Mountains and down to the Villages*. New Haven, CT: Yale University Press.

Brown, P., A. de Brauw, and Y. Du. 2009. "Understanding Variation in the Design of China's New Cooperative Medical System." *China Quarterly* 198:304–329.

Brownell, Susan. 1995. *Training the Body for China: Sports in the Moral Order of the People's Republic*. Chicago: University of Chicago Press.

Carpenter, Jennifer. *Generation Dance: Photography Exhibit by Jennifer Carpenter*. http://generationdance.weebly.com/photography.html.

Castells, Stephen, and Mark J. Miller. 2009. *The Age of Migration: International Population Movements in the Modern World*, 4th ed. New York: Guilford Press.

Chang, Gordon. 2015. *Fateful Ties: A History of America's Preoccupation with China*. Cambridge, MA: Harvard University Press.

Chang, Shih-Ming Li, and Lynn E. Fredericksen. 2016. *Chinese Dance in the Vast Land and Beyond*. Middleton, CT: Wesleyan University Press.

Chang, Sucheng. 1991. *Entry Denied: Exclusion and the Chinese Community in America, 1882–1943*. Philadelphia: Temple University Press.

Chi, Iris, Neena L. Chappell, and James Lubben. 2001. *Elderly Chinese in Pacific-Rim*

Countries: Social Support and Integration. Hong Kong: University of Hong Kong Press.
Chin, Tung Pok. 2000. *Paper Son: One Man's Story*. Philadelphia: Temple University Press.
Chinatown Atlas. Boston: Chinatown Atlas. www.chinatownatlas.org.
Chinatown Masterplan Oversight Committee. 2010. *Chinatown Masterplan 2010: Community Vision for the Future*. Boston: Chinatown Masterplan Oversight Committee.
Chow, Henry P. H. 2010. "Growing Old in Canada: Physical and Psychological Well-Being among Elderly Chinese Immigrants." *Ethnicity and Health* 15 (1): 61–72.
Chu, Julie. 2010. *Cosmologies of Credit: Transnational Mobility and the Politics of Destination in China*. Durham, NC: Duke University Press.
Chung, Tom Lun-nap. 2000. "Asian Americans in Enclaves—They Are Not One Community: New Modes of Asian American Settlement." In *Asian Americans: Experiences and Perspectives*, edited by Timothy Fong and Larry Shinagawa. Upper Saddle River, NJ: Prentice Hall.
Clifford, James. 1994. "Diasporas." *Cultural Anthropology* 9 (3): 302–338.
Coder, John, Lee Rainwater, and Timothy Smeeding. 2001. "Inequality among Children and Elderly in Ten Modern Nations: The United States in an International Context." *American Economic Review* 79 (2): 320–324.
Coe, Cati. 2012. "Growing Up and Going Abroad: How Ghanaian Children Imagine Transnational Migration." *Journal of Ethnic and Migration Studies* 38 (6): 913–931.
Cohen, Myron. 1976. *House United, House Divided: The Chinese Family in Taiwan*. New York: Columbia University Press.
Cohen, Robin. 1997. *Global Diasporas: An Introduction*. Seattle: University of Washington Press.
Constable, Nicole. 1999. "At Home But Not at Home: Filipina Narratives of Ambivalent Returns." *Cultural Anthropology* 14 (2): 203–228.
Constable, Nicole. 2007. *Maid to Order in Hong Kong: Stories of Migrant Workers*. Ithaca, NY: Cornell University Press.
Coutin, Susan. 2007. *Nations of Emigrants: Shifting Boundaries of Citizenship in El Salvador and the United States*. Ithaca, NY: Cornell University Press.
Da, Wei Wei. 2003. "Transnational Grandparenting: Child Care Arrangements among Migrants from the People's Republic of China to Australia." *Journal of International Migration and Integration* 4 (1): 79–103.
Davis-Friedmann, Deborah. 1991. *Long Lives: Chinese Elderly and the Communist Revolution*. Palo Alto, CA: Stanford University Press.
Deneva, Neda. 2017. "Flexible Kin Work, Flexible Migration: Aging Migrants Caught between Productive and Reproductive Labor in the European Union." In *Transnational Aging and Reconfigurations of Kin Work*, edited by Parin Dossa and Cati Coe, 25–42. New Brunswick, NJ: Rutgers University Press.
Dong, XinQi, E-Shien Chang, Ping Zeng, and Melissa A. Simon. 2015. "Suicide in

the Global Chinese Aging Population: A Review of Risk and Protective Factors, Consequences, and Interventions." *Aging and Disease* 6 (2): 121-130.

Dossa, Parin, and Cati Coe. 2017. "Introduction: Transnational Aging and Reconfigurations of Kin Work." In *Transnational Aging and Reconfigurations of Kin Work*, edited by Parin Dossa and Cati Coe, 1-21. New Brunswick, NJ: Rutgers University Press.

Eng, Kuah-Pearce K., and Andrew Davidson. 2008. *At Home in the Chinese Diaspora: Memories, Identities and Belongings*, edited by Kuah-Pearce, K. Eng, and A. Davidson. Basingstoke, UK: Palgrave Macmillan.

Espiritu, Yen Le. 2010. "Homes, Borders, and Possibilities." In *Asian American Studies Now*, edited by Jean Wu and Thomas Chen, 603-621. New Brunswick, NJ: Rutgers University Press.

Faier, Lieba. 2009. *Intimate Encounters: Filipina Women and the Remaking of Rural Japan*. Berkeley: University of California Press.

Farquhar, Judith, and Qicheng Zhang. 2012. *Ten Thousand Things: Nurturing Life in Contemporary Beijing*. New York: Zone Books.

Feng, Zhanlian, Heying Jenny Zhan, Xiaotian Feng, Chang Liu, Mingyue Sun, and Vincent Mor. 2011. "An Industry in the Making: The Emergence of Institutional Elder Care in Urban China." *Journal of the American Geriatrics Society* 59 (4): 738-744.

Field, Andrew. 2010. *Shanghai's Dancing World: Cabaret Culture and Urban Politics, 1919- 1954*. Hong Kong: Chinese University Press.

Foner, Nancy, and Joanna Dreby. 2011. "Relations between the Generations in Immigrant Families." *Annual Review of Sociology* 37:545-564.

Fong, Timothy. 1994. *The First Suburban Chinatown: The Re-Making of Monterey Park, CA*. Philadelphia: Temple University Press.

Fong, Vanessa. 2011. *Paradise Redefined: Transnational Chinese Students and the Quest for Flexible Citizenship in the Developed World*. Palo Alto, CA: Stanford University Press.

Fong, Vanessa. 2004. *Only Hope: Coming of Age under China's One-Child Policy*. Palo Alto, CA: Stanford University Press.

Freeman, Caren. 2011. *Making and Faking Kinship: Marriage and Labor Migration between China and South Korea*. Ithaca, NY: Cornell University Press.

Gilbertson, Greta. 2009. "Caregiving across Generations: Aging, State Assistance, and Multigenerational Ties among Immigrants from the Dominican Republic." In *Across Generations: Immigrant Families in America*, edited by Nancy Foner, 135-159. New York: NYU Press.

Glick Schiller, Nina, Linda Basch, and Cristina Blanc-Szanton. 1992. "Transnationalism: A New Analytic Framework for Understanding Migration." In *Towards a Transnational Perspective on Migration*, edited by Nina Glick Schiller, Linda Basch, and Cristina Blanc-Szanton, 1-24. New York: New York Academy of Sciences.

Gorfinkel, Lauren. 2017. *Chinese Television and National Identity Construction: The Cultural Politics of Music-Entertainment Programmes*. London: Taylor & Francis.

Guo, Man, Ling Xu, Jinyu Liu, Weiyu Mao, and Iris Chi. 2016. "Parent–Child

Relationships among Older Chinese Immigrants: The Influence of Co-Residence, Frequent Contact, Intergenerational Support and Sense of Children's Deference." *Ageing and Society* 36:1459–1482.

Guo, Zibin. 2000. *Ginseng and Aspirin: Health Care Alternatives for Aging Chinese in New York*. Ithaca, NY: Cornell University Press.

Haas, Heiko. 2013. "Volunteering in Retirement Migration: Meanings and Functions of Charitable Activities for Older British Residents in Spain." *Ageing and Society* 33:1374–1400.

Hall, Stuart. 1991. "The Local and the Global: Globalization and Ethnicity." In *Culture, Globalization and the World-System: Contemporary Conditions for the Representation of Identity*, edited by Anthony D. King, 18–39. Minneapolis: University of Minnesota Press.

Hershatter, Gail. 2011. *The Gender of Memory: Rural Women and China's Collective Past*. Berkeley: University of California Press.

Hess, Amanda. 2016. "Asian American Actors Are Fighting for Visibility. They Will Not Be Ignored." *New York Times*, May 25.

Ho, Elaine Lynn-Ee. 2019. *Citizens in Motion: Emigration, Immigration, and Re-Migration across China's Borders*. Palo Alto, CA: Stanford University Press.

Hochschild, Arlie. 2003. "Love and Gold." In *Global Woman: Nannies, Maids, and Sex Workers in the New Economy*, edited by B. Ehrenreich and A. Hochschild, 15–30. Dallas, TX: Metropolitan Press.

Hoe, Yow Cheun. 2013. *Guangdong and Chinese Diaspora*. New York: Routledge.

Hong, Phua Kai, and Alex He Jingwei. 2013. "Healthcare Reform: Where Is China Heading?" In *China's Social Development and Policy*, edited by Litao Zhao. New York: Routledge.

Horn, Vincent, and Cornelia Schweppe. 2016. "Introduction: Transnational Aging: Current Insights and Future Challenges." In *Transnational Aging: Current Insights and Future Challenges*, edited by Vincent Horn and Cornelia Schweppe, 1–15. New York: Routledge.

Horn, Vincent, and Cornelia Schweppe. 2017. "Transnational Aging: Towards a Transnational Perspective in Old-Age Research." *European Journal of Ageing* 14:335–339.

Hsu, Hua. 2015. "The Melancholy Pop Idol Who Haunts China." *New Yorker*, August 3.

Hsu, Madeline. 2000. *Dreaming of Gold, Dreaming of Home: Transnationalism and Migration between the United States and China, 1882–1943*. Palo Alto, CA: Stanford University Press.

Hsu, Madeline. 2015. *The Good Immigrants: How the Yellow Peril Became the Model Minority*. Princeton, NJ: Princeton University Press.

Hsu, Madeline Y. 2016. "Transnationalism and the Emergence of the Modern Chinese State: National Rejuvenation and the Ascendance of Foreign-Educated Elites." In *A Century of Transnationalism*, edited by Nancy L. Green and Roger Waldinger. Champaign: University of Illinois Press.

Huang, Claudia. 2016. "'Dancing Grannies' in the Modern City: Consumption and Group Formation in Urban China." *Asian Anthropology* 15 (3): 225–241.
Ikels, Charlotte. 2004. "Serving the Ancestors, Serving the State: Filial Piety and Death Ritual in Contemporary Guangzhou." In *Filial Piety: Practice and Discourse in Contemporary East Asia*, edited by Charlotte Ikels. Palo Alto, CA: Stanford University Press.
Ikels, Charlotte. 1983. *Aging and Adaptation: Chinese in Hong Kong and the United States*. Hamden, CT: Archon Books.
Ikels, Charlotte. 1996. *The Return of the God of Wealth: The Transition to a Market Economy in Urban China*. Palo Alto, CA: Stanford University Press.
Jackson, Lucy. 2015. "Intimate Citizenship? Rethinking the Politics and Experience of Citizenship as in Wales and Singapore." *Gender, Place and Culture* 23 (6): 817–833.
Jackson, Michael. 2013. *The Wherewithal of Life: Ethics, Migration, and the Question of Well-Being*. Berkeley: University of California Press.
Johnson, Graham. 2002. "Rural Development Patterns in Post-Reform China: The Pearl River Delta Region in the 1990s." *Development and Change* 28 (4): 731–752.
Ke, Jesper. 2019. "Filling the Empty Nest: Experiences of Chinese-Born Senior Migrants in the Greater Boston Area." BA thesis, Harvard University.
Kibria, Nazli 2003. *Becoming Asian American: Second-Generation Chinese and Korean American Identities*. Baltimore, MD: Johns Hopkins University Press.
Kim, Dohye. 2016. "Geographical Imagination and Intra-Asian Hierarchy between Filipinos and South Korean Retirees in the Philippines." *Philippine Studies: Historical and Ethnographic Viewpoints* 64 (2): 237–264.
King, Russell. 2016. "Afterword: Many Ageings, Multiple Migrations, and Ambiguous Homes." In *Transnational Migration and Home in Older Age*, edited by Katie Walsh and Lena Nare, 239–252. New York: Routledge.
Kleinman, Arthur. 2009. "Caregiving: The Odyssey of Becoming More Human." *Lancet* 373 (9660): 292–293.
Kleinman, Arthur, with Yunxiang Yan, Jing Jun, Sing Lee, Everett Zhang, Pan Tianshu, Wu Fei, and Jinhua Guo. 2011. *Deep China: The Moral Life of the Person*. Berkeley: University of California Press.
Kong, Lily, Brenda Yeoh, and Peggy Teo. 1996. "Singapore and the Experience of Place in Old Age." *Geographical Review* 86 (4): 529–551.
Kuehn, Julia, Kam Louie, and David M. Pomfret. 2013. "China Rising: A View and Review of China's Diasporas since the 1980s." In *Diasporic Chinese after the Rise of China: Communities and Cultural Production*, edited by Julia Kuehn, Kam Louie, and David M. Pomfret, 1–16. Vancouver: University of British Columbia Press.
Kuhn, Philip. 2008. *Chinese among Others: Emigration in Modern Times*. Lanham, MD: Rowman and Littlefield.
Kwong, Peter. 1987. *The New Chinatown*. New York: Hill and Wang.
Lai, Daniel W. L., and Cynthia Lee Andruske. 2014. "Uncovering the Hidden Treasures and Strengths: Contributions of Aging Chinese in Canada." *International Journal of Sociology of the Family* 40 (1): 71–96.

Lai, Daniel W. L. 2012. "Ethnic Identity of Older Chinese in Canada." *Journal of Cross Cultural Gerontology* 27:103–117.

Lai, Daniel. 2010. "Filial Piety, Caregiving Appraisal, and Caregiving Burden." *Research on Aging* 32 (2): 200–223.

Lamb, Sarah. 2007. "Aging across Worlds: Modern Seniors in an Indian Diaspora." In *Generations and Globalization: Family, Youth, and Age in the New World Economy*, edited by Jennifer Cole and Deborah Durham, 132–163. Bloomington: Indiana University Press.

Lamb, Sarah. 2009. *Aging and the Indian Diaspora: Cosmopolitan Families in India and Abroad*. Bloomington: Indiana University Press.

Lamb, Sarah, ed. 2017. *Successful Aging as a Contemporary Obsession: Global Perspectives*. New Brunswick, NJ: Rutgers University Press.

Lamb, Sarah, Jessica Robbins-Ruszkowski, Anna Corwin, Toni Calasanti, and Neal King. 2017. "Introduction: Successful Aging as a Twenty-First Century Obsession." In *Successful Aging as a Contemporary Obsession: Global Perspectives*, edited by Sarah Lamb, 1–23. New Brunswick, NJ: Rutgers University Press.

Lan, Pei-Chia. 2002. "Subcontracting Filial Piety Elder Care in Ethnic Chinese Immigrant Families in California." *Journal of Family Issues* 23 (7): 812–835.

Lee, Ching Kwan. 2007. "What Was Socialism to Chinese Workers?" In *Re-Envisioning the Chinese Revolution: The Politics and Poetics of Collective Memory in Reform China*, edited by Ching Kwan Lee and Guobin Yang, 141–165. Washington, DC: Woodrow Wilson Press, and Stanford, CA: Stanford University Press.

Lee, Erika. 2004. *At America's Gates: Chinese Immigration during the Exclusion Era, 1882- 1943*. Chapel Hill: University of North Carolina Press.

Lee, Erika. 2010. "The Chinese Are Coming: How Can We Stop Them? Chinese Exclusion and the Origins of American Gatekeeping." In *Asian American Studies Now*, edited by Jean Wu and Thomas Chen, 143–167. New Brunswick, NJ: Rutgers University Press.

Lee, Erika. 2015. *The Making of Asian America: A History*. New York: Simon and Schuster.

Lee, Heather. 2013. "A Life Cooking for Others: The Work and Migration Experiences of a Chinese Restaurant Worker in New York City, 1920–1946." In *Eating Asian America*, edited by Robert Ku, Martin Manalansan, and Anita Mannur, 53–77. New York: NYU Press.

Leong, Andrew. 2010. "The Struggle over Parcel C: How Boston's Chinatown Won a Victory in the Fight against Institutional Expansionism and Environmental Racism." In *Asian American Studies Now*, edited by Jean Wu and Thomas Chen, 565–580. New Brunswick, NJ: Rutgers University Press.

Leung, Genevieve Y. 2011. "Disambiguating the Term 'Chinese': An Analysis of Chinese American Surname Naming Practices." *Names* 59 (4): 204–213.

Levitt, Peggy. 2001. *Transnational Villagers*. Berkeley: University of California Press.

Levitt, Peggy. 2009. "Roots and Routes: Understanding the Lives of the Second Generation Transnationally." *Journal of Ethnic and Migration Studies* 35 (7): 1225–1242.
Li, Wei. 1998. "Anatomy of a New Ethnic Settlement: The Chinese Ethnoburb in Los Angeles." *Urban Studies* 35 (3): 479–501.
Li, Wei. 2009. *Ethnoburb: The New Ethnic Commodity in Urban America*. Honolulu: University of Hawaii Press.
Lim, Lena L., Weining Chang, Xin Yu, Helen Chiu, Mian-Yoon Chong, and Ee-Heok Kua. 2011. "Depression in Chinese Elderly Populations." *Asia-Pacific Psychiatry* 3 (2): 46–53.
Liu, Gordon G., with Samantha A. Vortherms and Xuezhi Hong. 2017. "China's Health Reform Update." *Annual Review of Public Health* 38:431–448.
Liu, Kang. 2004. *Globalization and Cultural Trends in China*. Honolulu: University of Hawaii Press.
Liu, Michael, and Kim Geron. 2008. "Changing Neighborhood: Ethnic Enclaves and the Struggle for Social Justice." *Social Justice* 35 (2): 18–35.
Liu, Tao, and Li Sun. 2016. "Pension Reform in China." *Journal of Aging and Social Policy* 28 (1): 15–28.
Lo, Shauna. 2006. "Profiles of Asian American Subgroups in Massachusetts: Chinese Americans in Massachusetts." Boston: Institute of Asian American Studies at the University of Massachusetts at Boston.
Lou, Vivian W. Q. 2015. "Active Ageing in Mainland China." *Active Ageing in Asia*, edited by Alan Walker and Christian Aspalter, 112–131. New York: Routledge.
Louie, Andrea. 2004. *Chineseness across Borders: Renegotiating Chinese Identities in China and the United States*. Durham, NC: Duke University Press.
Lowe, Lisa. 1996. *Immigrant Acts: On Asian American Cultural Politics*. Durham, NC: Duke University Press.
Lui, Mary Ting Yi. 2003. "Examining New Trends in Chinese American Urban Community Studies." *Journal of Urban History* 29:173.
Lulle, Aija, and Russell King. 2016. "Ageing Well: The Time-Spaces of Possibility for Older Female Latvian Migrants in the UK." *Social and Cultural Geography* 17 (3): 444–462.
Lynch, Caitrin. 2012. *Retirement on the Line: Age, Work, and Value in an American Factory*. Ithaca, NY: ILR Press.
Mahdavi, Pardis. 2016. *Crossing the Gulf: Love and Family in Migrant Lives*. Palo Alto, CA: Stanford University Press.
Manning, Elizabeth, with Stephen Connelly. 2013. *City of Quincy Demographic and Census Data Analysis*. Quincy, MA: City of Quincy.
Massey, Douglas S., Jorge Durand, and Nolan J. Malone. 2003. *Beyond Smoke and Mirrors: Mexican Immigration in an Era of Economic Integration*. New York: Russell Sage Foundation.
McKeown, Adam. 1999. "Conceptualizing Chinese Diasporas, 1842 to 1949." *Journal of Asian Studies* 58 (2): 306–337.

McKeown, Adam. 2008. *Melancholy Order: Asian Migration and the Globalization of Borders*. New York: Columbia University Press.

Mui, Ada C., and Suk-Young Kang. 2006. "Acculturation Stress and Depression among Asian Immigrant Elders." *Social Work* 51 (3): 243–255.

Mui, Ada C., and Tazuko Shibusawa. 2008. *Asian American Elders: Key Indicators of Well-Being*. New York: Columbia University Press.

Myerhoff, Barbara. 1978. *Number Our Days: Culture and Community among Elderly Jews in an American Ghetto*. Meridian Books.

Nare, Lena, Katie Walsh, and Loretta Baldassar. 2017. "Ageing in Transnational Contexts: Transforming Everyday Practices and Identities in Later Life." *Identities* 24 (5): 515–523.

Nee, Victor, and Brett De Bary. 2014. *Longtime Californ': A Documentary Study of an American Chinatown*. New York: Random House.

Newendorp, Nicole. 2008. *Uneasy Reunions: Immigration, Citizenship, and Family Life in Post-1997 Hong Kong*. Palo Alto, CA: Stanford University Press.

Newendorp, Nicole. 2011. "Chinese-Born Seniors on the Move: Transnational Mobility and Family Life between the Pearl River Delta and Boston, Massachusetts." Institute for Asian American Studies Publications, paper 26. Boston: University of Massachusetts Boston, Institute for Asian American Studies.

Newendorp, Nicole. 2016. "Negotiating Family 'Value': Caregiving and Conflict among Chinese-Born Senior Migrants and Their Families in the U.S." *Ageing International* 42(2): 187–204. doi:10.1007/s12126-016-9269-z.

Newendorp, Nicole. 2017a. "Boston's Chinatown." In *America's Changing Neighborhoods: An Exploration of Diversity through Places*, edited by Reed Ueda. Santa Barbara, CA: ABC-CLIO.

Newendorp, Nicole. 2017b. "Quincy, MA." In *America's Changing Neighborhoods: An Exploration of Diversity through Places*, edited by Reed Ueda. Santa Barbara, CA: ABC-CLIO.

Ngai, Mae. 2004. *Impossible Subjects: Illegal Aliens and the Making of Modern America*. Princeton, NJ: Princeton University Press.

Nyiri, Pal. 2010. *Mobility and Cultural Authority in Contemporary China*. Seattle: Washington University Press.

Oliver, Caroline. 2008. *Retirement Migration: Paradoxes of Aging*. Abingdon, UK: Routledge.

Oliver, Caroline. 2016. "Ageing, Embodiment, and Emotion in Orientations to Home: British Retirement Migration in Spain." In *Transnational Migration and Home in Older Age*, edited by Katie Walsh and Lena Näre, 188–200. Abingdon, UK: Routledge.

Ong, Aihwa. 1999. *Flexible Citizenship: The Cultural Logics of Transnationality*. Durham, NC: Duke University Press.

Ong, Aihwa, and Donald Nonini. 1997. *Ungrounded Empires: The Cultural Politics of Modern Chinese Transnationalism*. New York: Routledge.

Ono, Mayumi. 2015. "Commoditization of Lifestyle Migration: Japanese Retirees in Malaysia." *Mobilities* 10 (4): 609–627.

Osburg, John. 2013. *Anxious Wealth: Money and Morality among China's New Rich*. Palo Alto, CA: Stanford University Press.

Ossman, Susan. 2013. *Moving Matters: Paths of Serial Migration*. Palo Alto, CA: Stanford University Press.

Oxfeld, Ellen. 2001. "Imaginary Homecomings: Chinese Villagers, Their Overseas Relations, and Social Capital." *Journal of Socio-Economics* 30 (2): 181–186.

Oxfeld, Ellen. 2010. *Drink Water, But Remember the Source: Moral Discourse in a Chinese Village*. Berkeley: University of California Press.

Palmberger, Monika. 2017. "Social Ties and Embeddedness in Older Age: Older Turkish Labour Migrants in Vienna." *Journal of Ethnic and Migration Studies* 43 (2): 235–249.

Parreñas, Rhacel. 2001a. "Transgressing the Nation-State: The Partial Citizenship and 'Imagined (Global) Community' of Migrant Filipina Domestic Workers." *Signs* 26 (4): 1129–1154.

Parreñas, Rhacel. 2001b. *Servants of Globalization: Migration and Domestic Work*. Palo Alto: Stanford University Press.

Parreñas, Rhacel. 2005. "Long Distance Intimacy: Class, Gender, and Intergenerational Relations between Mothers and Children in Filipino Transnational Families." *Global Networks* 5 (4): 317–336.

Phillips, Judith. 2013. "Older People's Use of Unfamiliar Space." In *Environmental Gerontology: Making Meaningful Places in Old Age*, edited by Graham D. Rowles and Miriam Bernard, 199–224. New York: Springer Publishing.

Pieke, Frank N., Pál Nyíri, Mette Thunø, and Antonella Ceccagno. 2004. *Transnational Chinese: Fujianese Migrants in Europe*. Palo Alto, CA: Stanford University Press.

Polivka, Larry, and Baozhen Luo. 2013. "The Future of Retirement Security around the Globe." *Generations: Journal of the American Society on Aging* 37 (1): 39–45.

Poston, Dudley L., and Juyin Wong. 2016. "The Chinese Diaspora: The Current Distribution of the Overseas Chinese Population." *Chinese Journal of Sociology* 2 (3): 348–373.

Rodriguez-Galan, Marta B. 2013. "Grandmothering in Life-Course Perspective: A Study of Puerto Rican Grandmothers Raising Grandchildren in the United States." In *Transitions and Transformations: Cultural Perspectives on Aging and the Life-Course*, edited by Caitrin Lynch and Jason Danely. New York: Berghahn Books.

Rosaldo, Renato. 1994. "Cultural Citizenship and Educational Democracy." *Cultural Anthropology* 9 (3): 402–411.

Rowles, Graham D. 1993. "Evolving Images of Place in Aging and 'Aging in Place.'" *Generations* 17 (2): 65–71.

Rowles, Graham D., and Miriam Bernard. 2013. "The Meaning and Significance of Place in Old Age." In *Environmental Gerontology: Making Meaningful Places in Old Age*, edited by Graham D. Rowles and Miriam Bernard, 3–24. New York: Springer Publishing.

Rowles, Graham, and John Watkins. 1993. "Elderly Migration and Development in Small Communities." *Growth and Change* 24: 509–538.
S.D. 2018. "Why Universities Are Booming in China: Both Confucius and Mao Would Approve." *Economist*, August 16.
Sampaio, Dora, Russell King, and Katie Walsh. 2018. "Geographies of the Age-Migration Nexus: An Introduction." *Area* 50:440–443.
Sassen, Saskia. 2006. *Foundational Subjects for Political Membership: Today's Changed Relation to the Nation State in Territory, Authority, Rights: From Medieval to Global Assemblages*. Princeton, NJ: Princeton University Press.
Schein, Louisa. 2000. *Minority Rules: The Miao and the Feminine in China's Cultural Politics*. Durham, NC: Duke University Press.
Shelemay, Kay Kaufman. 1998. *Let Jasmine Rain Down: Song and Remembrance among Syrian Jews*. Chicago: University of Chicago Press.
Shen, Huifen. 2012. *China's Left-Behind Wives: Families of Migrants from Fujian to Southeast Asia, 1930s–1950s*. Honolulu: University of Hawaii Press.
Shen, Suyan, Fang Li, and John Kipkorir Tanui. 2012. "Quality of Life and Old Age Social Welfare System for the Rural Elderly in China." *Ageing International* 37 (3): 285–299.
Shenk, Dena, Kazumi Kuwahara, and Diane Zablotsky. 2004. "Older Women's Attachments to Their Home and Possessions." *Journal of Aging Studies* 18:157–169.
Sinn, Elizabeth. 2013. *Pacific Crossing: California Gold, Chinese Migration, and the Making of Hong Kong*. Hong Kong: Hong Kong University Press.
Sinn, Elizabeth. 2014. "Pacific Ocean: Highway to Gold Mountain, 1850–1900." *Pacific Historical Review* 83 (2): 220–237.
Siu, Lok. 2005. *Memories of a Future Home: Diasporic Citizenship of Chinese in Panama*. Palo Alto, CA: Stanford University Press.
Skeldon, Ronald, and Xiaohu (Shawn) Wang. 1994. *Reluctant Exiles? Migration from Hong Kong and the New Overseas Chinese*. London: Routledge.
Social Security Administration. *History of Social Security*. Accessed June 2018 at http://www.ssa.gov/history/chrono.html.
Sokolovsky, Jay, ed. 2009. *The Cultural Context of Aging: Worldwide Perspectives*, 3rd ed. Westport, CT: Praeger.
Sun, Ken Chih-Yan. 2014a. "Reconfigured Reciprocity: How Aging Taiwanese Immigrants Transform Cultural Logics of Eldercare." *Journal of Marriage and Family* 76 (4): 875–889.
Sun, Ken Chih-Yan. 2014b. "Transnational Health Care Seeking." *Global Networks* 14 (4): 533–550.
Sun, Ken Chih-Yan. 2016a. "Professional Remittances: How Ageing Returnees Seek to Contribute to the Homeland." *Journal of Ethnic and Migration Studies* 42 (14): 2404–2420.
Sun, Ken Chih-Yan. 2016b. "Changing Notions of Home across the Life-Cycle: How Ageing Taiwanese Return Migrants Rethink Their Relationship to the Homeland."

In *Transnational Migration and Home in Older Age*, edited by Katie Walsh and Lena Nare, 126–138. New York: Routledge.

Sun, Ken Chih-Yan. 2018. "Negotiating the Boundaries of Social Membership." *Current Sociology Monograph* 66 (2): 286–302.

Szonyi, Michael. 2005. "Mothers, Sons and Lovers: Fidelity and Frugality in the Overseas Chinese Divided Family before 1949." *Journal of Chinese Overseas* 1(1): 43–64.

Tatlow, Didi. 2015a. "China Promises Universal Pension Plan." *New York Times*, November 24.

Tatlow, Didi. 2015b. "China Fares 'Moderately' in Global Survey on Quality of Life for Older Adults." *New York Times*, September 24.

Teng, Emma. 2013. *Eurasian: Mixed Identities in the United States, China, and Hong Kong, 1842–1943*. Berkeley: University of California Press.

Terrazas, Aaron, and Jeanne Batalova. 2010. "Chinese Immigrants in the United States." Washington, DC: Migration Policy Institute.

Thang, Leng Leng, Sachiko Sone, and Mika Toyota. 2012. "Freedom Found: The Later-Life Transnational Migration of Japanese Women to Western Australia and Thailand." *Asian and Pacific Migration* 21 (2): 239–262

To, Wing-kai. 2008. *Chinese in Boston, 1870–1965*. Charleston, SC: Arcadia.

Toyota, Mika, and Leng Leng Thang. 2013. "'Lock In' or 'Run Away': Japanese Retirement Migrants in Southeast Asia." Paper presented at the Association of American Anthropology Annual Meeting, Chicago, November 23.

Treas, Judith. 2008. "Transnational Older Adults and Their Families." *Family Relations* 57 (4): 468–478.

Tsui, Bonnie. 2009. *American Chinatown: A People's History of 5 Neighborhoods*. New York: Free Press.

Tsui, Bonnie. 2014. "Chinatown Revisited." *New York Times*, January 24.

Tu, Wei-ming. 1994. *The Living Tree: The Changing Meaning of Being Chinese Today*. Palo Alto, CA: Stanford University Press.

U.S. Chamber of Commerce. 2016. "Immigration: Myths and Facts." Technical Report. Washington, DC: U.S. Chamber of Commerce.

Walker, Alan. 2015. "The Concept of Active Ageing." In *Active Ageing in Asia*, edited by Alan Walker and Christian Aspalter, 14–29. New York: Routledge.

Walsh, Katie. 2016. "'Expatriate Belongings': Traces of Life 'Abroad' in the Home-Making of English Returnees in Later Life." In *Transnational Migration and Home in Older Age*, edited by Katie Walsh and Lena Nare, 139–150. New York: Routledge.

Walsh, Katie, and Lena Nare. 2016. "Introduction: Transnational Migration and Home in Older Age." In *Transnational Migration and Home in Older Age*, edited by Katie Walsh and Lena Nare, 1–22. New York: Routledge.

Wang, Gungwu. 1980. *China and the Overseas Chinese: A Study of Peking's Changing Policy: 1949–1970*. Cambridge: Cambridge University Press.

Wang, Gungwu. 2002. *The Chinese Overseas: From Earthbound China to the Quest for Autonomy*. Cambridge, MA: Harvard University Press.

Watson, James L. 1975. *Emigration and the Chinese Lineage: The "Mans" in Hong Kong and London*. Berkeley: University of California Press.

Watson, James, and Evelyn Rawski, eds. 1990. *Death Ritual in Late Imperial and Modern China*. Berkeley: University of California Press.

Watson, Rubie S. 1986. "The Named and the Nameless: Gender and Person in Chinese Society." *American Ethnologist* 13 (4): 619–631.

Wei, Jianwen, Jie Zhang, Yuping Deng, Long Sun, and Ping Guo. 2018. "Suicide Ideation among the Chinese Elderly and Its Correlates: A Comparison between the Urban and Rural Populations." *International Journal of Environmental Research and Public Health* 15 (3): 422–432.

Whyte, Martin King, ed. 2010. *One Country, Two Societies: Rural-Urban Inequality in Contemporary China*. Cambridge, MA: Harvard University Press.

Wilcox, Hui. 2011. "Movement in Spaces of Liminality: Chinese Dance and Immigrant Identities." *Ethnic and Racial Studies* 34 (2): 314–332.

Wong, Bernard. 1982. *Economic Adaptation and Ethnic Identity of the Chinese*. New York: Holt.

Wong, Bernard. 1988. *Patronage, Brokerage, Entrepreneurship, and the Chinese Community of New York*. New York: AMS Press.

Wong, Sabrina T., Grace J. Yoo, and Anita L. Stewart. 2006. "The Changing Meaning of Family Support among Older Chinese and Korean Immigrants." *Journal of Gerontology: Social Sciences* 61B (1): S4–S9.

Wong, Sau-ling C. 2013. "Dancing in the Diaspora: 'Cultural Long Distance Nationalism' and the Staging of Chineseness by San Francisco's Chinese Folk Dance Association." In *Diasporic Chineseness after the Rise of China*, edited Julia Kuehn, Kam Louie, and David M. Pomfret, 126–148. Vancouver, Canada: UBC Press.

Xiang, Biao. 2015. "The Rise of China: Changing Patterns of Out-Migration and Identity Implications." In *Handbook of Chinese Migration: Identity and Wellbeing*, edited by R. Robyn Iredale, 278–294. Northampton, MA: Elgar.

Xiang, Biao, Brenda S. A. Yeoh, and Mika Toyota. 2013. *Return: Nationalizing Transnational Mobility in Asia*. Durham, NC: Duke University Press.

Xie, Xiaolin, and Yan Xia. 2011. "Grandparenting in Chinese Immigrant Families." Paper 82. Department of Child, Youth, and Family Studies, University of Nebraska–Lincoln.

Yan, Yunxiang. 2003. *Private Life under Socialism: Love, Intimacy, and Family Change in a Chinese Village: 1949–1999*. Palo Alto, CA: Stanford University Press.

Yan, Yunxiang. 2011. "The Individualization of the Family in Rural China." In *Boundary 2* 38 (1): 203–229.

Yan, Yunxiang, and Laura Bear. 2009. *The Individualization of Chinese Society*. Oxford: Berg.

Yang, Guobin. 2003. "China's Zhiqing Generation: Nostalgia, Identity, and Cultural Resistance in the 1990s." *Modern China* 29 (3): 267–295.

Yang, Philip Q. 2000. "The 'Soujourner Hypothesis' Revisited." *Diaspora* 9 (2): 235–258.

Yarris, Kristin. 2017. *Care Across Generations: Solidarity and Sacrifice in Transnational Families*. Palo Alto, CA: Stanford University Press.

Yu, Jiyuan. "Translation of Ren in Van Norden's Mengzi." *Journal of Chinese Philosophy* 37 (4): 660–667.

Yu, Kam-por, Julia Tao, and Philip J. Ivanhoe. 2010. *Taking Confucian Ethics Seriously: Contemporary Theories and Applications*. Albany: State of New York University Press.

Yoon, Sung Min. 2005. "The Characteristics and Needs of Asian-American Grandparent Caregivers." *Journal of Gerontological Social Work* 44 (3–4): 75–94.

Zelizer, Viviana A. 1985. *Pricing the Priceless Child: The Changing Social Value of Children*. New York: Basic Books.

Zhang, Hong. 2004. "'Living Alone' and the Rural Elderly: Strategy and Agency in Post-Mao Rural China." In *Filial Piety: Practice and Discourse in Contemporary East Asia*, edited by Charlotte Ikels, 63–87. Stanford, CA: Stanford University Press.

Zhang, Hong. 2009. "The New Realities of Aging in Contemporary China: Coping with the Decline in Family Care." In *The Cultural Context of Aging: Worldwide Perspectives*, 3rd ed., edited by Jay Sokolovsky. Westport, CT: Praeger.

Zhang, Li, and Aihwa Ong, eds. 2008. *Privatizing China: Socialism from Afar*. Ithaca, NY: Cornell University Press.

Zheng, Su. 2007. *Claiming Diaspora: Music, Transnationalism, and Cultural Politics in Asian/Chinese America*. Oxford: Oxford University Press.

Zhou, Min. 1992. *Chinatown: The Socioeconomic Potential of an Urban Enclave*. Philadelphia: Temple University Press.

Zhou, Min. 2009. *Contemporary Chinese America: Immigration, Ethnicity, and Community Transformation*. Philadelphia: Temple University Press.

Zhou, Min, and Guoxuan Cai. 2002. "Chinese Language Media in the United States: Immigration and Assimilation in American Life." *Qualitative Sociology* 25 (3): 419–441.

Zhou, Yanqiu Rachel. 2017. "The New Aging Trajectories of Chinese Grandparents in Canada." In *Transnational Aging and Reconfigurations of Kin Work*, edited by Parin Dossa and Cati Coe, 43–60. New Brunswick, NJ: Rutgers University Press.

Zong, Jie, and Jeanne Batalova. 2017. "Chinese Immigrants in the United States." Washington, DC: Migration Policy Institute.

INDEX

absent men, 37–38, 41–44, 46–47
acculturation of immigrants, 29
active aging: focus on in PRC, 13–14, 176, 178
adjustment factors, 29; loneliness, 178; racism as, 175; social role usage as, 179
adult children: busy working, 179; moving to be near, 7; pendular migration and, 177; under PRC hukou system, 188n15; as sponsors, 6, 45–46
advocacy: after 1990, 175; Chinese American seniors benefiting from, 180
affinity for U.S., defined, 28; emotional attachment, 28, 56–57; generational belonging and, 52–57, 74–75; in ideals of fairness, humanity, justice, 29; as primary place of belonging, 30
affinity to place, 29, 129–34, 173
agency/disempowerment, 17
Aging and Adaptation (Ikels), 11–12
aging in place concerns: Chinatown (Boston) and its boundaries, 125–29; Chinatowns as contested spaces, 122–25, 143–45; homemaking process, 122–25; as if in China, 29; physical insideness, 129–34; social insideness, 134–43; suicide rate in U.S., 188n19
aging populations: China having fastest growing, 176; in contemporary world, 179; demographic trend of increase in, 178; focus on senior well-being and, 176, 179; globalization and, 13–17; insecurities of, 179; negative effects of, 14; in new locations, 17; positive outcomes for senior mobility should be recognized, 180; worldwide, 176
amenity migration, 15, 16
Ang, Ien, 150
assistance migration, 15, 32

ballroom dancing, 30, 153–57, 157–63. *See also* performative cultural activities
belonging, sense of, 26, 28
blue sky metaphor, 74–75
Bulgarian senior migrants, 108–9, 110
Burma, 43

Canada, 190n27, 183n11
Cantonese language, inability to speak, 172
Cantonese speaking Chinese, 172, 185n9; global mobility flow engagement of, 171; immigration policy effects on, 11; in Quincy (Massachusetts), 185n58; in U.S., 10; methodological choice of, 20. *See also* Taishanese speaking Chinese; Quincy (Massachusetts)
capitalism, Chinese, 12
caregiving: Chinese family love in immigration context and, 102–10; Chinese grandparent caregivers, 19, 46, 190n27; family conflicts from tensions over, 173; family love and, 119–21; future of, 116–18; Nicaraguan grandmothers and, 14–15, 190n35; as paid/unpaid labor, 29, 178; as reason for

210   INDEX

migration, 46, 170; returns of, 110–16; time constraints from, 172. *See also* negotiating family values

Carpenter, Jennifer, 162, 192n1

CCP (Chinese Communist Party). *See* Chinese Communist revolution of 1949 (liberation)

challenges: daily, 180; of environment, 28; taking on new, 178

Chiang Kai-shek, 149–50

Chinatown (Boston): aging in place and, 125–29; ballroom dancing in, 30, 157–63; connections with, 192n21; as contested space, 122–25, 143–45; data collection in, 22; educational opportunities and, 172; employment and, 172; Ikels on, 11–12; local level structural support access in, 174; Mr. Lee (interviewee), 5–7; overview, 17–18, 19; resources of, 172; senior workers in, 7; socialization and, 127, 172; suburban areas, 19; travel to, 20

Chinatown (New York), 11

Chinatown (San Francisco), 11

Chinatowns (U.S.): razing of, 172; scholarly works on, 11–12; as unchanging, 191n3; as undesirable residential locations, 191n3

Chinatowns (worldwide): connections with, 171; networks of reception and, 172; work opportunities in, 7

Chinese Canadian seniors, 174

Chinese Communist revolution of 1949 (liberation), 40, 45, 58, 60–62, 63, 68

Chinese diasporic community: Chinese diasporic practices, 148; family dispersal, 37, 41; historical processes of, 192n9; performative cultural activities and, 29–30, 146–49, 167–69

Chinese Exclusion Act of 1882, xi, 6, 10, 39

Chineseness: conceptualizations of, 23; cultural production of, 149–53, 169; shared conceptions of, 163, 168; tied to nationalism, 27

Chinese senior migrants in U.S.: overview, 1–4; roles in fostering well-being in American communities, 4; with sense of affinity/active engagement in U.S., 4; social life, changes to, 176; sojourner trope (Chinese), 26

citizenship and language difficulties, 70–74

Coe, Cati, 38–39, 99–100

Cold War refugee categories, 10

compassionate behavior, 89–96

congregational dancing, 148, 153–57, 163, 164, 166–68

contemporary contexts of retirement in China and U.S., 80–84

contested spaces, aging in place and, 122–25, 143–45

Coutin, Susan, 56

Criminal Offender Record Information (CORI), 183n3

cultural issues: acculturation, 29; cultural capital, nationalism and, 27; cultural citizenship, 56; cultural connections, 26; cultural distance from mainstream American life, 173; cultural diversity, 27; cultural returns of caregiving, 110–16; cultural understanding of rootedness in/to China, 26; health care access and, 12; hybrid cultural forms, 25; performative cultural activities, 149–53; renegotiated cultural norms/ways of life, 29. *See also* aging in place; Chineseness; cultural values; family values

Cultural Revolution, xi, 45, 54, 67, 90, 93–94, 140, 187n14

cultural values: caregiving and, 102–10, 110–16; changing state of, 116–19; family love, 102–10, 119–21; filial piety, 99, 101, 104–5, 117, 119,

120–21; negotiating family values and, 99–102
culture of migration: in Ghana, 38; historical, 34–41; as reason for migration, 51–52; rural areas and, 38

daily schedules, lack of freedom of, 173
danwei system, 47, 80, 90, 97
demographics, study location and, 17–21
demographic shift: during 20th century, 10–11; characteristics of last ten years, 177; in Chinese community in Boston, 12; of contemporary migrants, 170; focus on senior well-being and, 176; globalization of retirement and, 13–17; scholarly work on, 12
Deneva, Neda, 108–9, 110
Deng Xiaoping, xi, 58, 60
depth of engagement after moving, 17
depth of integration after moving, 17
diasporic populations, 185n66; age-mate interactions of, 177; citizenship of, 193n12; community interactions of, 148–49; cultural production and, 149; diasporic lifeways, 28; emotional attachment to nation-states in, 56–57; family networks of, 3; interviewees as, 28; literature on, 25; pathways of, 20; Syrian Jews, 151–52; Taishanese families, 37; well-being through age-mate of, 177
disempowerment, 14–15
domestic migration, devaluing of elder care and, 179
Dossa, Parin, 99–100
Dreby, Joanna, 103

economic issues: in China, 172; conditions, 17; connections, 26; disparities of wealth in U.S., 180
economic capital, 27; economic disadvantages, 9; economic diversity, 27; economic-driven analyses, 8; economic gain and migration goals, 8; economic hardships in China, 43–44; economic injustices experienced by Asian Americans, 175; economic inequalities in economic opportunities, 176; economic returns of caregiving, negotiating family values and, 110–16; economic supports in U.S, 179: economic well-being, 178; nationalism and, 27; search for economic security goals, 181
educational opportunities, 15; Chinatown and, 172; graduate-level, 19, 170; as reason for migration, 10, 174; student migration pathway, 33, 186n21; Taiwanese seniors, 11
elder care: active promotion of in China, 13–14, 176; social transformations causing devaluing of, 179
emotional attachment, 28, 56–57, 57–58. *See also* affinity for U.S.
emotional hardships: cultural expressions of support, 13, 14; emotional returns of caregiving, 110–16
emplacement, sense of, 28
employment: blue-collar jobs in cleaning, caregiving, and food distribution, 172; Chinatown and, 172; for support, 174; white-collar worker migration pathway, 33, 170
engagement in migratory pathways: goals of well-being and, 178; as lens for understanding, 30; multitude of factors mattering in, 178; receptions in areas where they settle and, 29, 180; reshaping of life and, 178; social role usage and, 179
English language: citizenship and language difficulties, 70–74; lack of fluency in, 7; ESL programs, 20
exclusion laws/policies, 26, 34, 42, 44; Chinese Exclusion Act of 1882, xi, 6, 10, 39; Chinese exclusion era, 39–40;

effects on demographics, 10–11; exemptions from, 6, 186n21; Page Act of 1875, xi, 39; Taishanese speaking Chinese, 147
exercise as performative cultural activity, 163–67

family networks: 20; global mobility flow and, 40–41, 171; as senior resource, 41
family relationships: difficulties, 180; family conflicts, 28, 173; family histories of emigration, 28; family life changes, 176; unfolding after seniors' moves, 178
family reunion: after decades of separation, 29; key to migrations, 170; policy decisions and, 171; as reason for migration, 7, 31–34, 48–51
family separations: culture of migration and, 41–48; difficulties experienced through, 42–43; family abandonments, 44; family dispersal, 37, 41–42; family risk diversification, 173
family sponsorship: family preference categories, 178; perceived lack of contribution to country's economic growth from, 178; family ties as basis for legal entrance, 10
family values: changes to, 176; family love and, 119–21; practicing, 29. *See also* negotiating family values
Farquhar, Judith, 82–83, 87–88, 153
filial piety, 99, 101, 104–5, 117, 119, 120–21
Filipino residents in Quincy (Massachusetts), 185n58
financial support: financial goals, 174; financial precariousness, 176; legislation mandating adult children provide, 13, 14; unable to rely on adult children for, 175
flexible citizenship, 11, 41–42, 174
Foner, Nancy, 103

Fuzhounese villagers, 3

generational belonging in the nation-state: affinity for U.S. and, 52–57, 74–75, 174; citizenship and language difficulties, 70–74; exclusion from benefits in contemporary China, 179; searching for humane social atmosphere in China and U.S., 63–70; senior migrants' views of China, 57–63; social and political upheaval experiences and, 175
Generation Dance (photography exhibit) (Carpenter), 162, 192n1
Ghanaian culture of migration, 38–39
Ginseng and Aspirin (Guo), 12
globalization: active aging ideas and, 178; aging and, 13–17; critiques of processes of, 179; cutbacks on pensions/senior supports at global level, 176; globalization of retirement, as reframing lens, 17; literature focus on negative effects of, 14; of migration networks, 171; well-being and, 13–17;
global mobility: immigration restrictions, 14; family/peer networks and, 171; family preference categories, 178; increase in, 16; networks of trade/communication and, 40; neoliberalism and, 3, 179; migration patterns embedded in power structure of, 13; pathways as lens for understanding seniors, 30; physical limitations and, 14
gold rushes, xi, 35
grandchildren: busy working, 179; immigrating to care for, 11, 19; Nicaraguan grandmothers and, 14–15, 190n35; pendular migration and, 177
grandparents: immigration policy debates and, 9; as reason for migrating, 11, 19; Nicaraguan study, 14–15, 190n35; returning to China, 46

INDEX 213

Great Leap Forward campaign, 58–59
Guangdong Province: Chinese immigrants from, 5; historical culture of migration and, 34–41; migration increase from north of, 170; Pearl River Delta area, 35, 36, 52, 149, 171, 174
Guo, Zibin, 12

Hall, Stuart, 51
hardship struggles, 4, 8
Hart-Celler Immigration and Naturalization Act of 1965, xi, 9, 10, 11
health care: cultural negotiations and, 12; healthy aging promotion in PRC, 176; inequalities in, 176; senior navigation of, 12
Hershatter, Gail, 59–60, 62
homemaking process, 121, 122–25, 134, 141
homing process, 124–25, 143, 148, 180
Hong Kong: border closure during Maoist period, 40, 44–45, 54; ceding of, xi; criticisms against ballroom dancing in, 158; Ikels on aging and adaptation in, 11–12; migration corridors and, 36; Nationalists immigrate to, 149–50; returning to China from, 45, 154
household residency system (hukou system), 188n15
housing: flexibility in, 16, 174; household residency system (hukou system), 81, 98, 188n15
Hsu, Madeline, 40, 185n9, 186n18
Huang, Claudia, 148, 156
hukou system (household residency system), 81, 98, 188n15
humane social atmosphere in China and U.S., 63–70
humanization of migrants, 4, 174

identity formation, 17; complex views about, 25; role of Chinese dance in, 193n18
Ikels, Charlotte, 11–12, 94–95
immigration: future Chinese-born senior immigration decrease, 177; effects on Cantonese-speaking Chinese, 11; immigration policy debates, 9; longer waiting periods in U.S. today, 177; U.S. prohibitions on, xi
Immigration Act of 1924, xi

Jackson, Lucy, 56
Japan: as country of residence for overseas Chinese, 183n11; Japanese residents in Quincy (Massachusetts), 185n58; powerhouse economy in, 2; traditional family support in, 13
Johnson-Reed Immigration Act of 1824, xi

kinfare, 108–9
King, Russell, 124
kin work, negotiating family values and, 99–102
Korea: overseas Chinese in, 183n11; powerhouse economy in, 2; traditional family support in, 13; Korean residents in Quincy (Massachusetts), 185n58
Kuhn, Philip, 35

Lai, Daniel, 153–54, 174
Lamb, Sarah, 4, 179
language-based resources, 171 Chinese-language support services, 173; citizenship and language difficulties, 70–74; communication frustrations, 178
Lee, Ching Kwan, 64–70
Lee, Tunney, 192n24
Leung, Genevieve, 34, 139
Li, Wei, 191n3
liberation (Chinese Communist revolution of 1949), 40, 45, 58, 60–62, 63, 68

life stages: contradictions in experiences of, 16; life expectancy (life spans), 176; lifelong desire of family reunion, 48–51; lifestyle migration, 15; retirement as staggered/blended, 188n21

Long, Ho (interviewee), 146–47, 153, 192n1

low-income migrants, 20; as active community contributors, 17; as innovators of new ways of belonging in American communities, 17; homing processes participation of, 180; in Massachusetts, 184n22

mainstream American life: Chinese Americans as absent from, 27, 172; cultural distance from, 173; cultural practices differing from, 56, 123; cultural practices shed for acculturation into, 29; enclave areas as separate from, 172

Malden (Massachusetts), 192n21

Mandarin (language), 113, 162, 166

Mandarin-speaking Chinese seniors: in Boston area, 20, 139, 146; from mainland China, 147; migration increase of, 170; resilience of in adapting to life in U.S., 174; suburban migration of, 19, 177; support levels of, 177

Maoist period, xi; curtailing of emigration during, 40–41; dismantling of systems of collectivization of, 176; economic hardships, 43, 44, 58, 67; Great Leap Forward campaign, 58–59; Hong Kong border closure, 44–45; political hardships during, 44, 47, 48; restrictive policies of, 60–62; social injustices, 44, 64, 67, 172; social/political turmoil, 12

Mao Zedong, 40, 60; culture of the masses promoted by, 154

marginalization: of Asian immigrants, 172; from inadequate expansion of services for elderly, 14; including physically demanding work, dependence on ethnic social networks for everyday survival, 173; structural factors contributing to, 173

McKeown, Adam, 149, 151, 167

Medicare benefits, 69, 82, 175, 188n20, 189n23; eligibility requirements, 189n23

methodology: choice of Cantonese-speaking seniors, 20; data collection, 21–22; granular approach, 16; outsider status, 22–25; study location, 17–21

migration pathways: ambiguities of, 15, 180; complex views for aging adults, 16; engagement in, 4, 8; factors mattering in, 178; range of, 177; strategic use of, 179; typical trajectory, 36–37; for younger adult migrants, 33

model minority stereotype, 27

modernization, 14

morality, 66–68

motivations for migration: caregiving for grandchildren, 46; culture of migration and, 51–52; as family-centered, 31–34; family separation in 20th century, 41–48; historical culture of migration and, 34–41; for economic survival, 8, 173, 179; moving beyond, 29; realization of lifelong desire of family reunion, 7, 48–51; retirement age (China), 7; social activities, 7, 15; work activities, 7; life goal achievement, 16, 17

Mr. Cheung (interviewee), 36–38, 41, 44, 46–48, 51, 115, 186n15

Mr. Eng (interviewee), 129–32, 137

Mr. Ho Long (interviewee), 146–47, 153, 192n1

Mr. Lam (interviewee), 84–87, 89, 96, 97, 144

Mr. Lee (interviewee), 5–7, 11, 16, 20, 49–51, 117–18, 136–37, 184n20, 186n15

Mr. Moy (interviewee), 44–46, 47, 114, 186n15
Mrs. Chee (interviewee), 43, 48, 186n15
Mrs. Lung (interviewee), 110–12
Mrs. Tan (interviewee), 89–96, 97, 131
Mrs. Wong (interviewee), 60–62, 71–72, 94–96, 113–14, 135–36, 139–41
Mr. Wang (interviewee), 76–79, 89, 96
Mr. Wu (interviewee), 139
Mui, Ada C., 174
"My Chinese Heart" (popular song), 150, 193n14

nationalism: cultural capital and, 27; economic capital and, 27; immigration debates, 180; migration patterns embedded in national power structures, 13; social capital and, 27; structural support access, 174, 176; policies of restriction, 5
negotiating family values: caregiving and Chinese family love in immigration context, 102–10; caregiving future, 116–18; emotional, economic, cultural returns of caregiving, 110–16; family love, 119–21; kin work, 99–102, negotiating for power with adult children, 173. *See also* caregiving
neoliberalism, 176
network of support services, 14–15, 116, 190n35
Newton (Massachusetts), 192n21
New York, 11, 12, 41, 116, 129, 144, 174, 191n17
Nicaraguan study, 14–15, 190n35
nostalgia for past ways of life, 29, 57, 59, 174

older Americans, inability to retire statistics, 180
Oliver, Caroline, 57
one-child policy, 13, 33, 114, 176, 177
Ong, Aihwa, 11, 41–42

Opium War, first, xi, 36
Opium War, second, xi, 35
Oxfeld, Ellen, 68

Page Act of 1875, xi, 39
paid labor, seniors continuing, 189n21
paid/unpaid caregiving, 178
Palmberger, Monika, 148, 161
paradoxes of migration, 27
parental emigration, Nicaraguan grandmothers and, 14–15, 190n35
Pearl River Delta area (Guangdong Province), 35, 36, 52, 149, 171, 174
pendular migration, defined, 177
pensions, in postreform PRC, 175, 176
People's Republic of China (PRC): Cultural Revolution, xi, 45, 54, 67, 90, 93–94, 140, 187n14; establishment of, 12, 58; founding of, xi; government, 26; hardships during, 61–62; Hong Kong border closure, 36; liberation (Chinese Communist revolution of 1949), 40, 45, 58, 60–62, 63, 68; life changing over three decades, 12; modernization processes, 26; pension/medical policies to address income inequality, 176–77; postreform changes, 175, 176, 179; reform era under Deng Xiaoping, xi; searching for humane social atmosphere in, 63–70; senior migrants view of, 57–63; suicide rates in, 188n19; traditional family support in, 13; travel to, 48
performative cultural activities: ballroom/congregational dancing in Chinese past and present, 153–57; ballroom dancing in Quincy and Boston, 157–63; Chinese diasporic community and, 146–49, 167–69; cultural production of Chineseness, 149–53; group dancing and exercise, 163–67
personal independence, Western conceptions of personhood and, 179

personhood, Western conceptions of, 14, 179
physical insideness, 129–34
post-Mao China: exit policies in, 171; improvements under, 60
Poston, Dudley L., 192n9
poverty: in China, 13, 14; financial environment of post reform China, 175; poverty levels among U.S. elderly, 180
power structures: aging migrants' engagement with, 17; overlapping of historical, 25–26
precariousness: Nicaraguan grandmothers and, 14–15, 190n35; social precariousness, 176

Qin dynasty, 192n9
Quincy (Massachusetts): Asian American population of, 129; Asian residents of, 185n58; Chinese American residents of, 192n21; data collection in, 22; local level structural support access in, 174; network of service provision in, 133–34; overview, 17, 18–19; racist conflict in, 142–43; subsidized housing in, 132–33, 138, 142; travel to, 20

Race/racism: as adjustment factor, 175; immigration policies based on, 10; racial hostility, 27; social alienation and, 8
reconfiguration of retirement, 170–81
regional associations, 18, 126, 127, 139–40, 172
remittances, 35, 42, 44
residence: residency length, 17; retirement migration worldwide and, 12–13; suburban shift in, 12
resources: amenity migration, 15, 16; inadequacy of in China, 13; increased access to, 12
retirement: age for in China, 7; goals, 76–80; as lifestage in PRC, 176; lifestyles, 17, 174, 179; as reason for migration, 7; as staggered/blended life stage, 188n21
retirement meanings in U.S.: compassionate behavior, 89–96; contemporary contexts of retirement in China and U.S., 80–84; reconfiguration of retirement, 170–82; retirement goals, 76–80; retirement migration worldwide, 12–13; retiring well, 96–98; self-cultivation, 84–89; welfare support infrastructure, 29
retirement migration: amenity migration, 15, 16; assistance migration, 15, 32; family/peer networks and, 15; patterns of global movement, 17; return migration, 15, 124
return migration, 15, 124
Rosaldo, Renato, 56
routinization of emigration, 37–38
Rowles, Graham, 125, 130, 134
rural areas/urban areas: culture of migration and, 38; hukou system (household residency system), 188n15; inequalities between in economic opportunities and health care access, 176; policies addressing inequalities in PRC, 176–77; resources as inadequate, 13

sacrifice, cultural expression of, 14
San Francisco, 6, 11, 16, 35, 41, 43, 47, 49, 116, 144
Sassen, Saskia, 55–56
savings, 100, 120, 175
second-generation Asian Americans, 103, 126, 172
segmented labor theory, 173
self-cultivation, 79, 83, 84–89, 119
self-health movement, 82–83
Shelemay, Kay Kaufman, 151–52, 156
Shibusawa, Tazuko, 174
Singapore, 2, 183n11

Siu, Lok, 193n12
social affinity, 134, 136–37, 142
social atmosphere, 66–68, 70, 74, 141
social capital, 27, 171
social environment, 29, 66, 105, 131
social insideness, 134–43
social interaction, 134–43, 178–79
social marginalization, 8, 17, 27
social precariousness, 176
Social Security, 69, 81–82, 83, 85, 87, 109, 113, 174–75, 188n20, 189n23
social service organizations, 172; for advocacy and support, 175; Asian American community development and, 175; Asian American community organizing and, 175; Asian American community rights and, 175; in Chinatown (Boston), 126–28, 139; community development activists in, 96; group activities at, 164; recent migrants' access to, 172; rise in, 191n17; rise of, 191n17; support networks and, 20, 92, 117
social stability goals, 174; basic level of, 175; cultivation of interdependence and, 179; seniors continued search for ways to achieve, 181; seniors describe life in U.S. in positive terms, 8; social navigation, 4
social welfare infrastructures: 13; Medicare benefits, 69, 82, 175, 188n20, 189n23; Social Security, 69, 81–82, 83, 85, 87, 109, 113, 174–75, 188n20
split-family life, 37, 41–42
sponsorship: by adult children, 6, 45–46, 53, 177; by parents for adult children, 46, 177; by siblings, 177
subsidized housing, 18, 22, 38, 82, 84, 86, 87, 89, 127–28, 132–33, 135, 142, 166, 173, 174, 175
Sun, Ken Chih-Yan, 4
support networks: Chinese exclusion laws and, 40; time and effort establishing, 178–79

support service: Chinese American seniors benefiting from, 180; as context of reception for retirement as a stage of life, 29; increased access to, 12 senior support in China, 174, 176, 177
surname associations, 18, 126, 127, 139–40, 172

tai chi, 97, 147, 163, 164, 165, 167
Taishan County (China), 185n9, 186n18
Taishanese-speaking Chinese: among ballroom participants, 146–47, 162; Cantonese and, 34, 138, 172; caregiving, 116; in Chinatown (Boston), 129–30, 138; interpretation with, 24, 53; language difficulties, 113, 138–39; on Maoist era, 62; migratory traditions of, 37–38; organizations for, 126, 127; returning to China, 118; in U.S., 10, 11, 20, 147, 172, 185n9. *See also* Mr. Cheung (interviewee)
Taiwan, 193n12; ballroom dancing participants from, 153, 154, 157; criticisms against ballroom dancing in, 158; Mandarin-speaking seniors from, 147; Nationalists immigrate to, 149–50; returning to China from, 154; seniors returning for retirement in, 4, 16; Taiwanese American seniors, 4; Taiwanese refugees of Cold War, 10; returning to Taiwan after retirement, 15–16
Tang, Teresa, 160
third-generation Asian Americans, 144, 172
transnationalism, 5; Chinese exclusion laws and, 40; migratory pathways engagement, 8; Nicaraguan grandmothers and, 14–15, 190n35; pendular migration, 177; reconfiguration of identities within, 17
transportation, inability to access, 172
travel, return visits to China, 7, 8

Turkish migrants, 148, 161

undocumented migrants, 56
unequal benefit system (two-tiered system), 188n15. *See also* rural/urban areas
United States: beliefs about retirement in, 177; as country of residence for overseas Chinese, 183n11; suicide rates of Chinese American older women in, 188n19
urban areas/rural areas. *See* rural areas/urban areas

values. *See* family values
Vietnamese Chinese refugees, 147, 162, 185n58
vulnerability, 17

ways of being/belonging, 17. *See also* belonging, sense of
ways of life goals: achievement of, 28; as counterintuitive, 179–80; security, interdependence and opportunity to experience something new, 179
well-being promotion: affinity with physical spaces and, 29; critique of, 14; cultivation of interdependence and, 179; globalization of retirement and, 13–17; growing attention to seniors' experiences of, 12; of low-income seniors and those around them, 180; from moving to U.S., 8; personal independence and, 179; retiring well, 96–98; social engagement and, 28
white-collar worker migration pathway, 33, 170
Wilcox, Hui, 151–52
Wong, Bernard, 191n17
Wong, Juyin, 192n9
work/working: destinations, 26; policies addressing retirement age, 176–77; as reason for migration, 7; reasons for continuing, 189n21; time constraints from, 172
World War II, xi; effects on family separations, 36, 44; hardship struggles during, 44; Japanese occupation of China, 12, 36, 43, 58, 61; lifting of Chinese Exclusion Laws and, 10, 40

Yang, Guobin, 187n14
Yarris, Kristin, 14–15, 190n35
younger adult migrant pathways, 33
yumcha socialization, 189n29

Zelizer, Viviana, 101–2
Zhang, Qicheng, 82–83, 87–88, 153
zhiqing generation, 187n14